God After Darwin

A Theology of Evolution

John F. Haught

Westview Press
A Member of the Perseus Books Group

Copyright © 2000 by Westview Press, A Member of the Perseus Books Group

Published in 2000 in the United States of America by Westview Press, 5500 Central Avenue, Boulder, Colorado 80301–2877, and in the United Kingdom by Westview Press, 12 Hid's Copse Road, Cumnor Hill, Oxford OX2 9JJ

Find us on the World Wide Web at www.westviewpress.com

Library of Congress Cataloging-in-Publication Data
Haught, John F.
  God after Darwin : a theology of evolution / John F. Haught.
    p. cm.
  Includes bibliographical references and index.
  ISBN 0-8133-3878-6 (pbk.)
  1. Evolution—Religious aspects—Christianity.   I. Title.
BT712.H38   1999
231.7 ' 652—dc21
                                                             99–32621
                                                                  CIP

10   9   8   7   6   5   4   3

Praise for *God After Darwin*

"On the highly embattled issue of God and evolution, the most well-known positions tell us that God exists but evolution doesn't, that evolution exists but God doesn't, or that science and religion are completely different things. Jack Haught's *God After Darwin*, which regards evolution as "a gift to theology," presents an alternative vision—of a universe still unfinished and a Creator who, far from the omnipotent designer undermined by evolution, is the cosmic source of possibility, value, novelty, information, and beauty."

—David Ray, Griffin Claremont School of Theology;
author of *Religion and Scientific Naturalism: Overcoming the Conflicts*

"God is dead. At least the god of intelligent design is dead, gone the way of the god of the gaps. Daniel Dennett and Richard Dawkins need to re-tool their tedious and narrow theology. In *God After Darwin: A Theology of Creation*, theologian John F. Haught makes the exciting and compelling case that far from undermining the existence of God, Darwinian evolution points the way to a fresh understanding of God and the natural world. Creation is not finished and the future, so green with the promise of novelty, is not determined. . . . Drawing on the works of Pierre Teilhard de Chardin, Alfred North Whitehead, and Karl Rahner, among others, Haught has articulated an understanding of God that respects Christian orthodoxy but also resonates with the world of Darwin, Einstein, and Hawking. Can it be that theology owns its own "dangerous idea," namely that metaphysical materialism is incompetent to make full sense of the actual discoveries of evolutionary science?....As an evolutionary biologist, I have read Haught's book with excitement, admiration, and pleasure—though it will take me a long time to ponder all of the stimulating ideas."

—Peter Dodson, University of Pennsylvania;
President, Philadelphia Center for Religion and Science

"John Haught has a track record of presenting magisterial contributions to our understanding of how to regard the engagement of religion and science. In this book, he performs a twofold task: he shows how traditional thinking about God might take the measure of contemporary evolutionary science, and he also provides a resource for theologically serious thinkers in the ongoing work of reconstructing faith in a scientific age. His proposals carry the work to a new level."

—Philip Hefner, Lutheran School of Theology at Chicago;
director, Zygon Center for Religion and Science;
editor, *Zygon: Journal of Religion and Science*

To Evelyn

Contents

Preface

ANY THOUGHTS WE MAY HAVE about God after the life and work of Charles Darwin (1809–1882) can hardly remain the same as before. Evolutionary science has changed our understanding of the world dramatically, and so any sense we may have of a God who creates and cares for this world must take into account what Darwin and his followers have told us about it. Although Darwin himself beheld a certain "grandeur" in his new story of life, many of his scientific descendants, instead of taking his widening of the world's horizons as a springboard to a more exhilarating vision of God, have seen in evolution the final defeat of theism. Meanwhile, theology has generally failed to think about God in a manner proportionate to the opulence of evolution. I am convinced, though, that it has the resources to do so, and in the following pages I shall attempt to set forth some facets of a "theology of evolution."

If the idea of God is to arouse our instinct to worship, this idea cannot be smaller than the universe that science has made so conspicuous to us, especially after Darwin. But, as I shall argue, there is no good reason why the evolutionary news about nature should not be taken as an invitation for us to enlarge our sense of the divine. The understanding of God that many of us acquired in Sunday school is hardly expansive enough to incorporate the nuances of evolutionary thought. Moreover, the benign, ordering deity of traditional natural theology, as Darwin himself rightly concluded, scarcely accommodates the contingency and turmoil in the life process. A theology of evolution, on the other hand, will take into account all of the deviancy resident in the post-Darwinian representations of nature; and if this account compels us to relinquish comfortable ideas of divine order, we must accept the loss graciously. A theology of evolution must not sidestep, but instead tra-

verse, all the cliffs and abysses that so disturbed the religious preconceptions of Darwin and his contemporaries.

At the same time, however, it is not helpful for theology to talk
about God in vague terms that abstract from the particularities of our
faith traditions and their own ways of understanding ultimate reality.
Religious thinkers can deal with evolution in a meaningful way only if
they do so on the basis of their own experience of the sacred as medi-
ated through the faith communities to which they belong. Otherwise,
their discussions of "God" and evolution will drift so far from actual
religious experience as to be pointless and uninteresting. I shall propose here that fundamental aspects of biblical tradition, for example,
can initiate us into a way of experiencing and thinking about ultimate
reality that is not only religiously satisfying but also able to illuminate
the evolutionary character of the world. When the idea of divine creativity is tempered by accounts of God's vulnerability, and when nature itself is viewed as promise rather than simply as design or order,
the evidence of evolutionary biology not only appears consonant with
faith but lends new depth to it as well. A religiously adequate understanding of God not only tolerates but also requires the adventurous
extension of cosmic frontiers implied in evolutionary science.

An engagement of theology with evolution will be of benefit not
only to religious consciousness but also to the cause of science,
which has suffered immeasurably because the ideas of one of its
most brilliant thinkers have been taken by a great sector of the
world's population (including many American Christians) to be
completely irreconcilable with an appropriate sense of God. Much
of this distrust, of course, stems from the fact that evolutionary scientists themselves often present Darwinian ideas in an intellectual
guise that makes them appear inexorably irreligious or antitheistic.
And so, when faced with a choice *between* evolution and God, it is
hardly surprising that many among the religious will turn away from
the Darwinian alternative. It is very much in the interest of science
education itself, therefore, that we examine carefully whether such
an apparently forced option is the only one available.

However, it is not only the misunderstanding of religious experience by some evolutionists that forces the decision between God and
Darwin. A persisting distaste for evolution stems no less from ques-
tionable theological habits of identifying God with cramped notions
of order and design. I believe that we must look "beyond design" as
a first step in thinking responsibly about God after Darwin. Once

theological reflection has broken through an obsessive and restrictive association of God with cosmic and other forms of "order" it will then be able to place theology in its most appropriate setting—that of evolution itself.

John F. Haught

Acknowledgments

IN CHAPTERS 2 AND 4 I have borrowed material from my essay, "Darwin's Gift to Theology," which appears in *Evolutionary and Molecular Biology: Scientific Perspectives on Divine Action,* edited by Robert J. Russell, William R. Stoeger, S.J., and Francisco J. Ayala (used here with permission of the Center for Theology and the Natural Sciences). Chapter 3 amplifies a lecture given at Chicago's Field Museum (November 1997), another version of which appears in an in-house publication of the American Association for the Advancement of Science, *The Epic of Evolution,* edited by James Miller for the AAAS Program on Dialogue Between Science and Religion. Chapters 5 and 6 contain ideas first presented as the annual Russell Fellowship Lectures at the Center for Theology and the Natural Sciences (Berkeley, California, April 1996). Versions of these lectures appeared in the *CTNS Bulletin,* volume 18 (Winter 1998). I wish to thank Robert Russell, Richard Randolph, Ted Peters, and the staff at CTNS for the opportunity to share with them my thoughts on evolution and theology. Chapter 7 is revised from "Evolution, Tragedy, and Hope," which first appeared in *Science and Theology: The New Consonance,* edited by Ted Peters (Boulder, Colo.: Westview Press, 1998). And Chapter 9 modifies and extends an essay, "Ecology and Eschatology," that appeared in *And God Saw That It Was Good,* edited by Drew Christiansen, S.J., and Walter Grazer (Washington, D.C.: United States Catholic Conference, 1996), used here by permission of the United States Catholic Conference. Finally, I wish to acknowledge gratefully the efficiency of editors Laura Parsons, Sarah Warner, and Lisa Wigutoff of Westview Press in bringing this book to publication. And I owe a special thanks to David Toole for his many insightful suggestions and his exceptional editing skills.

J. F. H.

God After Darwin

I

Beyond Design

ABOUT A CENTURY AND A HALF AGO Charles Darwin surprised the world with his remarkable new theory of evolution. Theology has yet to come to grips with it. Even in the West, where many religious thinkers have given at least notional assent to Darwinian science, only a comparatively few have ever taken a long and deliberate look at it. And even those who claim to have faced up to the theory of evolution have often edited out some its most repellent features. When they have not rejected Darwinian ideas outright, theologians have mostly ignored them, content to nod at the platitude that "evolution is God's way of creating."

If theology has fallen short of the reality of evolution, however, so also has the world of thought in general. As Hans Jonas reminded us shortly before his recent death, philosophy also has yet to produce an understanding of reality—an ontology—adequate to evolution.[1] Materialism, the belief that lifeless and mindless "matter" alone is real, has provided the philosophical setting for most evolutionary science. Earlier in this century Alfred North Whitehead had already demonstrated that the reigning materialist metaphysics in Western philosophy choked out any sense of the emergent novelty in life's evolution, and he struggled to provide an alternative philosophical framework.[2] But only a minority of philosophers and scientists are familiar with or appreciative of Whitehead's thought, and to most evolutionists today there is still no persuasive alternative to materialism as an intellectual setting for their science.

Our concern here, though, is with theology, and I think it can be said safely that contemporary religious thought has yet to make a complete transition into a post-Darwinian world. To a great extent, theologians still think and write almost as though Darwin had never lived. Their attention remains fixed primarily on the human world and its unique concerns. The nuances of biology or, for that matter, of cosmology have not yet deeply affected current thinking about God and God's relation to the world. Although awareness of the eco- logical crisis has brought the natural world back into view for many sensitive people today, the story of nature's evolution is still not a consuming interest for most academic theologians and religious scholars, let alone for the general population of religious believers.

Scientific skeptics, of course, decided long ago that the only rea- sonable option Darwin leaves us is that of a totally Godless universe. That theology survives at all after Darwin is to some evolutionists a most puzzling anachronism. We would have to agree, of course, that if atheism is the logical correlate of evolutionary science, then the day of religions and theologies is over. But, as we shall see, such a judgment is hardly warranted. I shall argue in the pages ahead that Darwin has gifted us with an account of life whose depth, beauty, and pathos—when seen in the context of the larger cosmic epic of evolution—expose us afresh to the raw reality of the sacred and to a resoundingly meaningful universe.

Darwin's Theory of Natural Selection

Darwin claimed that all forms of life descend from a common ances- tor and that the wide array of living species can be accounted for by a process he called "natural selection." Members of any given species will, by sheer accident, differ from one another, and from the ensuing variety nature will then "select" only the "fit," those best "adapted" to their environmental circumstances, to survive and bear offspring. Over immense periods of time, selection of minute favor- able changes in adaptability will bring about countless new and dis- tinct forms of life, including eventually humans.

Darwin published *On the Origin of Species* in 1859, but today the majority of biologists still commend it for its general accuracy. In a synthesis known as "neo-Darwinism" they have simply added to Darwin's original ideas our more recent knowledge of genetics. Im- portant internal disputes still divide evolutionary biologists, but to- day there is an abiding appreciation of Darwin's genius and of the fundamental correctness of his ideas on life's common ancestry and

the mechanism of natural selection. Opinions differ about the respective roles in evolution of chance, adaptation, selection, genes, individual organisms, groups, struggle, cooperation, competition, and
so on. But most scientists today do not doubt that life has evolved—
at least roughly—along the lines that Darwin laid out so brilliantly.

Because of the role it gives to the elements of chance and blind selection in the unfolding of life, the Darwinian picture makes traditional ideas of a caring and almighty God seem superfluous and possibly incoherent. Even those theologians who have bothered to
examine the evolutionary terrain closely can hardly deny that it
raises difficulties about what our religions have come to call "God."
After weighing the now wellfounded accounts of life's lumbering
journey on Earth, any subsequent talk about a "divine plan" sounds
unbelievable. And the theological claim that life can be explained
adequately by divine "intelligent design" is especially suspect.

Of course, not everyone would agree. In his controversial book
Darwin's Black Box the biochemist Michael Behe, for example, offers
an interesting new pitch for the old theory that life is the result of
"intelligent design." He argues that Darwin's notion of a *gradual*
evolution from simplicity to complexity cannot explain life's intricate
patterns, even at the level of the cell. For most Darwinians even the
simplest living cell is a "black box" whose general functions may be
known but whose inner workings escape understanding. According to
Behe, however, biochemistry has now beamed its lights into Darwin's
black box, disclosing there a microworld of "irreducible complexity"
for which Darwin's theory has never given an adequate account.[3]

Darwin himself confessed that if it could ever be shown clearly
that life's variety comes about in any other way than by minute and
gradual modifications of undirected changes, then his theory would
be proven wrong. Highlighting Darwin's proviso, Behe seeks now to
show that the cellular constitution of living beings could not have
occurred incrementally, or step by step, as a pure Darwinian would
propose. The cell's complex inner components cannot function use-
fully unless they are all simultaneously present, working in tightly
integrated confederation. Hence, gradual emergence, which allows
the pieces of life to fall into place only one at a time, cannot really
explain even the living cell, let alone the larger world of life. Using a
simple analogy, Behe points out that a mousetrap will not work unless all of its constituent parts are present simultaneously. Take out
only one piece, and it won't catch mice. Likewise, cellular mechanisms

cannot function in the service of life unless all of their staggeringly complex and diverse components are assembled together and marching in unison.

Behe calls cellular mechanisms "irreducibly complex," meaning that they cannot be resolved into pieces or stages that have been assembled gradually over the course of time. It is hard to imagine how an enzyme or a blood-clotting mechanism, for example, could work at all without its many components being present together all at once. But if the cellular mechanism is not the product of a gradual accumulation of small changes, then, Behe concludes, the Darwinian explanation of life is demonstrably erroneous. The only alternative is "intelligent design."[4]

To many anti-Darwinians Behe's ideas are consoling. To Darwinians, however, whatever the merits of a biochemical analysis of the cell's complexity, the implicit appeal to theology in the pages of a book on science is a craven cop-out. The scorn with which some scientists have greeted Behe's rather guileless proposal is itself an interesting object of study. But what strikes the theologian after reading Behe's book is that if Darwinian theory is wanting in the full explanation of life, then so also is the notion of "intelligent design." "Intelligent design" smoothly passes over the disorderly, undirected aspects of evolution that are also part of the life-process. It ignores the darker hues in the Darwinian story that give a tragic cast to evolution and thereby strain the credibility of any theology.

Ironically, neither the proponents of "intelligent design" nor their materialist opponents actually deal with *life*. Both seek to purchase intellectual clarity only at the price of leaving out the *novelty* characteristic of living processes. Since by definition the ingress of genuine novelty always threatens to disturb present design, bringing about episodes of disorder, it is both intellectually and religiously tempting to deny that it exists. Materialist interpreters have typically dampened our intuitive sense of life's perpetual novelty by thinking of evolution only as the reshuffling of physical units (atoms, molecules, cells, or genes) already present. They have observed correctly that the emergence and flowering of life are constrained by the invariance of physical laws and that these laws are in no way violated by life's appearance. But from this truism they have wrested, without warrant, the extremely weak conclusion that since the evolution of life does not in any way violate the seemingly eternal laws of chemistry and physics, it therefore brings nothing really new into being.

Theological fixation on "intelligent design," however, is no less inclined to ignore the novelty essential to life. It sloughs off the fact that living systems require the continual *breakdown* of fixed order. It ignores the fact that life requires the dissolution of rigid "design," precisely in order to be alive at all. Instinctively, we all know this to be the case, but a theology based too securely on the notion of design abstracts habitually from this most fundamental truth. It ignores the *dissolution* that inevitably accompanies the appearance and extension of life. What is worse, by associating the idea of God only with the fact of order at the expense of novelty, a theology based on design is likely to attribute nature's disorder to the demonic. By exonerating ultimate reality of any complicity in chaos, such a theology removes God from the flow of life itself.

A theology obsessed with order is illprepared for evolution. But it is even less ready to embrace some of the more profound and disturbing aspects of religious experience itself, thus rendering it all the less capable of meaningful contact with the messiness of evolution. What makes evolution seem incompatible with the idea of God is not so much the startling Darwinian news about nature's struggle and strife, but theology's own failure to reflect deeply the divine pathos. What Darwin does—and this is part of his "gift to theology"—is challenge religious thought to recapture the tragic aspects of divine creativity. Evolutionary science compels theology to reclaim features of religious faith that are all too easily smothered by the deadening disguise of order and design.

Although they remain rancorous antagonists, both materialist scientists and "intelligent design" theorists share the compulsion to suppress a vibrant sense of life's openness to *new* creation. Almost by definition scientific materialism leaves out everything that common wisdom means by "life." But the focus by much religious thought on "intelligent design" likewise turns away from the novelty and instability without which life is reduced to death. By contrast, Darwin's own portrait of nature evolving is at least able to communicate a sense of real life with all the novelty, disturbance, and drama it involves. His science, when not suffocated by the stale climate of a materialist metaphysics, can give considerable depth and richness to our sense of the great mystery into which our religions attempt to initiate us.

Many good scientists, of course, will not see it this way. For a century and a half skeptics among them have found in evolution the

decisive confirmation of a strain of fatalism that has hovered over
modern science almost from the beginning. For an outspoken few,
Darwin has definitively laid to rest all the millennia of our species'
religious ignorance. To speak of an evolutionary "theology," as this
book does, will seem to be the most laughable of projects. To some
scientific thinkers, the evolutionary process is, in the words of David
Hull, "rife with happenstance, contingency, incredible waste, death,
pain and horror." Thus, any God who would oversee such a hash must
be "careless, indifferent, almost diabolical." This is not, says Hull,
"the sort of God to whom anyone would be inclined to pray."[5]

As long as we think of God only in terms of a narrowly human
notion of "order" or "design," the "atheism" of many evolutionists
will seem appropriate enough. Evolution does indeed upset a certain
sense of order; and if "God" means simply "source of order," even
the most elementary perusal of the fossil record will render this ancient idea suspect. But what if "God" is not just an originator of order but also the disturbing wellspring of *novelty?* And, moreover,
what if the cosmos is not just an "order" (which is what "cosmos"
means in Greek) but a still unfinished *process?* Suppose we look
carefully at the undeniable evidence that the universe is *still* being
created. And suppose also that "God" is less concerned with impos-
ing a plan or design on this process than with providing it with opportunities to participate in its own creation. If we make these conceptual adjustments, as both contemporary science and a consistent
theology actually require that we do, the idea of God not only becomes compatible with evolution but also logically anticipates the
kind of life-world that neo-Darwinian biology sets before us.

Such objections as Hull's notwithstanding, religion and evolution
can become the most natural of partners. During the many years I
have studied the so-called "problem" of science and religion, I
have grown increasingly convinced that a Darwinian (or, now,
"neo-Darwinian") view of nature answers to the deepest intuitions
of religion. In fact, a serious theological engagement with evolution
can bring us to a fuller and more satisfying understanding of the
many religious references to an "ultimate reality" than we might
otherwise have ever attained.

The understanding of ultimate reality that I shall be working with in
this book has been shaped primarily by my own Christian experience
of religious faith and theology. As a Roman Catholic I learned from
an early age that there can be no genuine conflict between scientific

truth and religious faith. I consider it my good fortune to have been advised throughout my life that believers in God should not look to biblical texts or religious creeds for information of a scientific nature.[6] For many Catholics and other Christians this simple instruction has been the source of both religious and intellectual liberation. By allowing us to distinguish clearly between the literal and religious senses of scripture, it implies that we do not have to place the cosmology of *Genesis* in a competitive relationship with Darwin's theory. The Bible is not trying to teach us science, but beneath and through its historically conditioned cosmological depictions it is inviting us to share a vision of ultimate reality that does not depend for its plausibility upon any particular view of nature. Throughout the past three thousand years, ideas about God have, in fact, outlived potential absorption into many different cosmologies.

Not all Christians or former Christians, of course, have found it so simple a matter to let the core teachings of faith slip out of their ancient cosmological apparel. For many, adherence to an ancient conception of nature is indispensable to the contemporary affirmation of religious doctrine. Surely, they would insist, the inerrant scriptures, of all things, would not give us a faulty picture of nature. Such anachronistic demands on the ancient texts may seem to be a distinctive mark of the religiously naive. Yet even scientific skeptics treat the Bible as a failure because it does not accurately present a "true" picture of nature. While reading sociobiologist E. O. Wilson's recent book *Consilience,* I was reminded of how deep-seated is the expectation that the Bible, if it is to live up to its reputation as the revelation of truth, should also be scientifically faultless. It was in college, Wilson says, that he first learned about evolution, and this knowledge liberated him from his former biblicist beliefs:

I had been raised a Southern Baptist, laid backward on the sturdy arm of a pastor, been born again. I knew the healing power of redemption. Faith, hope and charity were in my bones, and with millions of others I knew that my savior Jesus Christ would grant me eternal life. More pious than the average teenager, I read the Bible cover to cover, twice. But now at college, steroid-driven into moods of adolescent rebellion, I chose to doubt. I found it hard to accept that our deepest beliefs were set in stone by agricultural societies of the eastern Mediterranean more than two thousand years ago.

"Baptist theology," Wilson goes on to lament, "made no provision for evolution. The biblical authors had missed the most important revelation of all!"[7]

Especially noteworthy here is Wilson's implicit expectation that biblical authors and Baptist theologians should have been doing better *science*. And if they expected us to take them seriously, they should have done it much better than Darwin in the first place! Having apparently never shaken off the fundamentalist assumptions he brought with him to college, Wilson continues to reject biblical religion, ostensibly because it is scientifically unreliable. He puts Darwinian science into competition with biblical stories of origin, which have disappointed him by not providing a quality grade of information about the natural world. In this respect, the difference between his views and those of today's "creation scientists," therefore, is only that the latter judge the biblical accounts to be good science, whereas Wilson rejects them as inferior.

What I need to make clear at the outset is that theology does not have to share Wilson's assumption that "revelation" in science is of the same stripe as that testified to by religious believers. The two are not really comparable. Religious revelation can be encountered only by allowing oneself to be grasped by it, not by grasping it. Scientific discovery, as Wilson's writings insinuate, is a matter of our grasping hold of nature rather than of being grasped by anything. Deliberately pursuing Francis Bacon's Promethean ideal, Wilson claims that nature yields her secrets to us only if we seize her and, through the coercive powers of scientific method and technological know-how, deliver her of any pretense to mystery. Awareness of religious revelation, on the other hand, entails a sense of our being drawn into a great mystery that liberates the human spirit in a radical way from imprisonment in the mind's own sphere of competence, and in so doing places us in the clearing horizon of unending transcendence.

Theology's fundamental task, as I see it, is that of awakening us to the infinitely liberating openness and generosity of this mystery; theology should avoid enclosing discussion about God within a mundane preoccupation with "design." Contrary to what Wilson supposes, the mystery-oriented mission of theology in no way conflicts with science's effort to unfold—at its own level and according to its own distinctive method—the boundless secrets of nature. A wholesome expansion of our sense of divine mystery can exist in complete harmony with the scientific disclosure of previously hidden aspects of nature. And irrespective of continuing developments in Darwinian science's grasp of life's hitherto unmanifested intricacies, we can trust that there abides in the depths of the universe a forever fresh wellspring of novelty, unthreatened by the ongoing accumulation of scientific knowledge. It is to this faithful source of endlessly *novel* forms of life that a theology of evolution points, and to which the word "God" most appropriately refers.

In any case, the notion of God as an intelligent designer is inadequate. The God of evolution is an inexhaustible and unsettling source of *new* modes of being, forever eluding encapsulation in orderly schemata. Looking beneath the anxious quest for intelligent design, a theology of evolution seeks to highlight the disquieting—but ultimately fulfilling—presence of a promise and power of renewal that lives, in Gerard Manley Hopkins's familiar words, "deep down things." Such a theology is no threat to what Wilson speaks of as science's own work of "revelation." In fact, by envisaging a universe that satisfies science's implicit need for ever new frontiers of discovery, a theology of evolution points us toward the very soil within which science can forever find fresh nourishment.

Evolution and the Religions

Although this book is a Christian theologian's appreciation of evolutionary science, it will approach the topic with an eye to other religious outlooks as well. Since for many scientists today evolution clearly implies a meaningless universe, *all religions* must be concerned about it. Evolutionists raise questions not only about the Christian God but also about notions of ultimate reality or cosmic meaning as these are understood by many of the world's other religious traditions. If they looked closely at its contemporary scientific presentations, Jews, Muslims, Hindus, Buddhists, Jains, Taoists, native peoples, and others as well, would see that evolution is a shock to their belief systems. Almost all religions, and not just Christianity, have envisaged the cosmos as the expression of a transcending "order," "wisdom," or "rightness," rather than as an irreversibly evolving process. Most religions have held that there is some unfathomable "point" to the universe, and that the cosmos is enshrouded by a meaning over which we can have no intellectual control, and to which we must in the end surrender humbly. However, given the long, haphazard, and often cruel way in which evolution appears to work, is it still feasible for *any* of the religions to think of the universe as grounded in the ordering principle to which their ideas of ultimate reality generally point?

Sacred traditions have held consistently that the cosmos is here for a reason, even though they may not have been able to specify clearly just what this "reason" might be. Now, however, they must *all* respond to the claim made by Wilson and others that "Darwinism" has wiped away the many centuries of scientifically uninformed religious optimism. People of all faiths have to wonder whether their venerable teachings can honestly survive evolutionary portrayals of nature, humanity, ethics, and religion. The key word here is "honestly," for there is no question that religions still endure, and in some cases thrive, in most parts of the Earth. But is their persistence perhaps made too easy by a general ignorance of science and, especially, of evolution? What would religious people think about their central teachings, about the existence of a transcendent principle of meaning, or about the authority of their moral codes, if they were to become fully cognizant of evolution and the puzzling story of life that it narrates?

I think it is time for all religious communities to give these questions much more dedicated attention than they have done previously, especially now that Darwinian science is experiencing such a vigorous renewal in the contemporary intellectual world. Updated evolutionary interpretations of life, language, behavior, morality, and even religion have lately been gaining unprecedented acceptance by natural scientists, philosophers, linguists, ethicists, social scientists, and, more recently, the medical community. And so it seems both important and timely that the world's various faiths collectively and painstakingly examine just what the latest and most reliable versions of evolutionary science are telling us about life, the universe, morality, and religion itself.

Hasn't Darwin's evolutionary science placed in serious doubt the religious sense that we inhabit a meaningful universe? Or is it instead possible that what scientific skeptics often take to be the religiously ruinous consequences of Darwinian thought are in fact fresh openings to mysterious sacred depths of reality previously unfathomed? And in these depths will we find only an abyss of absurdity, or perhaps instead the sustaining presence of a truly living and renewing God, one who can command the fullness of our worship and one to whom we might still pray with love and confidence?

2

Darwin's Dangerous Idea

ACCORDING TO THE PROLIFIC AMERICAN PHILOSOPHER Daniel Dennett, Charles Darwin's theory of evolution by natural selection is a "dangerous idea." It is particularly threatening to religious believers because it wrecks any hope that the universe is here for a reason. Evolutionary science has shattered every pious illusion that life and human existence were planned from all eternity. It contradicts all the traditional religious intuitions that our universe is guided by divine wisdom and that a glorious destiny awaits it.[1]

Consequently, most of us, Dennett insinuates, will be afraid to look squarely at this "dangerous idea." Even when we think we have understood it, we probably have not really countenanced its appalling depths. Obviously theologians have not examined it closely, or else they would have abandoned their trade long ago. But, annoyingly, even many scientists carry on as though Darwin had not completely pulverized their pictures of an intelligently governed universe. Still clinging implicitly to the stories of meaning that beclouded our ignorant ancestors, some of our best naturalists, Dennett complains, refuse to face the darker implications of evolutionary science.

In laborious detail, Dennett argues that Darwin and his true followers have now demonstrated conclusively that biological evolution is an inherently meaningless process. It is only the working out of impersonal physical laws. The story of life on Earth requires nothing more than purely random genetic mutations, the deterministic laws of "natural selection," and enormous spans of time. There is no need for supernatural "skyhooks" to explain even nature's most impressive creations. The various animate forms result, one and all, from a purely mechanical kind of causation, lifting only from below.

Mathematically speaking, evolution takes place, Dennett goes on to say, in an open-ended "Design Space" comprised of all the logically possible forms of life. It meanders through "virtual" archives containing every conceivable arrangement of DNA, segments of which we call "genes." Within this "Library of Mendel" evolution toys with countless possibilities until it chances upon those that actually "work." The workable or "fit" genetic combinations are those that happen to be adaptive to their environments and thus are able, by way of the living organisms that unknowingly transport them, to survive and reproduce. Through selection of minute adaptive changes in organisms over a period of several billion years, this totally blind process can bring about all the diversity of life on our planet, including beings endowed with sight and consciousness. Even the human mind is an eventual—and perhaps inevitable—outcome of an utterly mindless sequence of physical occurrences.[2] The point is, there is no need for an "intelligent designer" to supervise the process.

This, according to Dennett, is the most "dangerous" implication of Darwin's idea, especially in its contemporary neo-Darwinian form. (Neo-Darwinism, once again, is essentially Darwin's original theory of selection, clarified and brought up-to-date by our more recent knowledge about genes and the molecular constituents of life, of which Darwin himself knew nothing.) If we had the fortitude to look closely at what this revised version of evolution tells us about life, we could have no doubt, Dennett insists, that any notion of divine influence in nature is cognitionally empty. Therefore, those biologists "who see no conflict between evolution and their religious beliefs" are refusing to face incontestable scientific facts.[3] If they took evolution seriously, they would see clearly that the natural world does not conform to humanity's traditional mythic, religious, or philosophical depictions. The cosmos in no sense bears the inscription of a cosmic orderer. If evolution has any message at all, it is that the universe is devoid of any message. The cosmos as a whole has no explanation—it "just is"—nor does the stream of life that accidentally appears and evolves within it. And nothing has ever "planned" for our own existence, either.

Hailed by Marvin Minsky as "our best current philosopher" and the "next Bertrand Russell," Dennett clearly holds a position of respect among contemporary American thinkers.[4] Even though many other scientists and intellectuals quietly share his reading of evolutionary science, Dennett's voice seems much louder than most others. He clearly relishes exhibiting what he takes to be the atheistic underside of Darwin's revolution. The sheer vehemence of his writing almost forces one to pay attention. For our purposes, his work has the advantage of spotlighting some of the suspicions that many other evolutionary biologists harbor but are usually reluctant to flash so publicly.

Dennett's depiction of evolution follows closely that of the well-known British zoologist Richard Dawkins. In *The Blind Watchmaker* and, more recently, in *River Out of Eden* and *Climbing Mount Improbable* Dawkins has argued that blind chance and natural selection working over long periods of time can account for life's creativity all by themselves.[5] The fundamental players in the game of life are not individual organisms or populations of organisms, as some Darwinians have held. Rather they are genes, coded segments of DNA. Evolution is primarily about "selfish" genes "trying" to survive, and only secondarily about the organisms and populations by which they perpetuate themselves. According to Dawkins, it is the nature of genes to maximize opportunities for survival and reproduction. Genes are driven by an impersonal physical necessity to secure their immortality, so they fashion to themselves individual organisms and a diverse array of species to function as "vehicles" that will carry them on to future generations. Even if it means invading innocent organisms and exploiting these in devious and destructive ways, the "selfish" genes must do all they can to endure indefinitely. It is this blind necessity, in combination with random genetic variations, that carries evolution along and allows it to execute all of its apparent magic.

Such a picture, Dawkins readily admits, "is not a recipe for happiness. So long as DNA is passed on, it does not matter who or what gets hurt in the process. It is better for the genes of Darwin's ichneumon wasp that the caterpillar should be alive, and therefore fresh, when it is eaten, no matter what the cost in suffering. Genes don't care about suffering, because they don't care about anything."[6] Maximization of the "utility function" of *DNA survival* can account for all the outcomes of evolution.[7] Life, therefore, has no need for an intelligent designer to provide it with its various profiles. The same impersonal momentum that rules atoms and stars also governs the selfish genetic units of evolution. Genes will seek to survive at all costs, and by whatever means available. They will even invent intelligent beings as vehicles to carry them on, unknowingly, to subsequent generations.

According to Dawkins, atheism has found in Darwin's ideas the firmest intellectual foundation it has ever had.[8] And Dennett fully agrees. He flaunts the gene's-eye interpretation of Darwinian selection as the definitive "scientific" refutation of theology. In this respect his work is an obvious challenge to all of us who are happy to accept modern science but who continue to embrace a religious vision of the universe. Ever since Darwin, of course, scientifically educated religious thinkers, especially the many who never interpreted their scriptures too literally in the first place, have talked approvingly, and at times even lyrically, about evolution. But have they ever looked closely at evolution's most "dangerous" features? If they had done so, Dennett claims, their theology could never have endured.

As I have already noted, Dennett's is by no means a lone voice. William Provine, a Cornell professor of scientific history who comes closer even than Dawkins and Dennett to equating evolution with atheism, allows that, prior to the "modern synthesis" of Darwinism and genetics, theological interpretations of evolution may have seemed plausible. But once science became aware of the imperial role of genes and molecular structures in the story of life, no room remained anywhere for the work of an ordering deity. Consequently, those evolutionary scientists who continue to think they can find room for God alongside of natural science must "check their brains at the church-house door."[9]

Dennett and Dawkins in particular have given fresh verbalization to a position that is by no means new, and so there has been no lack of response to it. Some rebuttals have taken the approach of insisting that Darwinian ideas are simply wrong, whereas others have looked for ways of rehabilitating the old arguments for intelligent design in spite of Darwinian complications. I believe, though, that such theological strategies are generally misdirected and apologetically fruitless. My own preference is to concede from the outset the general integrity of Darwinian *science* (which I would distinguish carefully from the materialist ideology in which it is often packaged). Certainly Darwinian ideas are not perfect. That evolutionary theory will continue to undergo revision, I have no doubt. Even today there is some discontent with neo-Darwinism in the scientific community. But out of respect for the thinking of most contemporary scientific experts, and especially the majority of biologists, in this book I shall take Darwin's version to be a reasonably close, though incomplete and abstract, approximation of the way life has developed on Earth.

In its conversations with science, theology should, I think, deal with all the untidiness of the Darwinian picture of life and not work with cleanly edited versions of it. For this reason I have chosen here to focus on the rather extreme views of Dawkins and Dennett. It is true, of course, that many biologists would themselves insist that these two neo-Darwinians exaggerate the role of genes and adaptation in the evolutionary construction of the forms of life. Both authors, I would also agree, have produced cleverly written books that make evolution look much simpler than it really is, and they do not by any means speak for all mainstream scientists. Nevertheless, even if their renditions of Darwinism are one-sided, they highlight aspects of evolution—especially its apparent randomness, blind experimentation, and impersonality—that are present at least to some degree in most other contemporary scientific renderings of the story of life. It is just these troublesome features that a theology in conversation with science must address today, and more carefully than it has done previously. Moreover, theology must grapple with the more extreme Darwinist interpretations simply because of their high public visibility and the shrillness of their assaults on the notion of God. For theologians simply to ignore these voices could be construed as an implicit submission to the apparent "deathblow" that Dawkins and Dennett think Darwin's science has dealt to religion.

The Sufficiency of Darwinism?

Has it, then, been conclusively established that Darwinian evolution rules out the existence of God? Is evolution inconsistent with the sense of cosmic purpose posited by many religions? Is the evolution of the universe and of life determined solely by a blind and mindless set of mathematical rules? Does the impersonal notion of "natural selection" provide us with a *sufficient* explanation of life's creativity? Is there no discernible directionality to evolution? Does evolutionary science adequately explain human existence, our place in the universe, and the reasons for our moral and religious behavior? Does neo-Darwinian biology give us the "ultimate" explanation of life?

If we listen to Dawkins and Dennett, we are led to believe that Darwin's scientific legacy provides so total an account of life that it removes any need for appeal to theological explanation *at any level* of understanding. Religious faith's intuition that a mysterious but infinitely intelligent creativity underlies biological process is now considered unacceptable, not so much because we can prove it is not there, but because science has apparently shown it to be superfluous. Before Darwin there may well have been logically sound reasons for invoking the idea of a divine designer, as even Dawkins agrees. But after Darwin it appears that blind natural selection deployed over the course of immense epochs of time is enough to account for the adaptive order in living beings, including the physiological complexity underlying human consciousness and behavior. Why seek multiple and complex explanations when a single, simple explanation—the Darwinian one—suffices? Why appeal to an "extraneous" divine causation if nature can so autonomously create itself, and if science can now tell us precisely how?

Evolutionary theory, at least to the scientific thinkers I have been considering here, provides a comprehensive account of life, of mind, and—especially in Wilson's writings—of morality and religion as well. Theology, therefore, even if it still gives comfort to the scientifically ignorant, must appear cognitionally inane to those who take Darwin's science seriously, especially the experts in our universities. "At least in the eyes of academics," Dennett contends, "science has won and religion has lost. Darwin's idea has banished the Book of Genesis to the limbo of quaint mythology."[10]

Adequately understanding evolution, according to Dennett, requires an uncompromising naturalism, the view that nature is all there is and that any talk of supernatural guidance or intervention is superfluous. What need is there for God if nature, when given enough time, can do the work of designing life all by itself? In his revolutionary book *On the Origin of Species*, Charles Darwin had already portrayed natural selection as a pitiless but nonetheless effective engineer of life's creations. Although he was for a time perhaps somewhat tormented by his findings, Darwin eventually arrived at the conclusion that the older theological notion of "creation by design" no longer had explanatory serviceability. Nature allows only those organisms to survive and reproduce that *by sheer chance* happen to possess physical variations more adaptive than "weaker" ones. In evolution, the feeble lose out and the reproductively fit survive. Mindless though the process may be, it has seemed to Darwin and many of his followers quite sufficient to account for the many kinds of life. Thus, the notion of an ordering and creative "God" loses out to a more elegant and parsimonious explanation.

Genetics and molecular biology have by now brought Darwin's "dangerous idea" into even sharper focus. Although the essentials of his vision may have been a good start for evolutionary science, they do not go far enough on their own. Darwin knew nothing about DNA or genes, and so he could understand evolutionary selection only in terms of organisms and populations. But for many evolutionary scientists today, the capacity of some organisms to survive and reproduce in any given environment can be explained more exactly if we also take into account the changes in gene frequencies within a given population. The neo-Darwinian joining of genetic knowledge to the implacably rigid law of natural selection is what biologists usually have in mind today when they refer to the "Darwinian" picture of nature. Thus, unless otherwise indicated, I shall follow the contemporary scientific practice of using Darwin's name in these pages as shorthand for what is now known more technically as the "neo-Darwinian synthesis."

In any case, the latest versions of Darwinism may seem even more religiously lethal than the master's original. According to Darwinian science, some individuals or groups in any given population of organisms can adapt to the challenges of their environment more readily than others. Out of this inequality, nature selects those whose genotypes are the most "fit," in the sense of possessing the highest probability of surviving and reproducing. Since only a few organisms will prove to be "fit" in this reproductive sense, nature will ruthlessly eliminate all the others. Mindless though this mechanism is, it appears to have been enough to bring about all the rich diversity and complexity we see in the fossil record and in living species today. And so, if nature is in this sense so *self*-creative, where is the need for a transcendent intelligence to act or intervene in evolution? Hasn't Darwin demonstrated that nature is inventive enough on its own, in need of no extrinsic "supernatural" support or ordering principle?

Whether in textbooks or philosophical essays on evolution, it is becoming increasingly routine for biologists to claim that all the diverse phenomena of the life-world can be explained in sufficient depth through the purely naturalistic concepts of evolutionary science. For example, in his latest book the revered Harvard zoologist Ernst Mayr repeatedly refers to neo-Darwinian science as the "ultimate" explanation of life.[11] Much earlier Gavin de Beer, in a major article in the *Encyclopedia Britannica,* where one might have expected more neutrality, even argued that Darwinism emphatically rules out the idea of God. "Darwin," his article concluded, "did two things: He showed that evolution was a fact contradicting scriptural legends of creation and that its cause, natural selection, was automatic *with no room for divine guidance or design.*"[12]

In a lucid summary of the Darwinian revolution, the noted biologist Francisco J. Ayala—who has, incidentally, authored the article on evolution in the current version of the same encyclopedia—also states that evolutionary science "excludes" the influence of God. If he had said explicitly that evolutionary science *methodologically* excludes any reference to God, there would be nothing controversial about such a statement. But Ayala writes that "it was Darwin's greatest accomplishment to show that the directive organization of living beings can be explained as the result of a natural process, natural selection, without any need to resort to a creator or other external agent. The origin and adaptation of organisms in their profusion and wondrous variations were thus brought into the realm of science."[13] If we take Ayala literally here, his wording can seem to imply that an adequate understanding of life has no need for any additional, nonscientific explanations. After Darwin, Ayala writes,

> the origin and adaptive nature of organisms could now be explained like the phenomena of the inanimate world, as the result of natural laws manifested in natural processes. Darwin's theory encountered opposition in religious circles, not so much because he proposed the evolutionary origin of living things (which had been proposed many times before, even by Christian theologians), but because his mechanism, natural selection, *excluded* God as accounting for the obvious design of organisms.[14]

Does this mean, then, that the concept of God can have no explanatory value at all as far as the evolution of life and its diverse patterns are concerned? It is not entirely clear, at least from the wording here, whether Ayala would allow for or exclude theological explanation at some other level of understanding. But at the end of his essay he gives at least the appearance of subscribing to a purely naturalistic account of evolution: "This is the conceptual revolution that Darwin completed—that everything in nature, including the origin of living organisms, can be explained by material processes governed by natural laws. This is nothing if not a fundamental vision that has forever changed how mankind perceives itself and its place in the universe."[15]

If Darwin had merely changed our understanding of life, this would itself have been compelling enough. But apparently, according to Ayala's understanding, the Darwinian revolution has gone much further than this: It has altered once and for all our standards of what should count as *adequate* explanation of life. Copernicus and other scientists had shown already that blind mechanical causation is sufficient to understand inanimate nature, but before Darwin we had been reluctant to apply the impersonal methods of science to the realm of living beings. Now we should know better. To understand life there is no need ever again to fall back on regressive religious explanations. Science alone suffices.

Contingency, Law, and Time

Many biologists now share the view that Darwinian science leaves no room at all for theological attempts at explanation. Apparently only three ingredients are needed for evolution to cook up the wide diversity of living beings: first, accidental, random, or *contingent* occurrences. These include, for example, the highly improbable chemical coincidences required for the very origin of life, the chance genetic mutations that make possible the diversification of life, and many other unpredictable events in natural history that shape the course of evolution (for instance, ice ages, volcanic eruptions, plate movements of the Earth, asteroid impacts, or the influence on populations by famines, earthquakes, floods, etc.). The second generic constituent of evolution is the determinism or so-called *necessity* implied in the "law" of natural selection and in the inflexible dictates of chemistry and physics that pertain throughout the universe. These remorseless rules lay out the boundaries within which life's contingencies can occur. They thicken what would be too thin a stew if evolution were only a matter of chance events. Lawfulness "constrains" randomness, placing it within limits, thus contributing order and consistency to life. Third and finally, biological evolution requires a stupendous span of *time*. Without a vast amount of temporal duration the many improbable products of evolution could never have come about. In the absence of an intelligent designer, after all, an enormous expanse of time is required to provide ample scope for the accidental emergence of those few genetic combinations that will permit survivable evolutionary outcomes.

According to many influential neo-Darwinians, the mixing and brewing of elements and occurrences bearing these three features— let us call them contingency, law, and time—are sufficient to account for the entire evolutionary stew. What explanatory enhancement, then, could religion or theology possibly add to this most economical of recipes?

The Problem of Suffering

Before I undertake in subsequent chapters a theological response to claims about Darwinian science's explanatory adequacy, I should take more careful notice of evolution's insensitivity to the pain of living beings, a fact that also seems logically incompatible with belief in the compassionate God to which many religions refer. "If Nature were kind," Dawkins writes, "she would at least make the minor concession of anaesthetizing caterpillars before they are eaten alive from within." Instead, he continues, "nature is neither kind nor unkind. She is neither against suffering nor for it. Nature is not interested one way or the other in suffering, unless it affects the survival of DNA.... The universe we observe has precisely the properties we should expect if there is, at bottom, no design, no purpose, no evil and no good, nothing but blind, pitiless indifference."[16]

Darwin, then, has done nothing to quiet the powerful complaint sensitive people have always aimed at the idea of God. How could a powerful and compassionate creator permit all the suffering, aimless wandering, and obscene waste that we behold in surveying the millennia of evolution? How could a lovingly concerned God tolerate the struggle, pain, cruelty, brutality, and death that lie beneath the relatively stable and serene surface of nature's present order?

Previous ages were not unaware of suffering, of course, but they had no sense of the millions of years of it that Darwin and his scientific progeny have uncovered, and which many of us have still not integrated fully into our benign cosmic visions. It is instructive, then, to feel the anguish of one whose religious feelings have been wounded so deeply by the Darwinian picture of life that belief in God is no longer an option:

Could an Almighty God of love have designed, foreseen, planned, and created a system whose law is a ruthless struggle for existence in an overcrowded world? Could an omnipotent, omniscient, and omnibenevolent God have devised such a cold-blooded competition of beast with beast, beast with man, man with man, species with species, in which the clever, the cunning, and the cruel survive?

How could a loving God have planned a cruel system in which sensitive living creatures must either eat other sensitive living creatures or be eaten themselves, thereby causing untold suffering among these creatures? Would a benevolent God have created animals to devour others when he could have designed them all as vegetarians? What kind of deity would have designed the beaks which rip sensitive flesh? What God would intend every leaf, blade of grass, and drop of water to be a battle ground in which living organisms pursue, capture, kill, and eat one another? What God would design creatures to prey upon one another and, at the same time, instill into such creatures a capacity for intense pain and suffering?[17]

These are the words of a former Christian clergyman who eventually came to be persuaded by Darwinian evolution that atheism is really the only honest response one can make to it. I could cite many such testimonies, and there can be no doubt that similar sentiments have at least occasionally crossed the minds of more than a few scientifically educated religious believers. Evolution not only threatens to make divine creativity an intellectually superfluous idea but also challenges us to confront more deliberately than ever the most intractable question of every age: How can we make sense of the universe, given the facts of suffering and eventual death? In a century that has witnessed the Holocaust, widespread warfare, genocides, political purges, and the prospect of ecological catastrophe, evolutionary science is hardly going to add much to what is already the most pestilent of all human and religious concerns, the problem of innocent suffering. However, even if it fails to deepen the wound, evolution clearly seems to widen it.

It is true that evolution is not just about competition and wasteful struggle. Evolution is also, as we are now beginning to realize more clearly, a story of cooperation among many diverse layers of organisms. Moreover, there is an inspiring beauty in the life-story that we can overlook easily if we focus only on the vulnerability of living beings to pain and death. Nevertheless, Darwin has extended the story of life's innocent suffering considerably, leading us down pathways of pain and bloodletting that stretch back through many millions of years. His "dangerous idea" has uncovered regions of terror and torture that we had never known about before. The picture of life he left us only fuels our perennial religious revolt against what seems to be God's indulgence of undeserved agony. By expanding the horizons of life's travail, Darwin gives unprecedented breadth to our sense of the tragic. His disquieting account of evolution intensifies our outrage at suffering and only adds to our consternation at the silence of God.

Nevertheless, as I shall argue in the following chapters, Darwin's challenge turns out to be a great gift to theology. It spreads out before us a panorama of life that can pilot us away from cheap and easy representations of the sacred such as that implied in a one-sided commitment to the notion of "intelligent design." The story told by evolutionary science may frighten us or confuse us, but we cannot deny what Darwin referred to justifiably as the "grandeur" of its vision. Those who prefer simple stories with fairy-tale endings will not relish the new narrative of life's troubled but creative journey here on Earth. If they are pious they may plug up their ears when scientists speak. And if they are skeptics, such as Dawkins and Dennett, they will flourish the facts of evolution before us as the definitive proof of religion's intellectual emptiness. But we shall see that Darwin's portrayal of the way the universe works actually invites us to think about God, once again, in a meaningful and truly inspiriting way.

3

Theology Since Darwin

ALTHOUGH DARWIN'S SCIENCE HAS YET to penetrate very far into the world's religious thought, at least some theological reflection during the last century and a half has grappled with the idea of evolution in one way or another. My sense, though, is that previous encounters of theology with evolution are still largely invisible to nontheologians, and uninteresting or irrelevant to most theologians. Little serious discussion of Darwin and theology—aside from the well-known fundamentalist condemnations of evolution—makes its way into the media or into church on Sundays. And in academic conversations with colleagues in the natural sciences, I have found that the notion of a "theology of evolution" is still completely foreign to the majority of them. Consequently, my attempt in these pages to provide the rudiments of such a theology should begin with at least a sketch of what has been accomplished already. What are the main ways in which religious thought has already greeted Darwin's science? I shall address this question here not by tracing the largely ignored history of evolutionary theology—which is too complex and diversified for us to cover here—but by setting forth three distinct and recurrent ways in which religious thinkers have been responding to Darwin.

It is important to note first, however, that Darwin gives us not one but two religiously "dangerous" ideas. The first is that all living beings share a common ancestry and are therefore historically and organically interconnected. This vision of a continuum of life seems to challenge the traditional religious sense of sharp ontological discontinuity between humans and the rest of nature. Evolution blurs the lines separating what we used to think of as distinct levels of being, making it more difficult than before to distinguish human from animal, and living from the nonliving. In Chapter 5 I shall say more about the apparent "danger" Darwinism poses to the traditional hierarchical way of understanding the universe. For now, I would note only that although the idea of an evolutionary continuum—today reinforced by the science of genetics—is disturbing to a certain kind of religious sensitivity, to many other religious believers it is a beautiful idea, confirming the biblical sense of the unity of creation and the interrelatedness of all members of the Earth community.

Darwin's second "dangerous" idea is his theory of natural selection, and for many it poses a much weightier challenge to classical theology than does that of common descent. Let us recall that according to standard evolutionary theory some organisms, by sheer chance, are better adapted to their surroundings than others. Those more suitably adapted obviously have a higher probability of surviving and producing offspring, and so nature "selects" only the reproductively fit, eliminating all other contenders. Accordingly, over the course of a very long period of time the natural selection of variations favorable to survival and reproduction brings about a wide diversity of species, including primates, among whom the human species now finds its own biological classification.

It should not be difficult to see why the theory of natural selection is so theologically troubling. For one thing, the variations that constitute the raw material for selection are said to be completely random, that is, undirected by any intelligent agency: This accidental or "contingent" aspect of evolution suggests that the universe is not governed by a divine providential intelligence after all. Next, the competitive "struggle" in which the weak (the reproductively unfit) are so ruthlessly eliminated reveals a universe apparently untended by divine compassion. And finally, the disinterested way in which natural selection works—Dennett refers to it as "algorithmic"— evokes the suspicion that we live in a remorselessly impersonal universe, hardly one residing in the bosom of a personal deity.

How then has theology greeted the difficulties posed by natural selection? I have found it convenient to organize its responses into three distinct types: *opposition, separatism,* and *engagement.* The first *(opposition)* holds, predictably, that theology is irreconcilable with Darwinian science. The second *(separatism)* argues that theology and evolutionary science differ so radically in their methods that they can neither compete nor logically conflict with each other. A third response *(engagement)* maintains that, on the contrary, theology cannot remain innocently unaffected by Darwinian biology, and that Darwin's "idea" is not so much a danger as a great gift to theology. Evolution, according to this third approach, even awakens in theology a fresh way of thinking about the central claims of traditional theistic faith. Let us examine each of these three responses more closely.

Opposition

Within the opposition camp we find several viewpoints, unanimous in their claim that theology and neo-Darwinian science are irreconcilable but mutually antagonistic in their assessment of which of these two options provides an *ultimate* explanation of the life-world.

Scientific Materialism

First, there are the "scientific materialists" represented in this book primarily by Dawkins and Dennett. Obviously theirs is an antitheological stance, but we can include it here because in seeing a conflict between Darwin and theism they concur with much religious sentiment today. As I have already noted, they claim that the Darwinian picture of life clearly renders any appeal to the idea of God indefensible. Darwin's notion of natural selection has now made "intelligent design," so dear to many theists, completely superfluous as far as any substantive explanation of life is concerned. William Paley's famous divine watchmaker has been replaced by the "blind watchmaker": natural selection.[1]

The two skeptics I have mentioned are by no means alone in rendering this judgment. The acclaimed Harvard paleontologist Stephen Jay Gould would seem to agree, although he is not the outspoken and hostile critic of religion and theology that Dawkins and Dennett are. He even states at times that religion and science do not conflict (although in order to do so he must first reduce "religion" to ethics). Nevertheless, it inevitably follows from the logic of Gould's position that Darwinism is antithetical to the most fundamental tenets of theistic faiths. Throughout his career Gould has argued that it is not Darwin's science as such that makes it so difficult for people in the West to accept it. Rather, he says, it is the unsettling "philosophical message" that comes along with Darwin's theory. This message is that life has no direction, that there is no purpose to the universe, and that matter is "all there is."[2] Nowhere in his voluminous writings, at least to my knowledge, does Gould ever allow that this "philosophical message" may in principle be disengaged from Darwin's scientific ideas. For Gould as well as for Dawkins and Dennett, then, only a materialist philosophy of nature can make appropriate sense of evolution.

However, if the ideology of materialism, with its inherent connotation of cosmic purposelessness, is indeed *inseparable* from the "science" of evolution, then Gould would also, logically speaking, have to agree that every possible brand of theism, and not just fundamentalist Christianity, is incompatible with evolution. For although theology can accommodate many different scientific ideas, it cannot get along with the notion of an inherently purposeless cosmos such as that entailed by the metaphysical materialism that Gould considers to be inalienable from Darwin's scientific ideas. No conceivable theology, by definition, could ever live comfortably with evolution if Gould's claim is correct that Darwin's theory inevitably entails a cosmos devoid of directionality and overall significance.[3]

Gould and other evolutionists have found apparent support for their association of evolution with cosmic pessimism in Darwin's own account of his gradual drift away from traditional theism as the result of long brooding over his discoveries. In his autobiography, Darwin had written that "disbelief crept over me at a very slow rate, but was at last complete. The rate was so slow that I felt no distress, and have never since doubted for a single second that my conclusion was correct."[4] To some contemporary neo-Darwinians such "disbelief" seems to be the most reasonable way in which to contextualize evolutionary science philosophically.

Creationism

Lying uncomfortably but nevertheless logically within the same king-sized bed (opposition) with the scientific skeptics are the so-called "creationists." These are predominantly Christian theists who agree with the skeptics that Darwinian evolution, if true, would logically rule out the idea of God and a purposeful universe. The difference is that they consider Darwinian biology to be completely fallacious. To creationists, contemporary evolutionary biology is much more than an innocuous set of scientific ideas devoid of theological implications. Neo-Darwinism, they concur with Gould, does clearly carry a "philosophical message," namely, atheism; and so it must be vigorously contested.

Moreover, the creationists often insist that Darwinian theory should be banished from public school education unless biblical creationism is simultaneously offered to students of biology as an alternative. The so-called "scientific creationists" propose that even on purely scientific grounds the biblical creation stories are superior to Darwin's. Evolution, they claim, is "merely a theory" inadequately supported by empirical evidence. When we observe the lack of transitional forms in the fossil record, for example, Darwin's gradualist theory does not stand up to the Bible's account of the fixity of species. The more plausible explanation of life is the theory of "special creation" by God.[5]

Phillip Johnson

Finally, brief mention should be made here of another prominent partisan of the "opposition" approach, namely, Phillip Johnson. A Berkeley law professor and born-again Christian, Johnson takes neo-Darwinism to be essentially a cultural weapon in modern secularism's warfare against religion.[6] Johnson would deny that he is a biblical literalist or a scientific creationist, and he admits the competency of science in areas other than that of neo-Darwinian biology. But he agrees with Gould that neo-Darwinism is soddened with the metaphysics of "naturalism," the view that nature is all there is and that the idea of God or the sacred is fictitious. By accepting contemporary evolutionary biology, he argues, one becomes locked into an inherently antitheistic position. Johnson is even grateful to the skeptics for their forthright admission that neo-Darwinism entails a radically materialist ideology. Gould's open admission that Darwinism brings with it the "philosophical message" of materialism and purposelessness simply confirms Johnson's claim that evolution is a subterfuge for atheistic propaganda.

If the alliance of Darwinism with atheism is insuperable, then of course any "evolutionary theology," such as the one I shall develop in subsequent chapters, would be an egregious compromise with atheism. As far as Johnson is concerned, any alliance of Darwinian science with religious truth-claims is a contradiction in terms, and proponents of evolutionary theology should understand that they too are really enemies of genuine religious faith. It is interesting to note in passing that Johnson has been eagerly adopted as an authoritative spokesperson by some political and religious neo-conservatives today who—often for other than purely scientific reasons—reject aspects of evolutionary science. To them neo-Darwinism is nothing more than just another flank in modernity's march against traditional cultural and religious values.[7]

Separatism

A second species of theological response to the Darwinian challenge seeks to save both evolutionary science and theology by rigorously and consistently insulating them against any close encounter with each other. "Separatism" claims that science as such is self-consciously limited to dealing with questions about the physical or mechanical causes of events, whereas theology, by definition, is more concerned with questions about the meaning and ultimate explanation of things. And since evolutionary theory is supposed to be scientific in nature, it should in principle pose no more threat to theology than do any other areas of science.

Science, by it very nature, methodologically restricts itself to non-theistic explanation. So any inferences from evolutionary biology that the universe is purposeless or Godless cannot possibly be categorized as scientific. Science deliberately allows itself from the outset to be denuded of any sensors that could detect signals of the divine even if they are present. And so, because there can be no real competition between evolutionary science and religion there can be no conflict between them either. The separatist is also a "compatibilist."

Because it seems so logically crisp and clean, the separatist approach appeals to many theologians and scientists. Apparently it allows the substance of theism to remain untouched by Darwin, and at the same time it forbids religion and theology to intrude into the business of science. However, one might protest immediately, can religious thought remain so utterly unaffected by evolution? Do not the randomness, struggle, and impersonality of the evolutionary process decisively refute theism, as the scientific skeptics have argued? Can we separate our theological convictions so cavalierly from what seem to be the spiritually devastating implications of evolutionary science?

A typically "separatist" response to such an objection would go something like this: First, "chance," "randomness," or "accident" (in genetic mutations and other contingencies of natural history) do not imply a Godless universe. These are simply terms we use to name events that are humanly and scientifically unintelligible, but that may still make good sense from the point of view of God's wider vision and wisdom. There is no need, then, to be disturbed by the evolutionist's inability to see the deeper meaning of life's contingent events, especially since science self-consciously limits itself to looking at things only in their empirical setting. And to insist that the scientific framework provides the only acceptable standard by which to measure the world's intelligibility, as the scientific skeptics do, is not itself a scientific claim, but one rooted arbitrarily in narrow-minded ideology.

Second, the separatist theologian would go on to argue that the struggle and suffering in evolution are not at all inconsistent with the existence of God. Indeed these experiences are quite compatible with the idea of a God who creates a world in which both life and humanity can thrive. If nature were in every sense benign and devoid of obstructions, after all, living beings would never evolve at all. Life must be continually presented with challenges that provoke it to go beyond any given status. Life needs obstacles precisely in order to affirm itself, and so to remain alive. For life to evolve, perhaps the prospect of suffering and even death is essential. Therefore, we can surmise plausibly that the evolutionary terrain described by Darwinian science is as good an ambience for the nourishing of life and the building of "soul" in humans as we could possibly imagine. Once again, there is no contradiction between Darwin and belief in God.

In his provocative book *The Seven Mysteries of Life*,[8] science writer Guy Murchie invites those who doubt that the evolutionary environment provided by our planet is an ideal "soul school" to experiment with the following hypothesis:

> Try to imagine that you are God. This may not come naturally to you. To be God of course you have to be a creator. And a creator, by definition, must create. So you, the creator, now find yourself creating creatures (a word meaning created beings) who have to have a world to live in. But what kind of world should they live in? Or, specifically, what kind of world will you decide to create for them?

Then Murchie asks us to "take a good look at Earth." We shall find there, he says, the most "educational" of any conceivable environment. Earth, of course, is teeming with all sorts of life: "Creatures are not only walking, creeping and slithering all over the land, but burrowing under it, climbing the trees above it, swimming in the seas around it, flying through the air, even dwelling invisibly within each other, trying out ... every imaginable mode of locomotion, of communication, of preying, eating, sheltering, and propagating their kind." Such an environment, Murchie says, is one that is also rife with "heartrending struggles with adversity" and, for humans, "social uncertainty." Nonetheless, Earth's evolutionary environment "excels in educating the spirit." It is "far and away the top-ranking Soul School available."

> Honestly now, if you were God, could you possibly dream up any more educational, contrasty, thrilling, beautiful, tantalizing world than Earth to develop spirit in? If you think you could, do you imagine you would be outdoing Earth if you designed a world free of germs, diseases, poisons, pain, malice, explosives and conflicts so its people could relax and enjoy it? Would you, in other words, try to make the world nice and safe—or would you let it be provocative, dangerous and exciting? In actual fact, if it ever came to that, I'm sure you would find it impossible to make a better world than God has already created.

Consequently, we are not compelled to envisage any real conflict between evolution and theology.

Third and finally, the separatist would insist that the apparently impersonal "law" of natural selection is no more theologically problematic than the laws of physics. The force of gravity pulls toward Earth both the strong and the weak, sometimes in a hurtful or fatal way; yet few have pointed to the law of gravity as an obstacle to theistic faith. Instead of ruling out a personal God, gravity's unswerving habituality can be interpreted just as easily as evidence of the non-capriciousness and fidelity of God.[9] Perhaps, then, theology can greet the invariant workings of natural selection no less politely than it does other laws essential for nature's consistency and intelligibility.

It is especially in the neo-orthodox and existentialist religious thought of the present century that we find the separatist distancing of Darwin from any close contact with theology.[10] We should not underestimate the appeal this approach has to many theologians and scientifically educated religious believers. By prohibiting any fusion of science with theology, the separatist approach has the advantage of interrupting the antagonism that occurs inevitably when we allow religious texts to serve as sources of scientific information, or when scientists carelessly overlay scientific ideas with materialist and other metaphysical assumptions.

Whatever its weaknesses may be—and the "engagement" position discussed below will point these out—the separatist approach provides an important rejoinder to all three representatives of the "opposition" standpoint described above. Separatists show clearly that the creationists, the scientific skeptics, and Phillip Johnson, all in their own ways, carelessly tolerate a simplistic conflation of science with ideological assumptions, whether these assumptions be religious or materialistic. It is just this melding of science with belief, rather than any inherent contradiction between science and religion, that lies at the root of the apparent sense of discord between theology and neo-Darwinism.

Let me clarify. Unfortunately, the scientific creationists, to take my first example, merge science with religion by situating the biblical creation stories alongside Darwinian evolutionary theory as a competing set of scientific ideas. To a rigorous separatist, such fusion of science with scripture not only threatens the integrity of science; what is worse, it also trivializes religion by placing sacred writings in the same genre as mundane scientific discourse. Ironically, the allegedly "literal" meaning that creationists find absolutely authoritative in the biblical creation stories is tacitly overlaid with a modern and nonbiblical requirement that all forms of truth should abide by scientific standards. Even though the relevant biblical texts were all composed in a prescientific age, before modern scientific method was even conceivable, the creationist—who is allegedly trying to be utterly "faithful to the text"—has already contaminated it with extraneous epistemological assumptions more characteristic of despised modernity than of idealized religious antiquity.

To turn now to my second example, the evolutionary materialists are no less guilty of commingling science with metaphysical belief than are the creationists. By coupling evolutionary science to the assumption that only mindless matter is truly real, Dawkins, Gould, Wilson, Provine, and Dennett transform neo-Darwinian science into an ideological alloy that, as Phillip Johnson rightly points out, is quite at odds with *all* versions of theism. The more cautious separatist position, on the other hand, objects to *any* wedding of science and belief, including belief in materialist metaphysics. So there can be no genuine conflict between theism and the *science* of evolution. Conflict lies only between theism and the gratuitous ideological coating painted over the scientific data by scientists and philosophers who already happen to have personal leanings toward materialist metaphysics.

At first it might seem, then, that Phillip Johnson escapes the separatist critique since he also apparently wants to distinguish science from "scientific naturalism." But in spite of his overt repudiation of materialist evolutionism, he ends up yielding to its proponents; for by refusing to let scientists separate evolutionary ideas from the materialist spin that scientific skeptics such as Gould put on them, he ironically ends up tolerating the very position he is trying to refute. Johnson, as we have seen, condemns what he calls "evolutionary theism" because he cannot see how anyone could conceivably distinguish Darwinian ideas from pure materialism. But in doing so he implicitly endorses as inevitable the conflation of science and belief characteristic of his adversaries. By maintaining dogmatically that neo-Darwinism is inseparable from materialism, he becomes in effect the ally of evolutionary materialists. As a matter of fact, however, both biologists and theologians (as we shall see later) can now easily and clearly distinguish evolutionary science from any materialistic overtones. By conceding Gould's and Dennett's claims that Darwin's ideas are theologically dangerous, Johnson merely adds fuel to his opponents' fire.

According to the separatists, Darwin's ideas would be dangerous only if we agreed with Dennett and Gould that they are inseparable from philosophical materialism. But there is absolutely no reason why evolutionary science cannot be methodologically naturalistic—following the proper decision of all science to leave out any appeal to nonnatural explanations—without being metaphysically materialistic. From the separatist point of view, Johnson unfortunately perpetuates the appearance of conflict by not allowing scientists and theologians to make such a distinction in the case of evolution.

Engagement

Even though the "separatists" have no objections to neo-Darwinian science as long as its followers stay out of metaphysics, their theological method holds evolution at arm's length. Separatism provides an essential moment of clarification, perhaps, but it does not give us an evolutionary theology. It tolerates evolution but does not celebrate it. A third family of theological responses to Darwin, on the other hand, after accepting the separatists' clear distinction of science from ideology, argues for the "engagement" of evolutionary science and theology. It refuses to hold Darwin's supposedly "dangerous idea" apart from theological understanding, but instead takes evolution into the very center of its reflections on the meaning of life, of God, and of the universe.

Generally speaking, Darwin's impact on this adventurous theology has been twofold. It has caused a noticeable shift in the character of "natural theology," an approach that looks for evidence of God in the natural world. And it has stimulated the emergence of what we may call "evolutionary theology," a radical reinterpretation of classic religious teachings in terms of Darwinian concepts. I shall say only a brief word about the first, and then go on to treat the second at more length.

Post-Darwinian Natural Theology

Before Darwin, as even Dawkins agrees, the best explanation for the ordered and adaptive features of living organisms seemed to be that of divine "intelligent design," the position William Paley made famous in his watchmaker analogy.[11] Suppose that while walking across a patch of ground you stumble across a watch. Upon opening up the timepiece and examining its interior structure, Paley observed, you would undoubtedly conclude that it was purposefully designed. Analogously you should be able to understand that the even more intricate design in living organisms must also point toward creation by an intelligent designer, the One whom theists readily identify as the creator God of biblical religion.

However, Darwin seems to have provided an adequate explanation of the design in living beings without resorting to theology at all. Natural selection of random variations, now called mutations, can explain life's "design," that is, if you just give it enough time. And scientists today think that life originated as long as 3.8 billion years ago, leaving more than enough opportunity for the seemingly improbable design in living beings to come about gradually in a purely naturalistic way. So the story of life does not require any special ad hoc interventions of the supernatural, and we can discard the design argument of natural theology.

We may note in passing that the evolutionary materialists are not alone in celebrating the apparent death of natural theology. Many mainstream theologians, both liberal and conservative, want nothing to do with it either. They view the design argument as an idolatrous attempt on the part of finite humans to grasp the infinite and incomprehensible God in rational or scientific terms. Rational arguments diminish the mystery of God, seeking to bring it under the control of the limited human mind. For religious reasons, therefore, we should be grateful to Darwinians for helping us get rid of the pretentiousness of natural theology.[12]

But natural theology has not gone away. It still lives on after Darwin, and under the stimulus of its encounter with evolutionary ideas, it has taken on new breadth and fresh confidence. Even though much of the revival of natural theology is now the work of scientists rather than professional theologians, it is an important instance of contemporary engagement of religious thought with evolution.

Instead of looking too closely and minutely at living organisms and their delicate adaptivity as the primary evidence of a designing deity, this revived natural theology today stands back and surveys with wider-angled lenses the larger cosmic story in which Darwinian evolution is only a relatively recent episode. For example, John Polkinghorne, an emeritus physicist at the University of Cambridge and now a practicing Anglican clergyman, argues that contemporary scientific advances in astronomy and physics place the whole story of life on our planet in an entirely new light.[13] We cannot divorce our understanding of the fact of biological evolution from its larger cosmic context or from the history of the universe as a whole. In the light of today's astrophysics, we have to account not only for life but also for the physical and cosmic conditions that made life possible in the first place.

Among these conditions is the existence of carbon and other heavy elements essential to the complex makeup of living beings. These elements were not yet present in the early universe, which featured only an abundance of hydrogen and helium; so if we are to understand the remote origins of biological phenomena, we need to review the process that eventually brought the chemical conditions for life into existence in the first place. Recently the physics of the early universe has provided us with a fascinating account of this process, one that seems—at least in Polkinghorne's updated version of natural theology—to point once again toward something like intelligent design at the very foundations of the universe itself. In the overall evolution of the universe, the eventual appearance of carbon and other heavy chemical elements depended upon cosmic features that had to have been precisely fixed during the first microseconds of the universe's existence at the time of the big bang. To a good number of scientists today, the initial conditions and fundamental cosmic constants of the universe seem so precisely bent toward the eventual production of carbon, and then life, that they suggest a new basis for natural theology, not in biology but in physics.

For life to be possible at all, the argument goes, the rate of expansion of the universe, the force of gravity, the ratio of electron to proton mass, and innumerable other cosmic birthmarks had to have been fixed infinitesimally close to their now established values. Otherwise the universe could never have produced hydrogen atoms, supernovae, carbon, and other ingredients essential to life. Details of this fine-tuning can be found in many scientific works today, and it is not necessary to discuss them any further here.[14] We need note only that natural theology's encounter with Darwin has not led inevitably to its death but, in some cases at least, to the search for a more expansive cosmic setting in which to look for signs of divine design.

As Polkinghorne argues, if life was eventually to come about, to evolve into the countless species, and eventually to become conscious in us humans, there must have been an extremely high degree of "improbable order" even at the very beginning of cosmic time. Human reason needs some intelligible account of this improbable initial ordering. Since such intricate and precise patterning was present already at the very beginning of cosmic history, it would not have had the "time" (since there was no time "before" the first cosmic moment) to come about by a process of evolution. Thus, Polkinghorne claims that the initial ordering of the cosmos strongly suggests the work of a supremely intelligent creator. Consequently, there is room even after Darwin for a revived and revised natural theology focusing on design in nature.

Of course, if you are truly addicted to the idea that our life-bearing universe is a purely random, undirected, and unintelligible occurrence, and that life within it *must* in no sense be the product of divine intelligence and wisdom, you may then imaginatively conjure up an endless series or proliferation of other "universes," so as to increase the probability that randomness rules. Though most of the alleged "universes" will be unsuited to life, you may still find it conceivable that, purely by chance, a life-biased set of initial conditions and fundamental physical constants such as we know to exist in our big bang universe might pop up eventually.

However, to Polkinghorne such unrestrained and purely ungrounded speculation is certainly less elegant, and indeed no less metaphysical, than the theological idea of "intelligent design." Polkinghorne admits that his revised natural theology is not a "knock down" argument for God's existence, but he views his work as strongly suggestive of the contemporary relevance and reasonableness of theistic explanation. In any case, we can see here that natural theology has been compelled by its encounter with evolutionary biology to seek a "wider teleology" than it did prior to Darwin.

Evolutionary Theology

A second and more important form of "theological engagement" with neo-Darwinism is "evolutionary theology." Evolutionary theology claims that the story of life, even in its neo-Darwinian presentation, provides essential concepts for thinking about God and God's relation to nature and humanity. However, it also agrees with Polkinghorne and others that all serious theological reflection on biological evolution today must be situated in the more expansive context of "cosmic evolution." It would be artificial in the extreme to relate theology to neo-Darwinian evolution without taking into account the entire physical universe that has sponsored the emergence of life.

Evolutionary theology, unlike natural theology, does not search for definitive footprints of the divine in nature. It is not terribly concerned about "intelligent design," since such a notion seems entirely too lifeless to capture the dynamic and even disturbing way in which the God of biblical religion interacts with the world. Instead of trying to prove God's existence from nature, evolutionary theology seeks to show how our new awareness of cosmic and biological evolution can enhance and enrich traditional teachings about God and God's way of acting in the world. In other words, rather than viewing evolution simply as a dangerous challenge that deserves an apologetic response, evolutionary theology discerns in evolution a most illuminating context for our thinking about God today. Here we may sample briefly some ways in which the Darwinian vision has already affected theological understanding of the notions of creation, eschatology, revelation, divine love (or "grace"), divine power, and redemption.

Creation.   The notion that God creates the world is, of course, central to the faith of millions. Traditionally, Christian theology spoke of three dimensions of God's creative activity: original creation *(creatio originalis)*, ongoing or continuous creation *(creatio continua)*, and new creation or the fulfillment of creation *(creatio nova)*. Prior to the scientific discoveries of cosmic and biological evolution, however, the latter two notions were usually eclipsed by the first. "Creation" meant primarily something that God did in the beginning. But even in the late nineteenth century a few theologians had already recognized that evolution implicitly liberates the notion of creation from confinement to cosmic origins.[15] And although today discussions between scientists and theologians about God and the big bang often assume that "creation" is only about cosmic beginnings, the idea of evolution forbids such narrowing of so powerful a notion.[16]

Indeed, the fact of evolution now allows theology to apprehend more palpably than ever that creation is not just an "original" but also an ongoing and constantly new reality. In an evolving cosmos, creation is still happening, no less in the present than "in the beginning." The big bang universe continues to unfold, and so every day is still the "dawn of creation." As Teilhard de Chardin put it, in an evolving universe "incessantly even if imperceptibly, the world is constantly emerging a little farther above nothingness."[17]

Moreover, evolution has allowed theology to acknowledge at last that the notion of an originally and instantaneously completed creation is theologically unthinkable in any case.[18] If we could imagine it at all, we would have to conclude that an initial creation, one already finished and perfected from the beginning, could not be a creation truly distinct from its creator. Such a "world" would simply be an appendage of God, and not a world unto itself; nor could God conceivably transcend such a world. It would be a world without internal self-coherence, a world without a future, and, above all, a world devoid of life. By definition, living beings must continually transcend, or go beyond, themselves. As Henri Bergson said long ago, life is really a *tendency* rather than something rounded off and complete.[19] An unfinished, or evolving, universe is essential to this tendency's actualization.

But if the universe is still unfinished, then we cannot demand that it should here and now possess the status of finished perfection. And if the universe is not perfect, then this can mean only that it is now imperfect. Moreover, if ours is an imperfect world, the appearance of evil (including the suffering and struggle depicted by Darwinian science) is not inconceivable. Evil and suffering could be thought of as the dark side of the world's ongoing creation.[20] To say that suffering is a logical possibility in an evolving universe, however, is not to claim that it is tolerable. For this reason faith and theology cry out for the completion of creation *(creatio nova)*. This brings us to the question of the meaning of eschatology in an evolving universe.

Eschatology. Biblical faith is concerned especially with what we humans may hope for, that is, with what awaits us as our final destiny and ultimate fulfillment. This branch of theology is known as *eschatology* (from the Greek word *eschaton,* which means "edge," or what is "last" or "final"). In an evolutionary context, however, our own human hope for final fulfillment must be situated within the wider context of the ongoing creation of the cosmos. The scientific epic of evolution invites us to extend our human hope outward and forward to embrace the entire cosmos, thus retrieving an often lost theme in the biblical wisdom literature and in the writings of St. Paul, St. Irenaeus, and many other religious thinkers who have also sought to bring the entire universe into the scheme of salvation.

The Jesuit scientist Teilhard de Chardin often pointed out that as long as nature seemed static or eternal it had no future of its own. Human hope for what is truly new and fulfilling, therefore, could lead us only to withdraw from the natural world in order to arrive, decisively after death, at an entirely different (supernatural) world situated "up above." But after Darwin and other recent scientific developments, the cosmos began to be perceived as itself moving, slowly perhaps, but nonetheless moving. And so the horizon of human expectations could begin to shift toward a future that includes the universe and the entire sweep of its evolution. In this way, evolutionary science has provided theology with a great opportunity to enlarge upon the ancient religious intuition—expressed so movingly by St. Paul—that the *entirety* of creation "groans" for ultimate fulfillment.[21] After Darwin we may speak more assuredly than ever about the inseparability of cosmic and human destiny.

Correspondingly, the sense of where the reality of God is to be "located" can also begin to shift from the One who abides vertically "up above" to the One who comes into the world from "up ahead," out of the realm of the future.[22] This new understanding of divine transcendence, as it turns out, actually corresponds—more closely than did our pre-evolutionary conceptions of the supernatural—to the God of the Bible, where God is the One who "goes before" the people, leading them to liberty. This is the God who turns the eyes of faith toward the future and "who makes all things new," as depicted by Second Isaiah and the Book of Revelation (Isa. 43:19; Rev. 21:5). The evolutionary portrait of life and the universe fits quite comfortably into the framework of biblical eschatology and in doing so gives it even wider compass than the biblical authors could have envisaged.

Revelation. Evolution also helps theology understand more clearly than before what is implied in the idea of "revelation." Indeed, as Catholic theologian Karl Rahner has suggested, the notion of revelation already anticipates an evolving cosmos.[23] Revelation is not fundamentally the communication of propositional information from a divine source of knowledge. Rather, it is at root the communication of *God's own selfhood* to the world. According to Rahner, the central content of Christian faith is that the infinite mystery of God pours itself generously, fully, and without reservation into the creation.[24] Put in simpler terms, the infinite gives itself away to the finite. But the fullness of divine infinity cannot be received instantaneously by a finite cosmos. Such a reception could take place only incrementally or gradually. A finite world could "adapt" to an infinite source of love only by a process of gradual expansion and ongoing self-transcendence, the external manifestation of which might appear to science as cosmic and biological evolution.

Grace. Reflection on evolution has helped some theologians, beginning in the last century, to illuminate the theme of divine love (or grace) and along with it the world's response to this grace. At the same time, a theology of grace can make intelligible the randomness, struggle, and natural selection that form the core of the Darwinian understanding of evolution. The doctrine of grace claims that God loves the world and all of its various elements fully and unconditionally. By definition, however, love does not absorb, annihilate, or force itself upon the beloved. Instead it longs for the beloved to become more and more "other" or differentiated. Along with its nurturing and compassionate attributes, love brings with it a longing for the independence of that which is loved. Without such "letting be" of its beloved, the dialogical intimacy essential to a loving relationship would be impossible.

Consequently, if there is any truth to the central religious intuition that God loves the world with an unbounded love, then God's "grace" must also mean "letting the world be itself." God's love would refrain from forcefully stamping the divine presence or will upon the world, much less dissolving the world into God. Indeed, this love might even take the form of a self-withdrawal, precisely as the condition for allowing the world to emerge on its own so as to attain the possible status of being capable of a deep relationship with God.[25] Nicholas of Cusa, in praying to God, asked: "How could you give yourself to me unless you had first given me to myself?"[26] It must be likewise with God's relation to the entire cosmos. Only a relatively independent universe, a universe allowed to "be itself," could be intimate with God. Theologically interpreted, therefore, the epic of evolution is the story of the world's struggle—not always successful or linearly progressive—toward an expansive freedom in the presence of self-giving grace.[27]

Evolution in all of its wandering, struggling, and temporally drawn out self-creating—as described by the neo-Darwinian accounts—is perfectly consonant with this notion of divine grace understood as God's "letting be" of the world. Indeed, if we reflect on cosmic process in the light of faith's assumptions about the selfless character of divine grace (impressed on Christians, for example, through the image of a crucified Goodness), we should *expect* to find a world percolating with contingency rather than one rigidified by necessity. Even St. Thomas Aquinas argued that a world devoid of chance or contingency could not really be distinct from its God. The world has to have aspects of nonnecessity or contingency in order to be a world at all: "It would be contrary to the nature of providence and to the perfection of the world if nothing happened by chance."[28] Thus, the randomness and undirected features of evolution are not just "apparent," as some of the "separatists" would argue. They are, in fact, essential features of any world created by a gracious God.

Divine Power.   Belief that the world can be finally redeemed from the evil and suffering that accompany its evolution requires special theological concentration on the notion of divine power. And of all the varieties of contemporary religious reflection on this doctrine of

faith it seems to me that "process theology" has been the most atten-
tive to evolution. It seeks, more directly than other kinds of theology, to show how God can be deeply involved with a world wherein
life meanders, experiments, strives, fails, and sometimes succeeds.
Using concepts of Alfred North Whitehead and his philosophical
followers, process theology seeks to interpret the teachings of biblical religion about God's creative and redemptive power in terms
consistent with the dynamic, evolutionary character of the world.[29]
Evolution, according to process theology, occurs in the first place
only because God's power and action in relation to the world take
the form of persuasive love rather than coercive force. In keeping
with the notion of grace mentioned immediately above, divine love
does not compel, but invites. To compel, after all, would be contrary
to the very nature of love.

But isn't the use of persuasion a sign of weakness rather than
power? After Darwin can theology still hold that God is a God of
"power and might"? Process theology responds that if power means
"the capacity to influence," then a persuasive God is much more
powerful than a hypothetical deity who magically forces things to
correspond immediately to the divine intentions. A coercive deity—
one that an immature religiosity often wishes for and that our scientific skeptics almost invariably have in mind when they assert that
Darwin has destroyed theism—would not allow for the otherness,
autonomy, and self-coherence necessary for the world to be a world
unto itself. Such a stingy and despotic forcefulness, by refusing to
favor the independence of creation, would clearly be less influential
in the final analysis than a God who wills the independence of the
world. A world given lease to become more and more autonomous,
even to help create itself and eventually attain the status of human
consciousness and freedom, has much more integrity and value than
any conceivable world determined in every respect by an external
"divine designer." If by persuasion rather than coercion something
greater than a puppetlike universe is permitted to come into being,
then we can say that persuasive power is more influential than
brute force.

A coercive divine power, furthermore, would be incompatible not
only with human freedom but also with the prehuman spontaneity
that allows the world to evolve into something other than its creator
over the course of billions of years. Thus, process theology finds
nothing religiously peculiar in the spontaneity manifested at the levels

of quantum indeterminacy, or in the undirected mutations in biolog-ical evolution that Darwinians refer to as random. Nor is its concep-tion of God inconsistent with all the other contingencies in life's open and undetermined history, or in the capacity for free choice that emerges during the human phase of evolution. Theologically speaking, process theology suggests that we should logically foresee, rather than be surprised, that God's creation is not driven coercively, that it is widely experimental, and that it unfolds over the course of a considerable amount of time. To those who object that process the-ology is hereby illegitimately redefining the idea of God's power in order to contrive a fit with neo-Darwinian theory, the reply is simply that no other conception of power is more consistent with the quite orthodox religious belief that God is infinite love. Neo-Darwinian evolution does not require that we abandon or modify the ancient biblical teachings about the unbounded generosity and compassion of God, but that we return to them more earnestly than ever.

Evolution occurs, according to process theology, because a God of love is the source not only of order but also of novelty. And it is the introduction of novelty into the world that makes evolution possi-ble. Thus, the obsession by creationists, Phillip Johnson, and scien-tific skeptics with the idea of God as an "intelligent designer" is en-tirely too narrow for—and in great measure irrelevant to—a genuine engagement of theology and science on the issue of Darwinian evo-lution. The idea of nature simply as "intelligent design" shares with mechanistic biology the trait of abstracting from the concrete reality of *life*. As the ultimate source of novelty in evolution, God must also be the cause of instability and disorder, conditions essential to life. There can, after all, be no process of ordering or reordering, such as that exhibited by life's metabolism and evolutionary transforma-tions, that does not also include aspects of instability or disorder. So it is simply inappropriate to think of God exclusively as a source of order (a distortion shared by much natural theology and scientific skepticism). God is also the source of novelty, and so God is also the reason for some disorder—and hence for the possibility of life.

According to process theology, evolution occurs because God is more interested in adventure than in preserving the status quo. "Ad-venture," in Whiteheadian terms, is the cosmic search for more and more intense versions of ordered novelty, another word for which is "beauty." God's will, apparently, is for the maximization of cosmic beauty. And the epic of evolution is the world's response to God's own longing that it strive toward ever richer ways of realizing aesthetic intensity. By offering new and relevant possibilities to the cosmos in every period of its becoming, God "acts" not only to sustain but also to create the world continually.[30] I shall develop this point in more detail later on.

Redemption.   Finally, process theology also highlights the hope for redemption that perennially lies at the heart of human longing and that comes to its most explicit expression in the world's religious traditions. But how can it conceive of redemption in a world of evolution, given the perpetual perishing that goes along with cosmic process? According to process theology, the answer is the same as that given in biblical and other traditions, namely, that God is infinitely *responsive* to the world as well as creative and nurturing of it. Following the pattern of love, God intimately "feels" the world, as the biblical narratives affirm over and over. God, it would seem, is influenced deeply by all that happens in the evolutionary process. Everything whatsoever that occurs in evolution—all the suffering and tragedy as well as the emergence of new life and intense beauty—is "saved" by being taken eternally into God's own feeling of the world. Even though all events and achievements in evolution are temporal and perishable, they still abide permanently within the everlasting compassion of God. In God's own sensitivity to the world, each event is redeemed from absolute perishing and receives the definitive importance and meaning that religions encourage us to believe in—always without seeing clearly. That we abide in darkness on something of such ultimate moment is itself consistent with the fact that we live in an unfinished, imperfect universe; in other words, the only kind of universe consistent with the idea of an infinitely loving and active God.

Conclusion

I shall come back later to several facets of the theological ideas I have just summarized. My intention in this chapter has been to give readers a sense of some of the responses theology has already made to Darwin's "dangerous idea." We have seen even in this brief digest that by embracing a generally Darwinian picture of nature, theology has the capacity to undergo considerable renewal. It is true that over the last century and a half much religious thought has rejected evolution *(opposition)*, or in other instances tried to ignore it *(separatism)*, but at least some theology has fully embraced it *(engagement)*. Doing so, however, is certainly not without difficulties, and so we need now to address these more deliberately. At the top of the list is the question of whether theology can make sense today of the epochs of suffering and struggle that the story of life's evolution has laid out before us. It is to this tormenting issue that we now turn our attention.

4

Darwin's Gift to Theology

THE DARWINIAN PICTURE of life's long struggle and travail gives unprecedented breadth to the so-called problem of theodicy, that is, how to "justify" God's existence given the fact of suffering and evil. How could a powerful and compassionate God permit all the agony, aimless wandering, and waste that scientific portrayals of evolution have laid out before us? In addressing this issue, I should stress once again that evolution is not unambiguously malign. In fact, as contemporary evolutionary science is bringing out more clearly all the time, the story of life on Earth is less one of competition among species and more one of their cooperation and interdependence than we used to think. Generally, neo-Darwinian models have failed to give sufficient attention to the ecological richness of the life-process.

Nevertheless, we cannot remain untroubled by the innocent suffering that evolution brings along with it. Because of the enormity of this suffering in nature, it seems to me that recent efforts to confront the challenge of evolution simply by restating or revising arguments for "intelligent design" are both apologetically ineffective and theologically inconsequential. One-sided appeals to the idea of God as an "intelligent designer" render the issue of theodicy all the more intractable. They lead us to ignore the more theologically challenging aspects of evolution. Rather than attuning theology and human life to the restlessness and ambiguity of an unfinished universe, advocates of "intelligent design" typically ignore the contingency, randomness, and struggle in evolution. But it is precisely the latter that a theology of evolution needs to take into account.

The idea of "intelligent design" is too restrictive, theologically speaking, to capture the deeper and ultimately more compelling meaningfulness that a robust theological vision may discern in an evolving universe. A reactionary focus on design filters out the tragic aspects of life. Fixation on nature's rational orderliness blunts our religious sense of the divine pathos. It ignores the "irrational" and anguished intimacy in God's whole long affair with the cosmos.

I suspect that only a theology that looks for concepts other than "design" and "order" can open us up—painfully, perhaps, but also salvifically—to the messiness, novelty, and chaos in Earth's life-story. An innocent preoccupation with design can obscure the theological riches we might recover by contemplating Darwin's "dangerous idea" in its rawness as well as its grandeur. Our facing openly and honestly the disquieting scientific accounts of life's evolution can expose us to the passionate and creative divine depths of nature much more nakedly than can a shallow skimming of isolated samples of order off of life's surface.

It is especially in this sense that the challenge by Darwin to theology—and I speak here from within a Christian context—may prove to be not so much peril as gift. Reflection on the Darwinian world can lead us to contemplate more explicitly the mystery of God as it is made manifest in the story of life's suffering, the epitome of which lies for Christians in the crucifixion of Jesus. In the symbol of the cross, Christian belief discovers a God who participates fully in the world's struggle and pain. The cruciform visage of nature reflected in Darwinian science invites us to depart, perhaps more decisively than ever before, from all notions of a deity untouched by the world's suffering.[1] Evolutionary biology not only allows theology to enlarge its sense of God's creativity by extending it over measureless eons of time; it also gives comparable magnitude to our sense of the divine participation in life's long and often tormented journey.

Hence Darwin's idea will indeed prove to be dangerous after all—dangerous not to theology as such but certainly to all the shallow theologies of order that ignore the divine attribute of co-suffering, or com-passionate involvement, in the life-process. After Darwin, we may still think of God as powerfully effective in the natural world, but we will have to do so in a manner quite distinct from that implied in much pre-evolutionary theology. Of course, in order to possess theological integrity our thoughts about God after Darwin must be continuous with the authoritative scriptural and traditional sources of faith. But our attending to the details of evolution invites us to appropriate these sources in a fresh manner today.

The Theological Task

How, though, can we accomplish such an objective in view of the position represented by Dawkins and Dennett on the one hand, and the reserve with which so many Christians and other religious believers have approached the topic of evolution on the other? Can theology after Darwin, instead of retreating from or only reluctantly accommodating Darwinian ideas, actually embrace them with enthusiasm?

Here I shall propose that the central and original content of Christian faith provides us with an image of God that is not only logically consistent with but also fruitfully illuminative of the Darwinian picture of life. I must emphasize once again, of course, that when I use the term "Darwinian" here I do not mean it in the materialistic sense often associated with it. Contrary to both Stephen Jay Gould and Phillip Johnson, I think it is quite possible to distinguish evolutionary science from the obsolete materialism that cripples both Darwin's and many of his followers' public presentations of it. Indeed, I would go so far as to say that when we look at evolutionary data in light of the biblical image of God, the life-process can make much more sense than when interpreted against the backdrop of materialist metaphysics. The undirected mutations, the process of natural selection, and the vastness of time required for the still unfolding story of life do not mandate the mechanistic conceptualization that Darwinians inherited from Newton and Descartes. Instead, the data of evolutionary science can be more intelligibly situated within a theological metaphysical framework centered around the biblical picture of "the humility of God."

The image of a vulnerable, defenseless, and humble deity may seem shocking to some, but it is crucial to the primordial Christian sense of the nature of ultimate reality. It is in a God who submits to crucifixion that Christian faith invites us to put the fullness of our trust. The portrait of God as a self-giving rather than self-aggrandizing mystery has always been implicit in the symbols of Christian faith. In fact, through its Trinitarian doctrine, Christianity has clearly made the crucifixion of Jesus an inner dimension of God's experience rather than something external to deity. But theologians and religious educators have often fled from this disquieting and revolutionary idea.

When Christianity entered Western culture, as Alfred North Whitehead rightly indicates, the image of Caesar rather than that of the
humble shepherd of Nazareth became the regnant model of God.[2]
And the specter of divinity as potentate still hovers over ideas about
the "intelligent designer" whose existence is so tediously debated by
creationists and evolutionary materialists.

Meanwhile, however, the ancient Christian sense of God's humility and vulnerability has begun to emerge more explicitly once again
in contemporary theology. It has by no means penetrated the sensibilities of all believers, and it is completely absent from scientific
skeptics' typical caricatures of "God."[3] But today a good number of
theologians consider it fundamental to Christian faith.[4] The image
of a self-effacing God, although always resident implicitly in Chris-
tology, is now—at least in the best of our theologies—beginning to
supplant the image of an invulnerable, immobile, and essentially
nonrelational God that seemed so antithetical to the world's evolutionary becoming and self-creativity.

At the center of Christian faith lies a trust that in the passion and
crucifixion of Jesus we are presented with the mystery of a God who
pours the divine selfhood into the world in an act of unreserved self-
abandonment. The utter lowliness of this image has led some theologians in our century to speak carelessly of God as "powerless." Diet-
rich Bonhoeffer, for example, wrote from prison that only a "weak"
God can be of help to us. And some process theologians, in their effort
to avoid crude notions of divine omnipotence, also speak of a powerless God. The Roman Catholic theologian Edward Schillebeeckx,
however, rightly argues that it is theologically unnecessary for us to
deny God's power when we acknowledge the divine participation in
the world's suffering. The image of God's humility does not imply
weakness and powerlessness, but rather a kind of "defenselessness" or
"vulnerability." These attributes, as Schillebeeckx claims, can powerfully and effectively disarm evil. Paradoxically, it is through the divine
humility that the power of God becomes most effective. Since
"power" means the capacity to bring about significant consequences,
the concept need not be abandoned, but instead endowed once again
with the meaning given to it by the properly Christian sense of God.
Schillebeeckx writes that "the divine omnipotence does not know the
destructive facets of the human exercising of power, but in this world
becomes 'defenceless' and vulnerable. It shows itself as power of love
which challenges, gives life and frees human beings, at least those who

hold themselves open to this offer."[5] Theological reflection on this image of divine defenselessness (which, I repeat, is not identical with powerlessness) can also help faith make sense of the ways of evolution, especially as these are depicted by neo-Darwinian biology.

The image of a self-emptying God lies at the heart of Christian revelation and the doctrine of the Trinity.[6] And it is just this surprising portrait of the divine mystery that allows us to situate intelligibly the process of the world's creation and evolution. Theologian Jürgen Moltmann, influenced by Jewish Kabbalistic speculation as well as classic Christian thought, argues that the creation of the universe itself is not so much a display of divine might as the consequence of God's self-restraint:

> [God's] ... creative activity outwards is preceded by his humble divine self-restriction. In this sense God's self-humiliation does not begin merely with creation.... It begins beforehand, and is the presupposition that makes creation possible. God's creative love is grounded in his humble, self-humiliating love. This self-restricting love is the beginning of that self-emptying of God which Philippians 2 sees as the divine mystery of the Messiah. Even in order to create heaven and earth, God emptied Himself of his all-plenishing omnipotence, and as Creator took ... the form of a servant.[7]

Moltmann is referring here to St. Paul's appreciation of the paradox that Jesus Christ, the Lord of all, "emptied himself" *(ekenosen seauton)* and became the servant of all. Jesus' selfless submission to death is the main theme in a very early Christian hymn interpolated into chapter 2 of Paul's letter to the Philippians. Subsequent theological reflection on this hymn has led many theologians to conclude that it is ultimately God's own being that undergoes "kenosis," or "emptying."[8]

In faith's response to this self-emptying or "kenotic" image of God there lurks, I think, a way of bringing new meaning not only to our perplexity at the broken state of social existence or individual human sufferings but also to our more recent bewilderment over the unfathomed epochs of wandering experimentation, struggle, apparent waste, and suffering that occur in the larger story of life as the result of evolution by natural selection.

The ways of nature take on a distinctively new definition when we view them in light of the vulnerability of God. In their apologetic response to evolutionary materialists, theists who focus exclusively on evidence of nature's design or order overlook the remarkable religious insight that divine influence characteristically manifests itself in "weakness." A truly responsive theology of evolution, therefore, must bring to the fore faith's sense of the self-outpouring God who lovingly renounces any claim to domineering omnipotence. The same self-withdrawal of God that, according to Moltmann's interpretation, makes creation initially possible *(creatio originalis)* also allows for the ongoing creation *(creatio continua)* of the world through evolution.

A theology of evolution need not lose sight of other aspects of revelation, but it will make central the theme of divine suffering love. Biblical teachings about God's word and promise, about exodus, redemption, covenant, justice, wisdom, the Logos made flesh, the Spirit poured out on the face of creation, and the Trinitarian character of God—these are all indispensable to Christian theology. But they disclose to us the nature of God only when they are joined closely to the theme of divine vulnerability, which, for Christians, assumes its most explicit expression in the life, death, and resurrection of Jesus.

The picture of an incarnate God who suffers along with creation is offensive to our customary sense of what should pass muster as ultimate reality. But perhaps this image can be called "revelatory" precisely because it breaks through the veil of our pedestrian projections of the absolute, and does so in such a way as to bring new meaning to all of life's suffering, struggle, and loss. This new meaning consists, in part at least, of the intuition that the agony of living beings is not undergone in isolation from the divine eternity, but is taken up everlastingly and redemptively into the very "life-story" of God.

Both scientific skeptics and anti-Darwinian Christian theists assume that the concept of the almighty as an "intelligent designer" scarcely permits such participatory, empathetic association with the messiness of nature. Though on opposite sides of the question of God's existence, they share the assumption that an ordering deity is incompatible with a universe in which the evolution of life occurs by way of natural selection. Both sides, however, refuse to grant that "belief in the divine self-emptying or condescension in Christ" is, in the words of theologian Donald Dawe,[9] "basic to Christian faith."

God in his creation and redemption of the world accepted the limitations of finitude upon his own person. In the words of the New Testament, God had "emptied himself, taking the form of a servant." God accepted the limitations of human life, its suffering and death, but in doing this, he had not ceased being God. God the Creator had chosen to live as a creature. God, who in his eternity stood forever beyond the limitations of human life, had fully accepted these limitations. The Creator had come under the power of his creation. This the Christian faith has declared in various ways from its beginning.

Unfortunately, however, as Dawe goes on to lament,

the audacity of this belief in the divine kenosis has often been lost by long familiarity with it.... The familiar phrases 'he emptied himself [heauton ekenosen], taking the form of a servant,' 'though he was rich, yet for your sake he became poor,' have come to seem commonplace. Yet this belief in the divine self-emptying epitomizes the radically new message of Christian faith about God and his relation to man.

An evolutionary theology, it goes without saying, expands this picture of God's suffering so as to have it embrace also the struggles of the entire universe and not just our own species' brief history here. God's empathy enfolds not just the human sphere but the whole of creation, and this can mean only that the vast evolutionary odyssey, with all of its travail, enjoyment, and creativity, is also God's own travail, enjoyment, and creativity. Nothing that occurs in evolution can appropriately be understood by faith and theology as taking place outside of God's own experience.

In the words of St. Paul, of course, such an understanding of God and God's ways amounts to "foolishness" in contrast to our conventional wisdom (1 Cor. 1:25). How strange an idea the "humility of God" is in the history of human attempts to understand the absolute. John Macquarrie comments:

That God should come into history, that he should come in humility, helplessness and poverty—this contradicted everything—this contradicted everything that people had believed about the gods. It was the end of the power of deities, the Marduks, the Jupiters ... yes, and even of Yahweh, to the extent that he had been misconstrued on the same model. The life that began in a cave ended on the cross, and there was the final conflict between power and love, the idols and the true God, false religion and true religion.[10]

We continue to resist the image of God's humility, even though, as Karl Rahner asserts, "the primary phenomenon given by faith is precisely the self emptying of God."[11] Evolutionary science invites us, however, to appropriate more solemnly than ever this way of thinking about the divine mystery.

The real stumbling block to reconciling evolution with faith is not the "dangerous" features of evolution that Dennett dwells upon, but the scandalous image of God's humility that comes right from the heart of religious experience and not from the logic of design arguments. In debates about "God and evolution" theologians have usually focused on the question of how to reconcile God's "power" and "intelligence" with the autonomous, random, and impersonal features of nature's evolution. Too seldom have we entered into such reflection by thinking first of nature in terms of how it might appear if the creator of all things is, in essence, suffering love. In its encounters with evolutionary science, theology has generally preferred to assume a typically dictatorial concept of divine power, and this bias has only led it to overlook or disavow those features of evolution that skeptics like Dawkins and Dennett consider to be most theologically lethal.

The reason, of course, that theology has resisted thinking of evolution in terms of the revelatory image of God's humility is that such an image seems to imply that God has too little power, and perhaps even no power at all, to act in nature. And since any coherent faith or theology rightly demands that God be actively involved in the world, such a vulnerable and defenseless God does not seem capable of providing an adequate foundation for our hope in redemption, resurrection, and new creation. Perhaps it is for this reason, as Macquarrie observes, that "the God of Jesus Christ, like Yahweh before him, has been turned back again and again into a God of war or the God of the nation or the patron of a culture."[12]

So we cannot help asking again: Is the Christian story of God's vulnerability really adequate to the religious need for a God whose power not only serves as the ultimate explanation of nature and its evolutionary creativity but also works to redeem an evolving world? Faith, it bears repeating, requires a God who is actively involved in the world. Yet our scientific understanding of the autonomously creative resourcefulness of natural selection, working over the course of immense periods of time, raises serious questions about whether and how God could be effectively operative in nature as science now understands it.

Why, we might ask with the Darwinians, do we need to posit any divine action at all if nature can create itself autonomously? After all, the main support for Dawkins and Dennett's atheism is the impression evolution gives them that life's astonishing creativity can be accounted for fully by the mindless filtering process known as "natural selection." And if nature is so *self*-creative, there is apparently no room for a providential, personal, and intelligent God to act or intervene in nature. In support of this conclusion, the skeptic might elicit even further confirmation from other branches of recent science, especially the new studies of complexity and chaos, which also feature the spontaneously "self-organizing" character of natural processes.

However, theology may still provide an *ultimate* explanation of why evolutionary creativity occurs in the spontaneous and self-creative manner that it does. For if ultimate reality is conceived of neither as mindless and impersonal "matter," as materialism sees it, nor simply as an "intelligent designer," but fundamentally as self-emptying, suffering love, we should already anticipate that nature will give every appearance of being in some sense autonomously creative (autopoietic). Since it is the nature of love, even at the human level, to refrain from coercive manipulation of others, we should not expect the world that a generous God calls into being to be instantaneously ordered to perfection. Instead, in the presence of the self-restraint befitting an absolutely self-giving love, the world would unfold by responding to the divine allurement at its own pace and in its own particular way. The universe then would be spontaneously self-creative and self-ordering. And its responsiveness to the possibilities for new being offered to it by God would require time, perhaps immense amounts of it. The notion of an enticing and attracting divine humility, therefore, gives us a reasonable metaphysical explanation of the evolutionary process as this manifests itself to contemporary scientific inquiry.

Such an "ultimate," theological account of cosmic and biological evolution in no way interferes with purely scientific explanations of evolutionary events. The theological explanation I have just proposed does not seek in any way to supplant the autonomy of scientific

discovery, nor to restrict the latter's scope. In fact, it shares with materialist evolutionism the need to place the results of all scientific discovery within at least some general understanding of the nature of
reality. To formulate such a general vision is the task of *metaphysics,*
some version of which we all carry with us, whether we are aware of
it or not. What I am arguing throughout this book is that since we
will inevitably situate our scientific understanding within one or another general vision of reality—or metaphysics—a most viable can-
didate is the theological conceptuality I am setting forth here. In my
own opinion, this theological metaphysics is superior to the materialist alternative both in explanatory power and in its respect for the
autonomy of evolutionary science.

Although the theology set forth here will not compete with evolutionary science as such, it will stand in strong opposition to the materialist and scientistic dogmas that so often accompany evolution's
public presentation, ironically much to the detriment of the advance
of science itself. In subsequent pages, I shall provide a more substantive clarification of this important point.

In any case, a theology of divine humility makes room for true
novelty to spring spontaneously into being—a feature logically suppressed by deterministic materialist interpretations, as well as by the
notion that the universe is simply the unfolding of an eternally fixed
divine design or plan. Moreover, God's unobtrusive and self-absenting
mode of being invites the world to swell forth continually, through
immense epochs of temporal duration and experimentation, into an
always free and open future, and to do so in the relatively autonomous mode of "self-creation" that science has discerned in cosmic, biological, and cultural evolution. Similarly, when framed by
such a theological interpretation, the "irreducible" biochemical
complexity that leads Michael Behe to reject Darwinian gradualism,
no more demands any special divine intervention in nature than is
already present in the self-ordering of atomic entities, crystals,
snowflakes, or other instances of "design." Autopoiesis becomes
more complex as we move from nonliving to living forms of matter,
but there is no need in the case of the latter to invoke special metaphysical principles and interventions. The compassionate divine concern for the world's internal integrity would make room for a considerable degree of autonomy and self-creativity on the part of the
entire cosmos, and it would do so in increasingly subtle ways at each
new stage of nature's evolution.

Of course, to the empirical eye and within the self-limiting scope of purely scientific "explanation," the whole idea of God will rightly be considered superfluous. Science as such need never resort to the "God-hypothesis." But when we ask the deeper, metaphysical question, "Why is nature permitted to evolve in a spontaneous, self-creative way?" a theology has every right to enter its own response as an alternative to materialism and "intelligent design theory." The metaphysics of divine humility, I am arguing, explains the actual features of evolution much more intelligibly than either of the main alternatives.

Consider, for example, the indefinitely extensive reservoir of genetic possibilities that we saw Dennett referring to earlier as Mendel's "library." Viewed against the metaphysical background of an ultimate self-sacrificing love, this virtual archive is an extravagantly overflowing abundance of possibilities rooted in God's compassionate concern that the world be given full scope to "become itself." Moreover, God's gift of allowing the world to "become itself" is entirely consonant with, and, in fact, renders plausible, evolution's experimental winding through an endless field of potentialities, its random groping for relevant new forms of being, and the autonomous creativity in the life-process set forth by evolutionary science.

Conclusion

Such an understanding of God's love and power is not inconsistent with the existence of pain and struggle in nature and in human existence. There is, I think, no easy answer to the problem of suffering. It is an open sore that theology can never pretend to heal. Inevitably, all theodicies fail. The fact of evolution, however, introduces a dimension that previous responses to the problem did not have available to them. This is the simple fact that the universe is still in the process of being created. It is not yet finished, and if it is not yet finished it cannot yet be perfect. An evolving universe may aim toward perfection, but at any moment prior to such an unimaginable fulfillment it will have to be not-yet-perfect. And if it is not perfect, then we cannot be altogether surprised that imperfection, including the fact of pain, will be a part of it.

As I have pointed out already, the alternative theological notion of a divinely directed, perfectly ordered world that corresponds to our narrowly human notion of "intelligent design" would be theologically incoherent. The only kind of universe compatible with a God who loves, and who therefore wills the independence of the creation, is one in which contingency is an essential ingredient. And to living finite beings, this contingency can only entail that along with the thrill of being alive there will also exist the possibility of suffering and eventual perishing.

Christian faith's image of a suffering God's eternal restraint, which allows for the world's self-creation, suggests to theology a notion of ultimate reality much more intimately involved with and powerfully effective in the world than a forcefully directive divine agency would be. God acts powerfully in the world by offering to it a virtually limitless range of new possibilities within which it can become something relatively autonomous and distinct from its creator. By giving the divine self away completely to the world, God encourages the world to develop as something radically "other" than the divine. This is how genuine love works, and the general picture of evolution that Darwin gives us seems to me to correspond intelligibly with a religious vision that sees God as the source and exemplar of selfless love.[13]

If God is essentially compassionate love, however, we must also assume once again that all of the sufferings, struggles, and achievements of the evolving world do not take place outside of God's own empathetic care. A vulnerable God, as the Trinitarian nature of Christian theism requires, could not fail to feel intimately and to "remember" everlastingly all of the sufferings, struggles, and achievements in the *entire story* of cosmic and biological evolution. By holding these and all cosmic occurrences in the heart of divine compassion, God redeems them from all loss and gives eternal meaning to everything, though in a hidden way that for us humans only faith can affirm. Such a theological understanding is not only faithful to religious tradition but also *ultimately* explanatory of the world, as the latter now shows itself in the light of evolutionary science.

5

Religion, Evolution, and Information

DANIEL DENNETT, RICHARD DAWKINS, and the other evolution-ary materialists we have met in the preceding pages claim that the "dangerous" idea of evolution has wrecked the ancient religious intuition that the universe is the expression of an eternal meaning. Darwin's science, they insist, has made it impossible for educated people to believe that nature is in any sense purposive. Biblical an-tiquity may have viewed the universe as an embodiment of divine "wisdom" or of an eternal "logos." And Eastern religious thought may have connected nature to a principle of "rightness," variously known as *Rta, Dharma,* or the *Tao.* But, according to our expert witnesses, Darwin has made all such ancient intuitions unbelievable.

Traditional religions thought of the cosmos as something like a great book or "teaching" that could be deciphered by those appro-priately initiated.[1] Within the book of nature there exists a hierarchy of distinct levels of being and meaning. At the lowest level lie inani-mate things such as minerals and liquids; above that we find the more elusive world of living beings, first the plants, and then the do-main of the animals where sentience and consciousness are promi-nent; then at the next level up we encounter the realm of human existence with its apparently unique capacity for reflective self-awareness, free choice, ethical aspiration, and religious longing.[2] And finally, presiding over all of these grades of being is the tran-scendent, inaccessible, and ultimate source of meaning, identified in theistic faiths as "God."

As we move up this "Great Chain of Being," the levels become increasingly harder to grasp in an objective way. Living organisms, for example, have an "intangible quality" that cannot be understood very well in terms of the lifeless things below them. Most religions, in fact, have perceived in living beings a mysterious empowering spiritual force, identified in biblical circles as the "Spirit of God." When we move up to the next level, that of the human mind, we discover a reality even harder to grasp. We find that our own mind cannot comprehend itself completely. As we try to master our own subjective consciousness objectively, the subjective or "inner" side of this same consciousness always slips safely beyond our grasp. The level of mind can never be unraveled objectively, and so it too becomes in religion an especially powerful symbol of the sacred mystery that grounds the universe's intelligibility.

Traditionally, intermediary levels of beings, such as angels, occupy the immense gulf between the human and the divine. But for our purposes it is sufficient to note only the nearly universal conviction prior to modern times that the whole cosmic hierarchy is overseen and permeated by an ultimate source of meaning whose reality can never be represented fully in terms of the lower levels.

Although today the term "hierarchy" may suggest obsolete ecclesiastical political structures or patriarchal oppression, this word's Greek roots imply simply that all things have their origin or principle of being (arche) in the domain of the sacred (hier). According to most religious traditions, a "purposeful" universe must have at least some form of hierarchical arrangement. In order to be the carrier of meaning, the book of nature has to consist of various levels, the lower open to being informed "from above" by higher levels of meaning and being. Moreover, the very notion of a purposeful cosmos requires that there be a "highest" level to inscribe intelligible meaning in the "lower" levels. Traditional religion and philosophy resisted almost unanimously the modern idea that reality can be reduced to a single, desacralized dimension.[3] Even the very lowest levels of nature in the "Great Chain of Being" somehow participate in their eternal source, and in various degrees all the levels symbolically represent the being of God. The entire cosmos, including its most humanly insignificant aspects, testifies to the power and munificence of an ineffable divine origin and principle of meaning.

The great attraction of the hierarchical scheme is that it embeds our own fragile lives and the whole fleeting temporal world within the larger framework of an eternal reality immune to transience and death. Participation in the imperishable permanence of God rescues the flux of transitory cosmic and human events from the oblivion of nothingness. The challenge evolutionary science poses to religion, therefore, consists in great measure of its apparent collapsing of the sacred hierarchy in which the sense of a purposeful universe has been positioned for ages. It is difficult to exaggerate the anxiety evolution can thus occasion. Darwin appears to have rendered untenable the whole classical hierarchical vision, along with any sense that the entirety of nature participates in a realm of perfect timelessness.

In modern evolutionary materialism, the inanimate level formerly thought of as the lowest of all is now identified as the most real or "fundamental." Lifeless and mindless "matter" is taken to be the metaphysical and historical source of all beings, including those now endowed with life and mind.[4] And since matter is thought of as inherently mindless, the cosmos that evolves from it must be *essentially* mindless also, even if evolution eventually and accidentally brings forth some beings with a capacity for thought. Clearly a mindless cosmos, taken as a whole, cannot possibly be the carrier of transcendent meaning. Instead of being a book or a "teaching" whose meaningful content would be transparent to the religiously awakened, the universe that evolves from dumb matter must be intrinsically pointless. The formerly lowest level, that of inanimate matter, is now the "ultimate" explanation of the "higher," and the "higher" levels of life and mind are derivatives of an inherently meaningless material underpinning. In the absence of any sacred hierarchical information flowing downward from higher to lower levels, the physical universe no longer symbolically represents an eternal significance. And so, no grounds remain for our attributing lasting value or importance to it.

Darwin's Other Dangerous Idea

As I noted earlier, Darwin gave us two "dangerous" ideas. Shocking enough, of course, was his theory of natural selection. But, at least for many of the religious, no less dangerous is his theory that all forms of life have a common ancestor, which itself arose accidentally out of a lifeless set of purely chemical occurrences. Evolutionary science has blurred the former lines between nonlife, life, humanity, and culture to the point where we can no longer decide clearly where one begins and the other leaves off. Evolutionary science posits a physical and historical *continuity* running through all those levels of nature formerly thought of as discontinuous and hierarchically distinct. In all of science nothing seems to have melted down the classic hierarchical vision more completely than has the evolutionary picture of nature. In combination with physics, chemistry, molecular biology, geology, and other sciences, neo-Darwinism has now made the traditional idea that nature leads upward to God by way of a series of hierarchically distinct rungs on the cosmic ladder seem quite unbelievable.

As we dissect the collapse of the ancient hierarchy, we find that the main causes of this collapse are the *atomizing* and the *historicizing* of nature. Atomism is the method of breaking organisms or other complex entities down into more elemental units such as genes, cells, molecules, and atoms. Once the complexity of nature has undergone granulation into irreducible particulate units, it becomes difficult for scientific thought to make out the formerly crisp hierarchical lines of demarcation that once separated the levels of material, living, and thinking beings. As the analytic method of science becomes fixated on the atomic constituents of things, our intuitive sense that some hidden integrating principle of coherence fashions these elements into ontologically discontinuous grades of being begins to dissolve. And so, all we have left are atomic, molecular, or (as in the case of Dawkins) genetic monads. The comprehensive wholeness that used to make organisms seem qualitatively different and hierarchically more elevated than their inanimate constituents vanishes as a ghost in the night.

Science, it is true, now allows that combinations of irreducible physical units may possess what are called "emergent" properties that do not appear at the level of the constituent parts. But any systemic or holistic features that appear to be ontologically discontinuous are, at least in the eyes of atomistic scientists, nothing more than "epiphenomenal" derivatives of purely accidental collocations of the constituent elements. Life, for example, is simply material stuff arranged in more or less "complex" ways. There is no room here for the ancient teaching that what is "really real" about things is their comprehensive wholeness and not their subordinate particulars. The modern dream that life and mind will eventually be made fully intelligible by the minute specification of their physical composition has caused many in our time to wonder if there is really any more to living and thinking beings than the atomic, molecular, or genetic activity that underlies them.

The second, and perhaps more serious, challenge by science to the religious sense of hierarchy lies in the *historicizing* conviction of Darwinians that life and mind—which used to be enshrined as relatively "higher" levels in the cosmic hierarchy—have emerged in a horizontally gradual manner over the course of time. That is, they have their origin *(arche)* not in the sacred *(hier)* but in the blank lifelessness of matter's physical simplicity, which vastly predates them in time. Life and mind do not appear in evolution until much later than their inanimate molecular ancestry. Consequently, it is difficult to elevate them to an ontologically "higher" plane than that of their material predecessors, from which they have inherited their being in the course of natural history. Viewed historically, life and mind now seem much more derivative than explanatory. If no traces of mind existed at the earlier stages of cosmic evolution, isn't mind itself explainable completely in terms of the "earlier" and inherently mindless physical routines out of which it has sluggishly, and apparently by sheer happenstance, emerged only quite recently?

The Vitalist Reaction

That the "higher" levels of life and mind can emanate from lower levels by purely Darwinian processes, and without any immaterial causal agency, seems irrational when viewed in terms of traditional religions and philosophies. The claim that lifeless matter might autonomously give birth to life violates the principle of causation, not to mention common sense. Surely, if we are to save the rudiments of sanity, we cannot reject the principle that "no effect can be greater than its cause." The emergence of living organisms from dead matter cannot be accomplished by matter acting alone but requires the informing causality of a "vital principle" to bring life and mind into being out of lifeless matter.

This view is known as "vitalism." Vitalism contends that the evolutionary emergence of life out of matter is the result of an intangible force or spiritual principle that lifts the lower level of matter up onto the higher plane of life. Life, in other words, is ontologically superior to sheer matter, even though in evolution it is chronologically posterior to the purely physical phases of cosmogenesis. Vitalism's most famous proponent, Henri Bergson (1854–1941), argued that matter, though earlier in cosmic history, is in fact merely ancillary and preparatory to life. Matter derives its being and meaning only from the fact that it somehow serves the eventual emergence of life and mind in evolution.[5]

Modern science, however, has seemingly demystified this vitalistic hypothesis. In the neo-Darwinian perspective, it now seems that "matter" is able, over the course of natural history, eventually to give birth to life and mind without any assistance from beyond. Life and mind have received their being from what people formerly took to be the very lowest level in the cosmic hierarchy. Now, when we look at nature in the historical-horizontal way suggested by evolution, blind and undirected material processes have an exalted causal status unimaginable in pre-evolutionary philosophies and theologies. Meaningless "matter" itself seems to be the mother of all things.

For Bergson it was still possible to posit the primacy of a supernatural kind of force—an *élan vital*—that surges through matter on the way to expressing itself creatively in all the diversity of living beings. But Bergson's vitalistic rescue operation has lost out to the intellectual cogency of the newer atomizing and historicizing of nature. Molecular biologists claim to have discovered the secret of life in the chemistry of amino and nucleic acids, that is, in lifeless chains of atoms. And the growing awareness that life arose and evolved in a historical manner *over an immense period of time* has helped snuff out the last gasp of supernaturalism in science. As a result, the hierarchical view of nature, and with it any sense of cosmic purpose, has also disintegrated.

Even before Darwin published his famous works on evolution, geologists had already known that the Earth itself had a much longer history than previously fathomed. But since Darwin's time the evidence that nature is historical, and that life's own journey on our planet is a surprisingly lengthy one, has only continued to accumulate. Given the enormity of time that evolution has had available to it, now estimated at about 3.8 billion years, what may have seemed initially improbable becomes increasingly more probable. A truly mammoth span of time provides opportunity enough for purely accidental coincidences to give rise to life in the chemical equivalent of Darwin's "warm little pond." Then, after life comes about by chance, evolutionary time provides room for an unimaginable number of purely undirected genetic mutations to occur so that out of them natural selection can gradually bring about adaptive living beings, eventually including those endowed with minds.

This, at least, is the argument of Dawkins and other evolutionary materialists. In the absence of our present awareness of the universe's temporal immensity the arrival of life may have seemed somewhat unlikely. And so, even as recently as the early years of the present century, at a time when Bergson's writings were highly respected, it seemed to make more sense than it does now to posit the exceptional intervention of a special creative agency to account for life (and mind). But in contemporary scientific portraits, the sense of cosmic time has become so unimaginably protracted that temporal magnitude itself has become the demiurge that transforms dead "matter" into living and thinking beings. Time's own largesse has eliminated the need to invoke anything miraculous or interventionist in order to understand nature and life's evolution.

Thus, along with the revival of atomism, the discovery of deep time has helped vanquish the intellectual need for a hierarchical cosmology. After Darwin, vitalism may have had a momentary appeal. By allowing us to posit a supernatural force as the creative source of life and evolution, vitalism temporarily fed our hunger for an adequate principle of causation and kept life ontologically elevated to a safe status above that of mere matter. In the scientific world today, however, vitalism has lost out, and time itself has quietly become—along with chance and the law of selection—a main ingredient in the explanation of life and evolution.

The Task of Theology After Darwin

To many scientists and philosophers, therefore, it now seems gratuitous to invoke the idea of a timeless, transcendent principle whose influence would, from up above, draw nature toward increasing levels of complexity. As Daniel Dennett has put it, there is no need for any such hierarchically construed "skyhooks" to explain what can be accounted for mechanically and horizontally simply by taking into account time's vastness.[6] To evolutionary materialists, the discovery of time's colossal reach now allows us finally to discard altogether our antiquated hierarchical habits of thought. Today what appears first in time—lifeless matter—also seems to be first in the order of explanation. In other words, all natural occurrences must submit to being deciphered exclusively in terms of a temporally *prior* series of mechanical causes. We are urged to look neither to a timeless Platonic realm above nor to a hidden cosmic finalism but to the misty abysses of the cosmic past for the fullest explanation of all things, including those aspects of nature that we value most: life and mind.

By collapsing the sacred hierarchy, modern evolutionary materialism gives every appearance of having pulverized the cultural, ethical, and religious formations around which human life on this planet has been organized for many thousands of years. It is impossible to exaggerate the enormity of this great drama of dissolution. Clearly, then, a central task of theology after Darwin is to face as honestly as it can the question of whether the hierarchical structuring that constitutes the very backbone of our religious traditions is in any substantive and coherent sense recoverable today.[7]

The formidability of such a challenge is manifested today in the number of ways in which the whole issue has been either swept under the rug or deemed impossible by religious thinkers. I will not even bother here to bring up once again the notorious repudiation of evolutionary science by Christian and other religious fundamentalists. It is worth noting in passing, however, that their negative reaction to Darwin is at least in part motivated by a strong impression that his ideas, if true, would destroy the precious hierarchy of being and value that they cherish so deeply and that, in fact, constitutes the inner core of all traditional theologies. What I shall now highlight, instead, is the fact that even some of our most sophisticated contemporary religious scholars, those who have no stake at all in scriptural literalism or right-wing politics, nonetheless have enormous difficulty reconciling the corrosive atomism and historical gradualism underlying the present scientific depiction of evolution with the ontological hierarchy that forms the backbone of their religious faith and ethical discernment.

Without slipping into logical contradictions or denying the clear results of natural science, can we still maintain that the universe is the sacramental expression of an absolute source of values? Put otherwise, can we hold clearheadedly that life evolved historically, and even that it can be scientifically broken down into genetic and atomic units, but that nonetheless it has its origin or *arche* in the realm of the sacred *(hier)*? And may we, without spurning the results of molecular biology and the evolutionary accounts of life's creation, continue to hold that some things in nature are more valuable than others, or that the cosmos is permeated by an eternal meaning?

Theology has not always dealt with these questions in a way that satisfies simultaneously the demands of logic, scientific integrity, and religious wisdom. Most modern theologians have concentrated so earnestly on purely human concerns that the seemingly irrelevant idea of an evolving cosmos has been effectively shoved into the background. In avoiding close attention to evolution, however, these theologians have tacitly invoked an obsolete dualism that segregates human persons from the natural world. By mentally distancing human life from its cosmic matrix, they have sought to render inconsequential the overwhelming evidence from science that all of life's variety, including humanity itself, has emerged from matter gradually, through identifiable transitional forms, over millions of years of adaptive evolution.[8]

There is also a suspicion, at least among some religious thinkers, that science's atomizing and historicizing of nature is not at all innocent, but that it is part of an insidious modern project to desacralize the natural world. And once every remnant of the sacred hierarchy has been removed, nature will then seem not only inherently purposeless but also vulnerable to despoliation by technologically proficient humans. Seyyed Hossein Nasr, one of the most eloquent contemporary defenders of the classic hierarchical vision, has been exceptionally sensitive to what he considers to be the sinister consequences of the post-Darwinian "horizontalizing" of the sacred hierarchy. He attempts boldly to safeguard the cosmic hierarchy from what he takes to be the nihilistic implications of Darwinian science. His voice is all the more impressive because it is combined with scholarly breadth, scientific erudition, and theological wisdom. It is important that we hear what he has to say.

A most distinguished philosopher and Muslim religious thinker, Nasr has been widely recognized for his voluminous writings on the religious implications of modern science. Some years ago he delivered the prestigious Gifford lectures on the theme of "knowledge and the sacred"; in these lectures he already expressed his objections to the leveling effect of neo-Darwinian ideas. More recently, however, he has set forth a no less poignant protest in his Cadbury lectures, *Religion and the Order of Nature,* from which the following summary is derived.[9]

Before the emergence of modern mechanistic science and its more recent Darwinian manifestations, Nasr maintains, the persistence of hierarchical visions of reality in religious cultures allowed people all over the Earth to locate both nature and humanity within a meaningful cosmos securely connected to a sacred principle of being. Nature was endowed with an order and meaning that expresses vividly the reality of its divine origin or *arche*. But modern science, especially evolutionary biology, now threatens to eclipse the ancient conception of a hierarchical cosmos and with it the capacity of nature to nourish the spiritual and intellectual lives of peoples the world over. The divine source of all life and mind has been removed from the sacred realm above (or from the metaphysical "center"), and its place as source of all has been taken over by the profane causal past. As a result, many modern thinkers find it difficult to view nature any longer as the visible representation of an eternal and absolute reality and meaning.

According to Nasr, the consequences of science's dissolution of nature's hierarchy are manifested most tragically in the unchecked contemporary worldwide destruction of Earth's life-systems. The collapse of the sacred hierarchical picture of the cosmos has made it nearly impossible for modernity any longer to attribute inherent value to life. As a result, the demystification of nature implied in the collapse of hierarchy leaves our planet vulnerable to an unrestrained economic recklessness and greed. Nasr's claim is that the current ecological crisis is an inevitable outcome of modern science's leveling of hierarchy and diminishing of life's value. The prospect of global ecological catastrophe, therefore, should alert us decisively to the functional nihilism implied in evolution's demolition of the ancient cosmic vision. But instead, Nasr claims, our intellectual life and educational processes remain uncritically submissive to scientific modernity's atomizing and historicizing of nature.

Nasr's own search for a postmodern, ecologically integral alternative to materialist evolutionism leads him straight back to tradition as encapsulated in the "perennial philosophy." The *philosophia perennis* (a notion first given currency by the philosopher Gottfried Wilhelm Leibniz, 1646–1716) is a synthesis of the shared central beliefs of the world's great religious and philosophical traditions. Foremost among the common core tenets of the perennial philosophy is the claim that the cosmos is grounded in a single ultimate reality and source of all being. Different traditions express their belief in an eminently sacred reality in culturally distinct ways, but they collectively witness to its presence and power. They also agree that this divine reality is "beyond all conceptualization and all that can be said of It."

> Even Its Name remains veiled and unutterable in certain traditions such as Judaism, but Its Reality is the origin of all that is sacred and the source of the teachings of each authentic faith. Like a mighty spring gushing forth atop a mountain, It gives rise to cascades of water that descend with ever-greater dispersion from each side, each cascade symbolizing all the grades of reality and the levels of cosmic and, by transposition, metacosmic reality of a particular religious universe. Yet all the cascades issue from a single Spring and the substance of all is ultimately nothing but that water which flows from the Spring at the mountaintop, the Reality which is the alpha of all sacred worlds and also the omega to which all that is in their embrace returns.[10]

The modern academic approach to religion, we should note, is largely unsympathetic to the perennial philosophy's hypothesis of a primordial monotheistic fountainhead of world religions. To most contemporary religious scholars the notion of a "perennial philosophy" is an abstraction that ignores the concrete historical and evolutionary factors in the genesis of sacred traditions. Nasr is aware of this objection, but I think he would simply reply that the academic study of religion has itself been taken hostage by the same scientific, horizontalizing evolutionary influences that seek to topple the traditional hierarchy. To view religion or the idea of God as having emerged only gradually from the ignoble historical origins posited by modern history and the various scientific studies of religion is to subject it to the same reductionist treatment that evolutionary thought has already accorded the cosmic hierarchy. The academic study of religion is not totally without value for Nasr, but it cannot put us in touch with the divine as it is understood from within the religions.

Along with its insistence on the metaphysical primacy of an absolute and ineffable sacred reality, the perennial philosophy also affirms the *irreducibility of the higher to the lower levels* in the hierarchy of being. Here also it apparently conflicts with the methodological agenda of modern science, which seeks to explain the things we spontaneously value most—living and thinking beings—in terms of lower-level atomic and molecular processes that in the traditional outlook have considerably less importance and less reality. To Nasr this reductionist ideal of explanation is especially pernicious because of its implied leveling of the hierarchy essential to religion and all genuinely ethical life. What we need instead of modern science, therefore, is a "sacred science," one that opens human awareness up to the totality of being rather than simply to the narrow scientific abstractions that modern intellectual life has identified pathetically with reality as such. Nasr does not seek the repudiation of science so much as its transformation into a discipline sensitive once again to the full hierarchical scale of being.

However, as much as it tries to widen the definition of "science" in order to appear intellectually open-minded, Nasr's proposal will impress most natural scientists today as entirely too selective in its dismissal of the empirical data supporting Darwinian evolutionary theory. While passionately defending a hierarchical cosmology against the attacks of narrow-minded reductionists, Nasr, it appears, ends up throwing away impartially assembled scientific information that a concern for truth should also take into account, no matter what adjustments this may require in our religious visions.

At the same time, however, Nasr must be credited with raising so pointedly an issue that religious thinkers who claim to have made their peace with evolutionary science and molecular biology need to face more explicitly than in the past: Is it both logically and metaphysically possible to embrace simultaneously religions' hierarchical sense of being and value on the one hand, and science's atomizing and historicizing picture of nature on the other? If so, how are we to embrace both science and religion in a convincing and coherent way? Can we subscribe to the notion that life and mind emerged chronologically out of "matter" without at least implicitly surrendering our traditional metaphysical sense of their sacred origin?

Whatever one may think of Nasr's own conclusions, he forces us to focus on this most important question. Is there a plausible way, both logically and metaphysically speaking, to save the essential concerns of the hierarchical vision without having to repudiate the new molecular and historical pictures of life? Here I shall deal only with the *logical* possibility of forming such a union. Then, in the following chapter, I shall suggest an alternative metaphysical framework that fits the requirements of both religion and evolutionary science and provides an alternative to the materialism that accompanies antihierarchical interpretations of evolutionary science.

The Presence of Information

I should begin by noting that even some theologians today consider the whole notion of a "hierarchy" of being to be a leftover from premodern, oppressively patriarchal cultures. It seems to them to be little more than the intellectual residue of outmoded social structures rooted in political and ecclesiastical domination. We should now abandon such a patriarchal notion, they insist, even when thinking about the natural world. Rather than envisaging things in terms of hierarchies, we should learn to think in more relational, cooperative, and democratic ways about the interconnections that make up the cosmos.[11]

Although I concur completely with the emancipative and ecological spirit manifest in this distaste for "hierarchy," there are three reasons why I think we cannot simply abandon the notion. In the first place, from both a theological and etymological point of view, the word "hierarchy," composed of two Greek roots—*hier* = sacred, and *arche* = origin—helps us hold onto the religious conviction that reality has its "origin in the sacred." This meaning—and here I agree with Nasr—is precisely what needs to be upheld in the face of contemporary evolutionary nihilism.[12]

In the second place, we need the term in order to emphasize that life and mind cannot be reduced without remainder to lifeless matter. Goodness, piety, and sanity all require that we hold firmly to the conviction that some dimensions of reality are more comprehensive, more real, and less derivative than others. Some things are patterned and others are patterning; some are included, whereas others are inclusive. Some are less fundamental, some are more so. Some are comprehended, others are comprehending. The notion of hierarchy clearly entails these distinctions. In defending the "hierarchical" vision of nature while simultaneously uniting it with evolution, my intention is to affirm the religious intuition that nature cannot be reduced to a one-dimensional level of being, as is logically implied in materialist metaphysics. To abandon hierarchical thinking altogether, therefore, even in the interest of political correctness, would be inconsistent with the fundamental beliefs of all the world's religions and ethical systems.

Third, "hierarchical" thinking is now experiencing a revival even within the world of science. Some of the most stalwart reductionists, in fact, acknowledge that "lower" levels of physical reality are nested within "higher" ones. Molecules enfold atoms; organisms incorporate cells; ecosystems contextualize individual organisms; and so on. Reference to the complex hierarchical arrangement of nature is becoming more and more a part of standard scientific discourse today. The spirit of reductionism, of course, is still very much alive, but it has been chastened by a fresh awareness among scientists of the practical impossibility of accounting for higher-level emergents or "comprehensive wholes" completely in terms of lower-level components. The suspicion is growing that more complex levels cannot be understood simply in terms of the less complex, for something will always get lost in such a facile translation. This "something" that will get lost if we try in a greedy way to reduce higher to lower levels is partially captured in the notion of "information."

By "information" I mean, in a broad and general sense, the overall ordering of entities—atoms, molecules, cells, genes, etc.—into intelligible forms or arrangements. The term "information," of course, has more specific and technical definitions in physics and engineering, but these need not concern us here. The point I wish to emphasize here is that the use of the metaphor "information" by scientists today is a transparent indication that they now acknowledge, at least implicitly, that something more is going on in nature and its evolution than simply brute exchanges along the matter-energy continuum. Though it is not physically separate, information is logically distinguishable from mass and energy. Information is quietly resident in nature, and in spite of being nonenergetic and nonmassive, it powerfully patterns subordinate natural elements and routines into hierarchically distinct domains.

The fact that information does not show up at the level of atomistic analysis does not mean that it is not really an aspect of nature or that it is somehow less real than atoms and molecules. Science today, at least implicitly, allows for a level of information hierarchically distinct from that of physical elements themselves. Moreover, discontinuous levels of information can exist within what may appear to chemistry, physics, or evolutionary biology as an unbroken material and historical continuum. Information—in a manner unspecifiable by physics or chemistry—insinuates itself into the universe without in any way violating "lower-level" laws of chemistry and physics. It does not interrupt ordinary physical routines but instead makes use of them in its ordering activity. Information, therefore, has the capacity to bring about hierarchical discontinuity among various levels, even though, when viewed in a purely historical or atomistic way, nature seems to be a closed and purely horizontal continuum.

By so characterizing the presence of information in nature, I do not intend anything mystical or supernatural. All I wish to emphasize at this point is that in its encounter with the informational component of nature, modern science has come up abruptly against something quite distinct from the mechanical or material causes with which it has been most at home.[13] Information, in the broad sense in which I am using the notion here, quietly orders things while itself remaining irreducible to the massive and energetic constituents that preoccupy conventional science. Its effects are clearly verifiable, but information itself slips through the wide meshes of science's mechanistic nets. Information, like mathematics, has a certain aspect of timelessness to it. It does not originate out of the historical past, nor does it undergo transformations in the same way that matter and energy do. It abides patiently in the realm of "possibility," waiting to be actualized in time. It is almost as though its various configurations have *always* dwelt "somewhere," anticipating appropriate opportunities to become incarnate.

The stamp of definiteness put on nature's various entities is the effect of information, but information as such lies in some sense outside of time, undevoured by the historical or horizontal scheme of physical causation. Information is sufficiently "real" to configure nature hierarchically, even though this structuring may be invisible to science's leveling depictions. Though beyond the grasp of science, information is not identifiable with pure nothingness. It comes from what we may call simply the realm of the possible. But possibilities, as Whitehead notes, must reside somewhere.[14] They could not arise out of sheer nothingness without violating every convention of rationality.

In the realm of scientific knowledge, the most obvious evidence of the presence of information in nature is found in the way DNA and RNA function in the living cell. Here information is present in a much stricter sense—namely, as meaning embedded in a code—than I have been using the term so far. In fact, for some scientific thinkers we should reserve the term "information" only for the coding that life introduces into the cosmos. In any case, in DNA it is not chemistry alone but the specific informational sequence of four acid bases (A, T, C, and G) that codes and figuratively sketches the distinctive shapes and identities of living beings.[15] The DNA molecule, although at a certain level of analysis appearing to be "just chemistry," is also, at another level of understanding, clearly distinguishable from the strictly deterministic chemical processes operative in it and in the living cell as a whole.[16] The *specific sequence* of the "letters" in the DNA of any particular organism consists of an informational arrangement that cannot be reduced without remainder to chemistry. This is necessarily the case, for if DNA were the product of chemical determinism alone there would be only one kind of DNA molecule, when in fact an indefinite number of arrangements of the "letters" in DNA molecules is chemically possible. In the nuclear DNA of the living cell, an informational ordering can steal onto the scene of nature in such an elusive way that it completely escapes the notice of a purely atomizing or historicizing focus.[17]

A simple analogy (adapted from Michael Polanyi) may help clarify this point.[18] Suppose I scribble meaningless scrawl with my pen on a piece of paper but then suddenly begin writing a coherent sentence. There is a physical and historical continuity between the scrawl on the one side and the sentence on the other when seen at a "lower" level of analysis. But viewed informationally, at a "higher" level, the arranging of letters in a code to form a sentence certainly introduces a radical discontinuity, abruptly propelling our attention onto another plane altogether. Physical continuity remains, but this continuity does not rule out an overriding logical and informational discontinuity. At the level of a purely chemical analysis of the bonding properties of ink and paper *nothing new is going on* when the informative sentence is introduced suddenly. From the point of view of physical science, things are the same as before. Yet from another kind of perspective, that of a human mind capable of reading written information, there is all the difference in the world.

Analogously, the arrangement of nucleotides in DNA does not violate, but instead relies on, the laws of chemistry and their uniform operation. And when we look at DNA from a purely mechanistic perspective, we will not observe any interruption of the laws of chemistry and physics. Moreover, we must admit that the *failure* of chemical processes to perform routinely and predictably would put an end to life (just as the failure of ink to bond with paper would prevent my expressing meaning informationally on this page). But even though determinism is present in the chemical bonding properties essential to DNA, there is enough overall openness or indeterminacy to allow the nucleotides ATCG to be arranged in any number of possible configurations. Hence, without any suspension of physical laws, DNA can function as a code and thus play an informational role at the level of life, one that virtually all biologists now acknowledge.[19] Philosopher Marjorie Grene comments:

> What makes DNA do its work is not its chemistry but the order of the bases along the DNA chain. It is this order which is a code to be read out by the developing organism. The laws of physics and chemistry hold, as reductivists rightly insist, universally; they are entirely unaffected by the particular linear sequence that characterizes the triplet code. Any order is possible physico-chemically; therefore physics and chemistry cannot specify *which* order will in fact succeed in functioning as a code.[20]

What needs emphasis here is that life's higher-level informational arranging of nucleotides in a DNA molecule can occur in such a way that no breaks or violations of nature's laws are noticeable in the continuum of invariant determinism operative in the lower-level chemical processes. Nevertheless, the cell's lower-level chemical functioning is not so rigid as to preclude its being hierarchically taken up into "higher" informational arrangements. A physically noninvasive introduction of information can bring about sharp ontological discontinuity, even though strict continuity of nature's regularities still prevails at the lower, chemical level. An unobtrusive informational discontinuity at one level can exist simultaneously with unbroken physical and historical continuity at another.[21]

It would follow, then, that if theology has any explanatory relevance as far as the evolution of life is concerned, it might be partially, though of course inadequately, represented in informational terms. God could be thought of as the ultimate source of the novel informational patterns available to evolution. If so, it is inappropriate for theology to specify the relation of God to the life-process in terms of the lower-level efficient and mechanical causes familiar to modern science. For that matter, even among the natural sciences themselves there is a hierarchical relationship that rules out any complete explanation in terms of chemistry or physics. Evolutionary biology, for example, does not have to account for such higher-level occurrences as speciation or the behavior of populations in terms of lower-level biochemical causes. Although the laws of physics and chemistry are presumed to be continually operative during natural selection, evolutionary explanation is not reducible to such material causes. Even some of the most reductionist scientific thinkers (Richard Dawkins, for example) now concede that evolutionary patterns appear at an autonomous level, hierarchically distinct from and, in their overarching formative features, unilluminated by physics or chemistry.[22] All the less, then, should theology be obliged to specify in terms of physical particulars just how God influences the natural world.

Nor should theologians involved in the science and religion conversation seek—in an overly eager spirit of accommodation—to render the notions of teleology or divine action intelligible in the same terms that scientific kinds of explanation employ. The informational analogy allows us to appreciate how the universe as a whole may have some overall meaning or "point" to it without this meaning or "point" needing to be displayed at the same level of investigation at which natural science functions. Whatever meaning the evolving cosmos might have from the point of view of religious faith and theology could never show up at the level of scientific specification.

How Does Information Work?

Some version of hierarchy, theology rightly insists, remains essential to any intelligible conception of cosmic meaning. To deny hierarchy altogether would be to plunge our lives and minds into a swamp of unqualified relativism, wherein religious and ethical claims would have no basis and nothing could plausibly be said to have any enduring importance. Hierarchical thinking, in which lower levels can be quietly informed by higher, is necessary to express the religious intuition that reality and human values have a sacred origin and a significance beyond what the physical sciences and biology can discern. Hierarchy is also essential if some things are to be considered more valuable and more real than others.[23]

However, the evolutionary portrait of nature seems to be so destructive of hierarchy that many religious people either reject Darwinism outright or refuse to confront it head-on. At the same time, the polemics of antitheists like Richard Dawkins and Daniel Dennett, based in what they take to be the materialist implications of Darwin's science, barely conceal a sophomoric delight in toppling ancient hierarchies that for centuries have structured the ethical and spiritual lives of millions. By placing matter, life, and mind on a historical and molecular continuum, they simply assume that evolution pancakes the illusory sacred hierarchy down to the one-dimensional plane of impersonal natural processes.[24] Puzzled about how to defend the classical religious traditions against the threat of such leveling, many theologians have found it convenient simply to ignore evolution altogether. What I am suggesting here, however, is that a study of the way information "works" can help us understand how a hierarchical shaping of meaning or purpose can become implanted in an evolving universe without having to be obvious at the level of scientific inquiry.

How then does information work? Such an awkward question would never have occurred to Plato and Aristotle, both of whom resisted atomistic simplism and gave prominent causal status to what they called "form" as essential to the very constitution of things. But standing as we do at the end of an age of mechanistic science, a period during which the ideal of explanation has become that of specifying only the efficient and material causes of things, the question of how information produces effects offers a fresh challenge. It has provoked a new generation of scientists, mathematicians, economists, computer scientists, linguists, anthropologists, and others to find the secrets underlying nature's puzzling tendency to organize itself "spontaneously." At the Santa Fe Institute in New Mexico, for example, whole careers are now being devoted to this pursuit.

Information "works," we can say at the very least, only by *comprehensively* integrating particulars (atoms, molecules, cells, bits, and bytes) into coherent wholes. Thus, any attempt to *specify* the *comprehensive* function of informational patterns in terms appropriate only to the comprehended particulars themselves is logically self-contradictory. Vague suggestions that the increasingly complex and comprehensive levels in evolution simply "emerge" or "bubble up from below" do not explain anything. This typical evasion (a confusion of description with explanation) is tantamount to claiming that the subordinate particulars of a phenomenon can integrate or comprehend themselves. Such bootstrapping, I would submit, is logical nonsense. By definition, a subordinate particular, or even a set of such particulars, cannot be concurrently both the integrated substituent(s) and the integrating totality that gives the particulars their subordinate identities. We may readily assume, therefore, that the origin of information and its *integrating* capacity resides in some other logical space than that of the atomic and historical particulars that natural science appeals to in its modern ideal of explanation.

To reply that information is just our own mental abstraction and that it has no real existence in nature is also refutable. Guy Murchie, referring to the universal patterning of natural phenomena, lists "abstraction" (which for him includes what I am calling form or information) as one of the great "mysteries" of life.[25] I agree with him that information as such is a mystery that science cannot comprehend through its atomizing reductions. However, "abstraction" is the wrong word. We usually contrast "abstract" with the term "concrete" and accord the latter the status of being "real," whereas we view abstractions as mere constructs of the human mind that evaporate as soon as we stop thinking about them. Information, on the other hand, inheres concretely in nature. It is not an abstraction that vanishes when we stop thinking about it but is, rather, the very real (though scientifically unspecifiable) foundation of anything being actual at all. Form or pattern, as philosophers from Aristotle to Whitehead have noted repeatedly, is a metaphysical aspect of things, one without which they would have no actuality at all.[26]

Informational patterning, in other words, is a *metaphysical* necessity; for in order for anything to be actual at all, it must have at least some degree of form, order, or pattern. Otherwise a thing would be indefinite, and whatever is indefinite is no-thing. To be *some-thing* at all an entity has to be informed in a definite way. This is a requirement both of things within the universe and of the universe as a whole. Beings would have no actuality without being informed, and this means limited, in a certain way. True, the human mind, especially by using mathematics, can *logically* pull aspects of form apart from the concrete fabric of nature into which it is woven, leaving the remainder to crumble imaginatively into a pile of atoms. And in the purely logical form of having been mentally noted, science may, of course, call information an "abstraction." But if information were literally taken out of the world, then the world and its inhabitants— at all levels—would cease to be at all. Neither would there be atomic units, for these too must be patterned, limited, and "informed" to be actual themselves.

Information subtly weaves the world into patterns, then gathers these into still more comprehensive wholes, and always slips silently out of our grasp. It hides itself, even while performing its integrative and hierarchical chores. We murder it whenever we dissect it. Modern thought, in its compulsion to grasp things materially and mechanistically, has considerable trouble dealing with the slippery unobtrusiveness of information, even though the notion is now indispensable in disciplines ranging from physics to biology. Information's inaccessibility to empirical scrutiny or mechanical analysis makes it seem "mystical"; hence it is intellectually safer for many scientific thinkers to call information an "abstraction" and to give the status of "reality" only to the physically specifiable particulars that are "accidentally" integrated into coherent wholes over the course of time.

However, science in general and biology in particular always find themselves already swimming in a river of information. One must agree with Murchie that in coming up against this fact of information we are entering into one of what he calls the great "mysteries." We do not grasp it so much as it grasps us. It always at least partly eludes us. We cannot get our minds around it since it somehow already enfolds our own minds. Science, as even Einstein was willing to admit, must admit defeat at this point, for the capacity to do science at all requires an assumption in advance that nature is informed intelligibly and that the mind itself is informed in such a way as to attune itself to at least some of the world's intelligible patterning.

A Taoist Interpretation of Information

Once again, then, how does this mysterious dimension—broadly called "information"—really work? Do we have any analogies by which to clarify how something so reserved and concealed from our focal vision can be powerful enough to endow things with their very identities, and perhaps the cosmos with an overall meaning? As I have just argued, we cannot find useful analogies in conventional scientific terms. Perhaps, though, we might derive some illumination from the world of religious thought.

Let us look, for example, at the ancient Chinese body of wisdom known as Taoism. In Taoism, ultimate reality, called the Tao, is thought of as energetically passive while remaining informationally active. Paradoxically, the very inactivity of the Tao is what gives rise to structure and function in the world. The Tao "works" in the world by way of *wu wei,* an untranslatable term for "active inaction" or what we might call "noninterfering effectiveness." Perhaps information "works" in an analogous way. In a manner similar to the modesty of the Tao's effectiveness, information can order nature in such a subtle way as to render discontinuous and hierarchical what we perceive, at the level of evolutionary and atomic understanding, to be purely continuous and horizontal.

The *Tao Te Ching,* a text attributed to Lao-Tzu (sixth century B.C.E.) portrays the Tao (or the "Way") as like water, or a valley, or an uncarved block. All of these are said to accomplish much while remaining unobtrusive and passive. Is it possible that something like this self-concealing power influences the whole of the cosmos? Physical science is able to observe only things that are prominent and mechanically "forceful." Lao-Tzu, however, stresses the power of the negative, of that which is not forceful and does not stand out noticeably. The Tao that informs nature is so empirically withdrawn that one cannot even name it. It recedes behind or beyond all phenomena and cannot be located among the manifold of things we experience sensibly. Yet it is, paradoxically, powerful in its self-withdrawal. The "Way" of nature, according to Lao-Tzu, is noninterference. The regions of our experience governed by force or active energy are therefore superficial in comparison with the silent informational depths of the universe.

Here once again we encounter something along the lines of the divine *kenosis,* which in the preceding chapter I identified as the *ultimate* explanation of evolution. The self-limiting Tao may even be spoken of as "nonbeing," since it does not fall among the classes of things we normally call "beings." In a sense it is "no-thing." But precisely as "no-thing" it exercises its power:

> *Thirty spokes are joined at the hub.*
> *From their non-being arises the function of the wheel.*
> *Lumps of clay are shaped into a vessel.*
> *From their non-being arises the functions of the vessel.*
> *Doors and windows are constructed together to make a chamber.*
> *From their non-being arises the functions of the chamber.*
> *Therefore, as individual beings, these things are useful materials.*
> *Constructed together in their non-being, they give rise to function.*[27]

The Taoist philosopher Wu Cheng (1249–1333) comments: "If it were not for the empty space of the hub to turn round the wheel, there would be no movement of the cart on the ground. If it were not for the hollow space of the vessel to contain things, there would be no space for storage. If it were not for the vacuity of the room between the windows and doors for lights coming in and going out, there would be no place to live."[28]

I am suggesting, then, that information can pattern the universe, and even endow it with hierarchically distinct features, in a similarly noninvasive, utterly humble manner. And it may do all of this without interrupting in any way what from a purely scientific point of view must appear as an unbroken continuum of atomic elements or historical becoming.

However, Taoism teaches us that if there is a hierarchical arrangement to evolutionary phenomena, and an overarching meaning to the universe, then we will become sensitive to its presence only if we ourselves have first learned the wisdom of *wu wei* and allowed our own lives, in a deeply personal way, to be informed by the Tao's humility. The impersonal methods of modern science, by way of contrast, are a much coarser, controlling way of understanding. They fix our focal gaze only on the wheel's spokes, the potter's clay, or the window and door frames, rather than on the self-effacing power of the "void" or "no-thing" at the center that makes these entities functional at all. Any real awareness of cosmic hierarchy or of cosmic meaning, therefore, can occur to us only after we too have undergone—at least in some measure—a personal transformation, whereby a Taoist sensitivity to the power of humility can take root and become the guiding ideal of our own lives.

Christianity, though obviously different from Taoist philosophy, shares with it and with some other traditions a kindred intuition that what is most real is also the most hidden and subdued—even to the point of seeming to be completely absent.[29] In Christianity, as St. Paul came to believe, God's "power is made manifest in weakness." I have no desire here to reduce Taoism to Christianity or vice versa. But it seems to me that the Taoist insight at least points in the same general direction as the often suppressed intuition of Christian faith that God creates and acts in the natural world in the manner of humble self-restraint rather than crude intervention. Taoism expresses its similarly paradoxical sense of ultimate reality in this way:

Gaze at it; there is nothing to see.
It is called the formless.
Heed it; there is nothing to hear.
It is called the soundless.
Grasp it; there is nothing to hold on to.
It is called the immaterial.
Invisible, it cannot be called by any name.
It returns again to nothingness.[30]

In other words, ultimate reality has the capacity to influence the world as a consequence of, and not in spite of, its nonavailability. Therefore, perhaps we should not be too eager to specify the meaning or "point" of the cosmos. To seek clarity and certitude here is inappropriate. The logic of both Taoism and kenotic theism deflates the requirement, especially dear to modern scientism, that everything truly real must make itself available in an empirically obvious manner. The assumption that all of reality should subject itself to our cognitional control in this manner is a most impoverishing attitude.

Contemplate the ultimate void.
Remain truly in quiescence.
All things are together in action,
But I look into their non-action.[31]

Conclusion

Nasr's thought is illustrative of the challenge theology faces in mapping evolutionary science onto the classical hierarchy of being to which the "perennial philosophy" tightly adheres. My objective in this chapter, however, has been to show that we need not conclude, with either Nasr or his materialist opponents, that evolution *logically* rules out a hierarchical metaphysics. Science's own growing awareness of the explanatory role of information in nature's constitution allows us to embrace consistently both a religious vision—including a sense of cosmic meaning—and the carefully established results of evolutionary biology. In the next chapter, I shall look for a metaphysics, that is, a general sense of reality, that will enhance our appreciation of this felicitous alliance of theology and evolution.

6

A God for Evolution

TOWARD THE END OF HIS LIFE the famous Jesuit paleontologist Teilhard de Chardin (1881–1955) observed that traditional theological reflection has conceived of God's influence on nature too much in terms of Aristotle's notion of a prime mover pushing things from the past *(a retro)*. Evolution, Teilhard said, requires that we think of God not as driving or determining events from behind or from the past, but as drawing the world from up ahead *(ab ante)* toward the future. Teilhard goes on to say that "only a God who is functionally and totally 'Omega' can satisfy us." But, he asks, "where shall we find such a God?... And who will at last give evolution *its own* God?"[1]

Almost half a century later we still struggle with the same questions. It is not yet evident that theology has thought about God in a manner consistent with the data of evolution. Powerful voices in the religious world continue to hold the idea of an absolute reality as far away from evolution as possible. And even theologians who have assented notionally to the compatibility of Darwin and theology have often failed to address the difficulties involved in such a novel union of ideas. A complete consummation of Teilhard's hopes for a vision of God deeply resonant with evolution still eludes us.

Probably no modern thinker has been more persistent than Teilhard in seeking to transform our theological sensibilities in a way that takes evolution seriously. Long before most of his fellow believers, he realized that the intellectual plausibility, as well as the renewal, of Christian faith in our day depends upon a sustained encounter with Darwinian ideas. Teilhard himself struggled for many years to spell out what he thought would be the invigorating spiritual outcome of such an engagement. And in terms of sheer inspirational force, it is hard even today to surpass the depth and passion of his own contributions to this venture.

But is Teilhard's religious thought itself adequate to Darwinian science? There have been considerable refinements in the scientific understanding of evolution since his day, especially in the areas of genetics and molecular biology. Moreover, his notion of evolutionary "progress" has led some neo-Darwinians to write him off as an outdated ideologue. The paleontologist Stephen Jay Gould, for example, is so certain that evolution is devoid of the directionality Teilhard discerned in it that he has attempted to destroy completely the famous Jesuit's scientific reputation by making him appear to be an accomplice to the notorious Piltdown hoax.[2] Gould's scurrilous attack, incidentally, has been thoroughly debunked; but, to my knowledge, he has never publicly retracted his claims, in spite of clear evidence that Teilhard could not have been involved.[3]

Daniel Dennett, who is not always in sympathy with Gould on some of the finer points of neo-Darwinian evolution, in this case expresses even more bluntly what Gould may be trying to say in his attack on Teilhard. After devoting several pages of *Darwin's Dangerous Idea* to a crude caricature of Teilhard in order to make him seem scientifically incompetent, Dennett adds: "The problem with Teilhard's vision is simple. He emphatically denied the fundamental idea: that evolution is a mindless, purposeless, algorithmic process."[4]

This is not the place to debate the merits of either Teilhard's scientific reputation or his scientific understanding of evolution, nor is it necessary to do so. Suffice it to say that Gould's and Dennett's charges have been refuted decisively and that Teilhard had the reputation in his day of being an excellent scientist; had he lived to the end of this century there is no question that he would have kept up with the latest developments in biology.

What is worth talking about is Teilhard's call for a new metaphysics in which to situate our understanding of evolutionary science. All scientists have at least an implicit metaphysics. Every scientific idea is presented against the backdrop of general assumptions about the nature of reality (which is what "metaphysics" is all about). Even in the case of the "purest" Darwinian accounts, metaphysical convictions are impossible to suppress. Teilhard wanted simply to make sure that the implicit metaphysical beliefs that scientists bring with them to the study of life do not blind them to what is really going on in an evolving universe. And, like Bergson and Whitehead, he understood instinctively that the materialist metaphysics that frames the "scientific" ideas of many modern biologists is simply inadequate to the full reality of evolution.

Although science must be distinguished carefully from metaphysics, what scientists actually decide to focus on or leave out of their scientific pictures is deeply determined by their general visions of what is real and what is not. Thus, Teilhard would certainly argue that materialism, instead of leading scientists to see the evolutionary data more clearly, actually closes them off to the most obvious feature of evolution, namely, its bringing about new being, or what we shall call "novelty." In the case of Gould and Dennett, both of whose "scientific" thinking is determined in great measure by an a priori commitment to materialist metaphysics, it is not Teilhard's science that really arouses their disdain, but his demand for an alternative metaphysics. They are disturbed by Teilhard's own "dangerous idea," namely, that metaphysical materialism is incompetent to make full sense of the actual discoveries of evolutionary science. The extravagant lengths to which they have gone in order to distort Teilhard and his ideas is an indication that something much more contentious is occurring here than merely scientific disagreement. What really repels them is Teilhard's suggestion that a metaphysically adequate explanation of any universe in which evolution occurs requires—at some point beyond the limits that science has set for itself—a transcendent force of attraction to explain the *overarching* tendency of matter to evolve toward life, mind, and spirit.

However, this postulated divine "force," or the "Omega," which Teilhard identified with the Creator God of his Christian faith, was never intended to be taken as a strictly scientific explanation. Teilhard does not introduce the notion of God simply to fill up a "gap" in scientific exploration. Rather, his appeal to a theological metaphysics is undertaken precisely so that our background assumptions, unlike those of materialist evolutionism, will allow *all* of the data of evolution, and especially the fact of emergent novelty, to stand out.

A "Metaphysics of the Future"

What Teilhard seemed to be looking for is what we might call a "metaphysics of the future." "Metaphysics" is the term philosophers use to refer to the general vision of reality that one holds to be true. As Teilhard acknowledged explicitly, our religious thought has been dominated by a metaphysics of *esse* (or "being") that has obscured the obvious fact of nature's constant "becoming" and its perpetual movement toward the future. The metaphysics of "being" that we find in Plato and Aristotle was taken over in one form or another by Christian, Jewish, and Islamic theology, and it still forms the intellectual setting of much religious reflection in the West. An exclusivist preoccupation with "being" may have seemed appropriate to a static cosmos and to the classic hierarchical pictures of the cosmos reviewed in the preceding chapter. But evolution requires that we now entertain an alternative understanding of reality, one that stresses the prominence of the future.

Teilhard called his proposed alternative a "metaphysics of *unire*," that is, a conception of reality in which all things are drawn perpetually toward deeper coherence by an ultimate force of attraction, abstractly identified as Omega, and conceived of as an essentially *future* reality.[5] Evolution, to put it as directly as I can, seems to require a divine source of being that resides not in a timeless present located somewhere "up above," but in the future, essentially "up ahead," as the goal of a world still in the making. The term "God" in this revised metaphysics must once again mean for us, as it did for many of our biblical forbears, the transcendent future horizon that draws an entire universe, and not just human history, toward an unfathomable fulfillment yet to be realized. This, I think, is what Teilhard means when he says that God must become for us less Alpha than Omega.

Teilhard, therefore, surely would have endorsed the contemporary German theologian Jürgen Moltmann's persistent reminder that in the biblical view of things the word "God" means, before all else, "Future."[6] And he would have applauded the suggestions by another famous Jesuit scholar, Karl Rahner, who spoke of God as the "Absolute Future."[7] Likewise he would be in sympathy with the Lutheran theologians Wolfhart Pannenberg and Ted Peters, who think of God as the "Power of the Future."[8] Since Teilhard's own lifetime, exegetical rediscovery of the prominent role of hope in biblical religion has made it more theologically appropriate than ever to think systematically of ultimate reality in terms of the dimension of "future."

Nevertheless, in spite of this century's reacquaintance with biblical eschatology and a God who relates to the world primarily in the mode of promise, Christianity's conversion to the metaphysics of the future implicit in its biblical foundations is still far from complete. This, I think, is the main reason why evolution does not yet have "its own God." After many centuries of domination by Platonic and Aristotelian philosophical concepts, a considerable portion of Western theology and spirituality is still ruled by a metaphysics of the "eternal present," according to which the natural world is the always deficient reflection of, if not a perverse deviation from, a primordial perfection of "being" that exists forever in a fixed realm generally pictured as "above" creation, untouched by time. In accordance with this traditional "metaphysics of the eternal present," the inevitable "becoming" that occurs in evolution can be interpreted only as meaningless straying from a timeless completeness, rather than as genuinely *new* creation.

Accordingly, when the idea of evolution made its appearance in Europe a century and a half ago, the new historical sense of nature-in-process ran up against a still Platonically soddened theological mind-set incapable of accommodating a deep sense of the future. In spite of the biblical hope for new creation, what seems to have dominated our religious preconceptions is a strong suspicion that the future somehow must not be allowed to invade and transform the present. Aside from occasional apocalyptic expressions of hope for radical renewal, Western religious sensibilities still carry at least some residue of the pre-evolutionary prejudice that cosmic time can bring about nothing that has not already been fully realized in a perfection existing from all eternity.[9]

Nostalgia for this lost perfection persists deeply in the souls of all of us. It is not surprising, then, that evolution is still taken by many theologians as a relatively inconsequential process of becoming. After all, if being is a *fait accompli,* fully realized from all eternity, then evolution, when interpreted within the classical framework of *esse,* can be relegated easily to the same order of relative unimportance that pertains to all temporal occurrence. One must wonder, therefore, whether evolution will ever find "its own God" as long as theology and spirituality remain hostage to this brand of metaphysics.

It is worth noting once again that biblical literalists are not the only ones who cannot make room for evolution in their religious thinking. As I observed in the previous chapter, intellectually sophisticated devotees of the "perennial philosophy," with their notion of a "Great Chain of Being," have denied vehemently that evolution can be harmonized with the hierarchical vision of reality essential to religion. Instead of revising this hierarchical metaphysics, with its static sense of graded levels of being, proponents of the perennial philosophy have found it more efficient to ignore, where they have not completely renounced, Darwinian science.[10]

For its part, the typically materialist reading of evolution, following what might be called a "metaphysics of the past," also logically rules out the coming of a genuinely new future. Evolutionary materialism locates the source and substance of life's diversity in the purely physical determinism that, allegedly, has led, step by fateful step, out of the dead causal past to the present state of living nature in all its profusion of complexity. Such a metaphysics no more allows for the emergence of real novelty in evolution than does a religious metaphysics fixated on the eternal present. The extravagant proliferation of living beings on this planet over the past several billion years, clear evidence of evolution's inclination to bring about unprecedented novelty, is for the pure materialist nothing more than a reshuffling of lifeless stuff that has always been there. Materialist versions of neo-Darwinism claim that all events in nature, including the story of life and mind on Earth, were coiled up implicitly in lifeless primordial cosmic conditions. Nature needed only to undergo the somewhat incidental drama of gradually unfurling over the course of time in order for life and mind to make their unremarkable appearance. Conceived of in this way, the entire life-process, rather than being evidence of nature's openness to the arrival of genuine novelty, is only the explication of what was fully latent already in lifeless matter from the time of cosmic beginnings.

It is not hard to find examples of this "metaphysics of the past" in contemporary pessimistic interpretations of evolution. Once again, perhaps the most overt example is Daniel Dennett's convoluted argument that evolution is nothing more than an "algorithmic" process, fully explainable by tracing present outcomes back to their determining physical causes in the past. All we need in order to understand the present, Dennett argues, is to practice "reverse engineering." This is the procedure of figuratively taking apart complex things, such as living beings, piece by piece in order to disclose how the implacable laws of nature assembled them over the course of time without anticipating any future goal. Reverse engineering will show that the deterministic laws of nature, not any attraction to the future, fully explain how evolution happens.[11]

I have found Dennett's position especially worth noting in this book not because it has much light to shed on the evolutionary process, but because it sets forth so nakedly the materialist metaphysical assumptions espoused by many distinguished neo-Darwinian scientists.[12] Dennett's fatalistic vision, not unlike the tragic stoicism that has haunted much modern scientific thought, resolutely prohibits in principle the emergence of true novelty. Dennett, no doubt, would reply that the virtual archive of yet untried genetic combinations is enough to guarantee the perpetual renewal of life. However, as I indicated in the preceding chapter, the existence of life and the process of evolution require an informational coefficient that does not itself originate in any past series of mechanical causes and that therefore cannot be accounted for by the method of reverse engineering. By definition, an atomistic, reductive method of inquiry into the past "causes" of life will abstract from the very organizational principles and informational patterns that give living beings their characteristic identities in the first place.[13]

I would submit here that the novel informational possibilities that evolution has available to it arise from the always dawning future. It is the arrival of the future, and not the grinding onward of an algorithmic past, that accounts for the novelty in evolution. Without the persistent coming of an unrehearsed future, the present and the past would have no opening onto the path of transformation. Evolution is rendered possible only because of the temporal clearing made available when the future faithfully introduces relevant new possibilities. The apparent "contingencies" (in the sense of undirected occurrences) in natural history, which appear to shape evolution in all of the serendipitous and unpredictable ways that Gould's writings highlight, are themselves made possible only because of the temporal gift of an open future. Contingent events, then, are not themselves ultimately explanatory of evolutionary novelty, for their own occurrence is itself dependent fundamentally on time's opening toward the future. It is not the occurrence of contingency that brings about the future; rather, it is the arrival of the future that allows events to have the status of contingency, that is, to be more than just the inevitable outcome of past deterministic causes.

Evolutionary materialism's picture of things has attained its intellectual appeal only at the price of abstracting from the concrete actuality of nature in process. What it leaves out is a sense of the "coming of the future" as the fundamental "force" in evolutionary occurrence. Following the ideas of Wolfhart Pannenberg and Ernst Bloch, as well as giving voice to what I think are the sentiments of Teilhard, Rahner, Moltmann, and many process theologians, I would argue that we need to situate our understanding of nature's evolution within a "metaphysics of the future."

A metaphysics of the future is rooted in the intuition, expressed primordially in the biblical experience of what is "really real," that the abode of ultimate reality is not limited to the causal past nor to a fixed and timeless present "up above." Rather, it is to be found most characteristically in the constantly arriving and renewing future. Such a vision, conceptually difficult though it may be, can suitably accommodate both the data of evolutionary biology and the extravagant claims of biblical religion about how a promising God relates to the world.[14]

We need a vision of reality that makes sense of the most obvious aspects of life's evolution, in particular the fact that it brings about *new* forms of being. Dennett's mechanism-materialism may seem to provide an appropriate set of background assumptions for explaining some aspects of evolution, but it is too abstract to encompass and account for the novelty that emerges in evolution. For example, the assumptions of materialist metaphysics can provide no illumination regarding the surprising emergence in evolution of what we all know immediately as the experience of our "subjectivity." Materialist interpretations of evolution have so far shed no light whatsoever on the question of why living beings have developed something like an "inner sense." And it is especially in the ongoing intensification of inwardness that what I am calling "novelty" enters into the material universe.[15]

This inability to take the fact of subjectivity into account is indicative of the more general incapacity of materialism to adjust itself to novelty as such. Materialism is closed a priori to the prospect of there arising in evolution truly new being, since by definition it has identified being with the mindless "matter" already present prior to life's evolution. Most materialists, of course, will allow that *unprecedented* arrangements of mindless matter appear in evolution constantly. But the underlying being or *reality* of all such configurations, including entities endowed with a high degree of subjectivity, consists of lifeless and mindless atomic constituents rather than of the elusive informational patterns by which they are ordered and in which their novelty is realized.

The Power of the Future

An alternative view of reality, one more commensurate with the evidence provided by evolutionary novelty, is a metaphysics that gives priority to the future rather than to the past or the present. But what exactly do we mean by this oddly named "metaphysics of the future"? I am compelled, in a way, to resist the invitation to clarify. For to "clarify" something almost always means—at least in academic circles—to situate it in terms of either the classical metaphysics of *esse* or, in a more modern vein, the metaphysics of the past that hovers over scientific materialism. By definition, the futurity of being cannot be translated into these alien provinces without in the process having its very heart cut out of it.

Let me emphasize, therefore, that the notion of a metaphysics of the future has an irreducibly religious origin. Such an admission will undoubtedly lead anyone committed to either of the other two metaphysical frameworks to judge my commitments as an evasion of "reality." However, I would simply respond that the metaphysics I am espousing here is rooted deeply in the *experience* that people have of something that to them is overwhelmingly and incontestably real, namely, what may be called metaphorically the "power of the future." Of course, it is perhaps only by adopting the religious posture of hope that they have been opened to the experience of this power. But that they are prepared for such an experience by participation in a particular religious tradition, one that encourages them to place their trust in the promise of a surprising future fulfillment, need not be taken a priori as sufficient reason for our suspecting its veracity.

Faith, at least in the biblical context, is the experience of *being grasped* by "that which is to come." Any theology that seeks to reflect such faith accurately, therefore, is required to attribute some kind of efficacy to the future, difficult though this may be to conceptualize clearly. A metaphysics of the future is already implicit in a certain kind of religious experience. Paul Tillich describes it as a sense of being grasped by the "coming order": "The *coming* order is always coming, shaking *this* order, fighting with it, conquering it and conquered by it. The coming order is always at hand. But one can never say: 'It is here! It is there!' One can never grasp it. *But one can be grasped by it.*"[16]

In the experience of faith, it is the "future" that comes to meet us, takes hold of us, and makes us new. We may call this future, at least in what Rahner calls its "absolute" depth, by the name "God." In biblical circles, the very heart of authentic faith consists of the total orientation of consciousness toward the coming of God, the ultimately real. Beyond all of our provisional or relative futures there lies an "Absolute Future." And since our own experience cannot be separated artificially from the natural world to which we are tied by evolution, we are permitted also to surmise that "being grasped" by the Absolute Future pertains not just to ourselves but to the whole cosmic process in which we are sited. Theology can claim legitimately, along with St. Paul (Rom. 8:22), that the *entire universe* is always being drawn by the power of a divinely renewing future. The "power of the future" is the ultimate metaphysical explanation of evolution.

The sense of being grasped by the power of the future is palpable to religious experience, but it cannot be translated without remainder into scientifically specifiable concepts, precisely because science typically attributes efficacy only to what lies in the causal past. Nevertheless, if we follow Whitehead's pertinent metaphysical reminder that an investigation of human experience provides rich concepts that can be applied by analogy to the events that make up the rest of nature, then theology can infer that the same "power of the future" that grasps us in faith also embraces the entire cosmos.

If this all sounds too metaphorical to be scientifically palatable, we may recall here the role that metaphor also plays in scientific explanation. Evolutionary biology in particular has to employ metaphorical language. Even a scientist as reductionistic as Richard Dawkins complains of the "physics envy" among some of his fellow biologists who seek to escape metaphor by collapsing nature's hierarchical structure down to the level of physics, where only mathematics is appropriate.[17] The explanatory success of Darwinian biology, Dawkins insinuates, has occurred *because* of, not in spite of, its reliance on foggy but still illuminating metaphors such as "adaptation," "cooperation," "competition," "survival," and "selection."

To admit that the notion of the "power of the future" is also metaphorical, therefore, is in no sense to diminish its explanatory competence. Accordingly, by a "metaphysics of the future," I mean quite simply the philosophical expression of the intuition—admittedly religious in origin—that all things receive their being from out of an inexhaustibly resourceful "future" that we may call "God"; this intuition also entails the notion that the cosmic past and present are in some sense given their own status by the always arriving but also always unavailable future.[18] If such an idea at first seems difficult, we need only observe that even our most ordinary experience readily corresponds to this way of thinking about reality. Only a brief reflection suffices to convince us that the past is gone and remains irretrievable, and the present vanishes before we can ever grasp hold of it. The "future," on the other hand, is always arriving faithfully at the green edge of each moment, bringing with it the possibility of new being. What has already been consigned to the fixed past is not itself enough to explain the novelty of evolutionary occurrences. We can look only to the future to find the ultimate source from which new life and new species of life arise.

It should not be too hard for us to appreciate, therefore, why a religion that encourages its devotees to wait in patient hope for the fulfillment of life and history will interpret ultimate reality, or God, as coming toward the present, and continually creating the world, from the sphere of the future "not-yet." Such an idea, I once again admit, will not make sense to everyone immediately. In fact, many of us think intuitively of the future as quite "unreal," since it has not yet arrived fully. The past and the present may seem to have more "being," in the sense of fixed reality, than does the future, which apparently has the character of not-yet-being. So the idea of a *metaphysics* of the future will probably seem confusing, at least at first.

However, perhaps this confusion is the result of our having been bewitched by a metaphysics either of the past or of the eternal present. Modern scientific thinking, which has affected all of us deeply, is not ready to abandon its passionate allegiance to the explanatory primacy of the causal past. Consequently, it seems to scientistic thinkers such as Dennett that everything that occurs in cosmic or biological evolution is simply the unfolding of what has already gone before. We are compelled to acknowledge, I think, that in such a view of reality there is no room for the emergence of anything truly new or in principle unanticipated. There is something very safe, but also very stale, about such a vision of things. It thoroughly suppresses the possibility of any real informational novelty and surprise that might disturb the prospect of complete scientific prediction, or that might challenge us, as part of the evolving universe, to let new creation occur in our own lives.

At the same time, however, I think we must also confess that many of our traditional theologies and spiritualities are equally reluctant to terminate their long affair with the Greek philosophical world's metaphysics of the eternal present, a way of thinking about the real that also forbids the occurrence of anything truly new. The traditional hierarchical vision—according to which all the levels of finite being are held up from above and sacramentally permeated by an eternal, timeless *arche*—is certainly preferable to the modern materialist metaphysics of the past. Materialism, after all, is nothing less than what Paul Tillich has perceptively called an "ontology of death," a way of thinking that gives the status of "reality" only to lifeless units of "matter."[19] However, as far apart as the traditional hierarchical view of being is from the modern materialist metaphysics, it unfortunately joins with the latter in its cadaverous tendency to nullify the future.

The interior logic of both of these prominent metaphysical options—and indeed what may partially explain their appeal—is their aversion to the future or, in other words, their shared inclination to shut out the disturbing arrival of genuinely new possibilities. Both modern science, with its Newtonian sense of the theoretical reversibility of time, and the traditional hierarchical depiction of the sacred think of what is "really real" in terms that make the passage of time, and hence the coming of a new future, more or less inconsequential. Even though the new studies of complexity and chaos call for an alternative metaphysical horizon for science, there is still enormous resistance to most efforts to supplant the mechanistic worldview.[20]

The Oxford physical chemist Peter Atkins, for example, declares that all the variety in the life-world is merely simplicity *masquerading* as complexity.[21] As this formula implies, the present complex state of nature is mere appearance concealing the lifeless physical simplicity that for Atkins is the only true *reality* underneath and temporally prior to the masquerade. Here the accomplishments of time and the constant arrival of the future are discounted as purely incidental, concealing the harsh truth that only past simplicity is fundamental. Such a way of looking at things ignores the reality of time and implies that the emergent novelty in evolution is only a charade. The limitless possibilities lurking in the future are here disregarded, since only physically simple constituents originating in the past can claim to be causally real.

Steven Weinberg's well-received reflections on contemporary physics share the same tendency to abstract from time and the resourcefulness of the future. Weinberg argues that in the field of particle physics, science is inching ever closer to an irreducibly simple and comprehensive understanding of nature. Once we have acquired a firm hold on the "fundamental" simplicity of which science "dreams" so feverishly, we will be in a position to write a "final theory" of the universe. All that will be left for science to do afterward is merely to describe in more and more refined detail how the ultimate simplicity has led to the astounding complexity we see all around us. But the real work of scientific discovery will be over.[22] Along the same lines, science writer John Horgan recently garnered the impression from interviews with several other well-known contemporary scientists that we are at last reaching the "end of science."[23] Horgan claims that science has almost completed the long human quest to understand the makeup of the universe, so science as we know it may be about to disappear. Explanation is going to give way to pure description. As Peter Atkins puts it: "When we have dealt with the values of the fundamental constants by seeing that they are unavoidably so, and have dismissed them as irrelevant, we shall have arrived at complete understanding. We are almost there. Complete knowledge is within our grasp."[24]

That such a thought occurs at all is testimony to the uncritical allegiance some scientific thinkers have had to the imprisoning and depressing "metaphysics of the past" that has governed so much of modern thought. As long as we keep looking "back there" in the cosmic past for what is most "fundamental"—as physicists, biologists, geneticists, astronomers, and other scientists are accustomed to doing—we close our eyes to what is most obvious to all human experience, namely, the arrival of an always unprecedented future; and we inevitably rob science of its own future as well. For this reason, I would suggest that a metaphysics of the future not only allows scope for the hopes of religion but also provides an open-ended and more realistic framework for the ongoing adventure of scientific discovery. For our purposes here, such a metaphysics allows us to make better sense of Darwinian science than does the mechanistic framework that typically swamps and distorts much of the novel information that we associate with evolution.

An Ultimate Explanation of Evolution

Once again, I would not deny that a serious commitment to the metaphysical primacy of the future may be possible only if we first

learn personally to dwell within a tradition or a faith community
that enables us to develop the skills of seeing things in a hopeful
rather than pessimistic way. Obviously those who idealize a kind of
knowing allegedly devoid of any such commitment will claim that a
consciousness attuned to the sense of reality's promise is hopelessly
subjective and incapable of being "objective." However, as I have
noted already, commitment to a metaphysics of the past or to a
metaphysics of the eternal present is no less a matter of belief than is
the one that I am defending here. I think that honesty compels us to
acknowledge the inevitably personal, fiduciary, and passionate
commitments that underlie all of our knowing, including the alleged
"realism" of modern scientific materialism. And so I am proposing
merely that, with respect to contextualizing evolutionary phenomena, the sense of promise in which biblical religion seeks so earnestly
to implant our hearts, and by which it also seeks to orient our lives
and thoughts, entails a vision of the real that can claim a legitimacy
far exceeding the conventional alternatives. In addition, I would argue that it is precisely the implied metaphysics of the future that
can best account for the three cosmic qualities—chance, lawfulness, and temporality—that allegedly provide the raw stuff of biological evolution.

No doubt there is a risk involved in the kind of commitment I am
proposing here as the appropriate framework for understanding
evolution. But it is only by allowing ourselves to be imprinted by the
sensibilities of a specific religious tradition—and not by remaining
safely uncommitted, and hence allegedly neutral or presupposition-
less—that we can gain an appreciation of the ultimate futurity of being.[25] We may never experience fully the ontological power of the
future without first "indwelling" a specific narrative history, wherein
a saving future invades the present unpredictably and opens up the
world to undreamed possibilities. When the Bible speaks of the dramatic action of God in the world, it is giving expression to generations of human experience in which an unpredictable and surprising
future has often interrupted the normal course of events, confound-
ing all "realistic" expectations. Our visions of reality today have
been so hamstrung by a metaphysics of the past or a metaphysics of
the eternal present that we may no longer feel instinctively the competence of the biblical stories to open us up to what is truly new. Indeed it may even seem irrational, given conventional standards of

rationality, for us to allow our consciousness to be enfolded by the biblical narratives of promise and hope.

However, it seems to me that we can get the point of the biblical narratives, and thus be grasped by their meaning, not when we look *at* them, as our objectifying intellectual criticism compels us to do obsessively, but only when we look *with* them—in the here and now of our own lives—to a future that may interrupt our own present in as surprising a way as the stories themselves claim to have happened in the lives of our religious ancestors. Biblical accounts of the "mighty acts of God," whatever judgments we make regarding their historical facticity, are at least the clear records of generations of religious openness to clues that point us toward a future coherence that can potentially conquer our own present lostness and confusion.[26] At the same time, these biblical accounts empower us to expect—in a way that goes beyond the predictions of science, without contradicting them—that the cosmic process will finally be redeemed from the insignificance that alternative metaphysical outlooks logically expect.

It is to such an anticipated but not yet fully actualized coherence that a metaphysics of the future points. And this anticipated integration is the goal and ground not only of our human hopes but also of cosmic and biological evolution. I am convinced that much of the contemporary resistance to situating evolution within a futurist metaphysics is rooted in established beliefs about reality, according to which the natural world is constituted either eternally from above or deterministically *a retro*. In the one case, evolutionary developments provide us only with flashes or reminiscences of a lost eternal and perfect world; and in the other, evolution is merely the impersonal unfolding of a mathematical simplicity that first appeared at some remote (and usually unspecified) time long ago in nature's past.

If mechanism-materialism makes the cosmic past the crucible in which all present and future states of nature's evolution are fashioned, a religious metaphysics of *esse* is no less inclined to cover up the possible emergence in creation of what is truly new. In both cases, it bears repeating, being is *already* virtually given in full, whether eternally from above or implicitly in the indefinite cosmic past. There is no room in either standpoint for the emergence of real novelty, and so both standpoints imply that the future will be inherently barren. In these lusterless conceptions, the future is nothing more than the predictable "outcome" of what has gone before in time or eternity. In either set of metaphysical beliefs, no cognition, but only *re-cognition*, is possible. Hence, my suggestion that the coming of the future into the present might be the ultimate ground of evolutionary novelty will hardly sit comfortably in the world of conventional religious and scientific thought.

And yet, I am convinced that numerous puzzles that arise in our reflections on evolution will simply fall away as pseudoproblems if we situate the Darwinian picture of things within the framework of a theological metaphysics of the future. Why is nature ordered and yet open to disorder? Why doesn't contingency or chance, so prominent in evolution, prevent order from emerging? Why is natural selection so rigorously lawful and yet open to indeterminate new creation? Why does the world have the temporal character that allows evolution to occur at all? These are all questions that remain without answer when we view them through a metaphysics of the eternal present or of the deterministic past. But if we place them within the horizon of the coming of the future, then evolution not only begins to make scientific sense but also —at last—to have "its own God."

I realize, of course, that such a readjustment of our vision of reality may not occur without a certain degree of anxiety, not to mention intellectual bewilderment.[27] The idea that the future, the realm that Ernst Bloch referred to as *not-yet-being,* is what powers evolution will make little sense within the framework of the tacit metaphysics underlying current scientific notions of causation and explanation. If the future is not yet available, how can it be explanatory or have metaphysical priority? Isn't the future itself a mode of nonbeing, incapable therefore of grounding the being of nature and its evolution? A metaphysics of the future, and of a God who creates out of the future, seems a contradiction in terms.

Here, though, it may be illuminating to recall ideas I mentioned in previous chapters about the creative and redeeming potency that resides, paradoxically, in the humility of God and the "informational" Taolike character of divine action. I have emphasized already that theology may assume that ultimate reality is informationally effective only by being hidden from the arena of causation familiar to science:

> *Invisible, it cannot be called by any name.*
> *It returns again to nothingness.*

The Taoist intuition is that nature is informationally shaped by the noninterfering effectiveness of ultimate reality. Similarly, as I have proposed along with other Christian and Jewish theologians, it is the "self-withdrawal" of any forceful divine presence, and the paradoxical hiddenness of God's power in a self-effacing persuasive love, that allows creation to come about and to unfold freely and indeterminately in evolution. It is in God's self-emptying humility that the fullest effectiveness resides.

Consistent with these religious intuitions, a theology of hope also attributes the deepest kind of potency to what is not yet available, in this case the Absolute Future. We may even speculate that the arena into which God "withdraws" in order to allow for the relatively autonomous self-creation of evolution is that of the unavailable but infinitely resourceful future.[28] Because God is the world's future, we cannot discover God by scrutinizing only the past and the present. And for this reason, ultimate reality lies off-limits to any scientific verification oriented toward the past alone. But the empirical unavailability of God is consistent with the effectiveness of divine humility and the infinite generosity of God's futurity.[29]

Once again, I suspect that this biblical notion of God as the world's future may seem novel because our minds have been so thoroughly shaped—perhaps I should say misshaped—by the alternative ways of thinking about the real as either fundamentally past or eternally present. We are not accustomed to envisaging the realm of power as that which lies up ahead rather than behind us or up above us in a timeless place of Platonic perfection. And yet a metaphysics of the future should not be completely foreign to any of us who have been formed religiously by the traditions that come down from Abraham, the exemplar of all who live out of the future. Arguably, the most distinctive and precious contribution of biblical religion to human life and consciousness is its impression that reality is shaped by promise, a notion that naturally brings the horizon of futurity into view. By urging us to "wait upon the Lord," to live in trust and hope, the biblical vision inevitably locates the fullness of being in an arena that we can locate only "up ahead" and not "up above" in a timeless heaven of total perfection, nor behind us in the fixed routines of past physical causation.

Today even science seems almost on the verge of a revolutionary shift away from its characteristic understanding of causation only in terms of the impact of the past on the present. Recent scientific descriptions of the self-organization, chaos, and complexity in nature often barely conceal the haunting premonition that these occurrences are all *anticipative* in nature. Somehow drawn toward an indeterminate future, these events are more than just the predictable unfolding of a determining past series of causes. Even if chaos is taken to be physically deterministic—in the sense that, from the point of view of physics, chaotic phenomena do not violate the rigid laws of nature—unpredictable novelty can still take up residence in these systems at higher hierarchical and informational levels. Most natural systems are open to indeterminate outcomes without violating the laws of physics and chemistry. In ways that we do not yet understand fully, complex physical systems unfold in time almost as if they "know" where they are going. Their future states, though not yet realized in actuality, exercise a quietly formative effect on them in every moment of their evolution, shaping their trajectories *in absentia,* as it were. Our metaphysics of the future provides an appropriate setting for these phenomena, as well as for Darwinian evolution.

The metaphysical relocation of transcendence into the future—Teilhard's *ab ante*—will not appeal to those who are satisfied with the way things are, or to those who seek to restore intact some past epoch in the history of nature, culture, or religion. And the horizon of futurity will possibly loom more faintly for those of us who *have* than for those who *have not.* However, for the destitute and dispossessed, for the wretched of the Earth, for the *anawim* of Yahweh, there remains only the future to sustain their lives and aspirations.

A major part of the message of prophetic religion is that the dreams that arise among the poor are not naive illusions but compelling clues about the true nature of the real. The seeds of our metaphysics of the future are sown in the fields of the fortuneless. Perhaps only by allowing our own lives to be integrated into the horizon of their dreams and expectations, that is, by our own "solidarity with victims," can we too make ourselves vulnerable to the power of the future. Religious infatuation with the past or romantic nostalgia for an ahistorical eternal present, on the other hand, can allow us all too easily to legitimate the miserable circumstances of the afflicted and thus close us off to the future that their own suffering opens up.

What I am proposing here, then, is that the metaphysics implied in this religious vision of an unsettling but redeeming future also provides a coherent framework for *theologically* locating and understanding the fact of biological and cosmic evolution. The "power of the future" sensed most palpably by the poor and oppressed, the future to which we also are invited to look for renewal and freshness of being, must—theologically speaking—also be the *fundamental* explanation of nature's evolution.

The prominence of the divine future in shaping our own religious "mentality" provides theology with an inkling of how God relates to the rest of nature as well. Theologically speaking, we may surmise that evolution occurs at all only because in some analogous sense all of nature is being addressed by the future that we call God. Evolution happens, ultimately, because of the "coming of God" toward *the entire universe* from out of an always elusive future. And just as the arrival of God does not enter the human sphere by crude extrinsic forcefulness but by participating in it and energizing it from within, we may assume that it does not enter coercively into the prehuman levels of cosmic and biological evolution either. The coming of God into nature, like the nonintrusive effectiveness of the Tao, is always respectful of the world's presently realized autonomy. God's entrance into the present and invitation to new creation may be so subtle and subdued as to go completely unnoticed by a science oriented only toward the temporal past, and unappreciated by a philosophical theology that turns us only toward a timeless and already completed plenitude of being.

Our metaphysics of the future can also provide an ultimate explanation for the contingency, lawfulness, and temporality that have sometimes been identified as the "raw ingredients" of Darwinian evolution. Darwinian evolution, as I think most scientists would agree, can occur only in a certain kind of universe, one that already possesses just the right proportions of randomness, regularity, and temporality. The fascinating evolutionary story of life could never have taken place in a world where, for example, chance wiped out all regularity, or where lawfulness allowed no room for contingency, or where sufficient time for adaptational experimentation was not abundantly available. The universe in which evolution has in fact occurred is one that contains a congenial blend of contingency, predictability, and duration. Explaining in an *ultimate* way why the universe has these generic features, and why it has them mingled in a way that allows for the evolution of life, is a legitimate function of theology.

Contingency

Let us look first at nature's contingency, a feature that allows for what evolutionary scientists refer to as random, accidental, or chance occurrences. I would suggest, as others have done previously, that theology can interpret the *contingency* (or nonnecessity) of natural occurrences such as genetic mutations as signals of nature's fundamental openness to new creation.[30] The very same events that appear purely random or absurd when viewed only in terms of a scientific method oriented toward the fixed causal past can be understood theologically as openings to the incoming of an indefinitely renewing future in this presently unfinished and perishable cosmos.

In the Abrahamic religions it is toward the future that one looks to discover the full meaning of past and present events.[31] Only the coming of a radically new and unpredictable future can give genuine definition to what has gone before. But in order for this identity-bestowing future to come about, the present order has to give way. And so, what evolutionary scientists refer to as random, contingent, or accidental events are—at least from the perspective of an eschatologically grounded metaphysics—instances of present order making way for new forms of order. Without the occurrence of contingent events, nature's regularities (the laws of physics and natural selection, for example) would freeze the cosmos into an eternal sameness immured against the future.

In our futurist metaphysics, the world is in a sense not yet real, and therefore it is not yet intelligible, at least in a complete way. And so the existence of the perplexing "contingencies" in evolution that Gould features so colorfully is just what one should expect in an unfinished universe whose real character cannot be grasped adequately in the present.[32] Both the religious metaphysics of *esse* and the materialist metaphysics of the past, on the other hand, are unwilling to wait in hope for an intelligibility not yet visible to us. They insist on present clarity, an obsession that leads inevitably to truncated explanation. They manifest an impatience reminiscent of Gnosticism's unwillingness to let reality unfold at its own pace. A metaphysics of the future, on the other hand, allows for an inevitable uncertainty and ambiguity in every present. Certain events in life's history, whether neutral genetic mutations or occasional asteroid impacts, render the future trajectory of evolution incalculable, humanly speaking. But rather than consigning such contingencies to the realm of sheer "absurdity" for not fitting into what humans understand *presently* as appropriate order, a metaphysics of hope is willing to wait for a wider intelligibility—even indefinitely. It looks toward a future in which the fuzziness of present chaos may be resolved into meaningful patterning, though perhaps only in the eschatological long run.

If left on its own, natural science, to the extent that it is ensconced currently in a pre-evolutionary materialist metaphysics, can talk about the future only in terms of lines of causation that it determines to have occurred *already*. Inevitably, the orientation of science is going to be influenced by analogies and conclusions pertinent to previous calculations. Whatever predictions science makes about the future are restricted by what it has observed to be the case antecedently. Consequently, if certain events deviate significantly from familiar patterns of physical activity, they are relegated to the status of "accident," and often the inference is made that the whole evolutionary process is therefore inherently meaningless. Viewed theologically, however, such events—even the most painful and tragic—may be consistent with the unfinished character of a universe that can become fully intelligible only when it opens itself completely to the coming of the future.

As pictured by science since the time of Newton, the world *should* be dominated completely by necessity and therefore devoid of inherent uncertainty. It *should* be ruled by linear processes captured easily by mathematical reasoning. Conceived of in this way, nature and its evolution can be imaginatively reduced to an "algorithmic" process, as depicted by Dennett's obsoletely mechanistic ruminations. Thus, when novel, unpredicted events do occur they are considered absurd, or the result of inaccurate measurements and scientific ignorance. Such a universe is so rigid in its obsequiousness to eternal laws that within it nothing could ever happen that cannot be anticipated on the basis of scientific knowledge of the past.[33]

Obviously, however, nature is stubbornly unpredictable in its actual evolutionary outcomes. The eventual emergence of life and consciousness in evolution, for example, could never have been forecast from even the closest scrutiny of the early phases of cosmic becoming. And so we need to go beyond the epistemological assumptions of scientism and the metaphysics of materialism and determinism in order to understand why such novel forms of being can emerge in evolution. We need to give an integral place to contingency.

Contingency is not a mask for a hidden necessity not yet understood. Rather, it is the way in which the cosmos breaks out of complete subordination to habitual routine and opens itself to the future.
Contingent events are an essential part of any world open to evolutionary novelty. And they are exactly what we should expect in a
world whose ultimate ground and source favors the world's emerging independence as it opens itself to the future.

Law

What are we to say, then, about the remorseless regularity of laws of
nature such as natural selection? Isn't the deterministic invariance
that we attribute to the laws of physics, or to the inexorable filtering
of DNA by natural selection, a clear sign of an ultimately impersonal
universe, one ruled only by blind necessity and therefore "pointless"
in the same sense as that depicted by the ultra-adaptationist Darwinians? How could such an unforgiving propensity of nature as we
find in the "law" of selection, which always protects the strong and
eliminates the weak, ever be reconciled with the faith that we live in
an ultimately purposeful universe cared for by a compassionate
God? Is not natural selection a purely deterministic, "algorithmic,"
pitiless, and meaningless process, as Dawkins and Dennett have argued? Above all, doesn't the inflexibility of nature's lawful determinism close it off to any truly new future?

For the moment let us grant that natural selection is just as mindless and impersonal as, say, the law of gravity. Does this element of
unbending necessity in natural selection, or in any other uniform set
of natural occurrences for that matter, mean that nature is so driven
by mindless determinism that a truly new and unpredictably meaningful future is ruled out? Not at all. Lawfulness at one level of nature's hierarchically emergent structure is essential for the emergence
of novelty and indeterminacy at another. Try to imagine a universe
devoid of the predictable routines that modern science has uncovered. Such a world would be so utterly bereft of order and identity
that no *new* emergence would be possible at all, since there would be
nothing definite enough to undergo transformation. Evolutionary
novelty cannot become implanted in absolute chaos, for then there
would be nothing to distinguish the new from the old. If an aspect of
contingency is essential for nature's being open to new creation, it is

no less true that some degree of regularity and predictable order, such as we find in the recurring laws of physics or natural selection, is essential for the world's remaining consistent and durable enough even to have a future. A world open to the future without also possessing the reliability of lawful "necessity" would be as unimaginable as one devoid of contingency. Nature's lawfulness and predictability are needed to keep natural processes continuous enough to avoid decaying into utter caprice.[34]

Time

Finally, the fact of irreversible time, our third essential condition of evolution, can also be given a most satisfying explanation by a theological metaphysics of the future. Ultimately it is *the arrival of the future* that allows each present to retreat irreversibly into the fixed past so that other new moments may arise in its place. In this sense, the past, out of which science seeks exclusively to explain the present, is itself the "residue" of the openness of nature to a futurity that had formerly come to pass. The past is therefore a gift whose very stability as fixed facticity is ultimately due to the "fidelity" of an always new future; for without the consistent and faithful coming of the future there would be no pushing of the present into the past, and consequently no temporal sequence of moments in which evolution could occur. And there would be no fixed past that could enter causally into the present.

In summary, then, the synthesis of randomness, regularity, and temporality that makes for biological evolution is actually characteristic of all natural beings. Everything in the universe, including our own existence, participates in contingency, that is, in events that are not inherently necessary; in lawful "necessity," the predictable patterns that organize events into identifiable and intelligible actualities; and in temporality, the succession of moments that allows for continually new kinds of being and for the creative transformation of present forms of order.

When we look for an *ultimate* explanation of evolution, we must account for the cosmic blend of contingency, predictability, and temporality that make evolution possible and that science, limited as it is in its method of inquiry, does not ask about, as such. It has been my contention here that the metaphysics of the future entailed by the biblical vision of a cosmos sustained by the promise of an Absolute Future provides a most plausible metaphysical grounding of these three aspects of our world. Without in any way intruding into the specifics of scientific work itself, such a vision of reality provides us with an *ultimate* explanation of evolution.

7

Evolution, Tragedy, and Cosmic Purpose

A T THE END OF HIS IMPORTANT BOOK *The First Three Minutes,*
physicist Steven Weinberg remarks grimly that the more comprehensible the universe has become to modern science the more
"pointless" it all seems.[1] Many other scientists would agree. Alan
Lightman has collected several of their reactions to Weinberg's oft-
repeated claim. Astronomer Sandra Faber, for example, states that
the universe is "completely pointless from a human perspective."[2]
Physicist Marc Davis adds: "Philosophically I see no argument
against [Weinberg's] attitude, that we certainly don't see a point. To
answer in the alternative sense really requires you to invoke the principle of God, I think. At least, that's the way I would view it, and
there's no evidence that He's around, or It's around."[3] And Margaret
Geller, a Harvard astronomer responds: "Why should [the universe]
have a point? What point? It's just a physical system, what point is
there?"[4]

Although scientists do not deny the existence of design in the universe, science as such has no need to posit the existence of an intelligent designer. The complex patterning of life, as we now know,
emerged only gradually in nature, by way of a long, drawn-out
process of evolution that included a good deal of random, blind experimentation and a lot of what we humans would consider sheer
waste. It is easy to look at the potholed pathway of life and conclude
that the absence of direct and unambiguous design renders ours a

purposeless universe, one incapable of fitting into any of our traditional theologies.

However, the question of whether there is a point or purpose to the universe is not answered simply by reference to evidence for or against a designer. Purpose is a much wider notion than design, and it can live much more comfortably with chance, disorder, and the abyss of cosmic time than can the all too simple notion of design. Thus, it is not fruitful for a theology after Darwin to counter the sense of nature's apparent absurdity simply by cataloging more and more apparent evidence of design. Evolutionists themselves are already quite aware of the order in nature. They are simply convinced that a purely naturalistic explanation of order is much more appropriate than the apparently superfluous appeal to an intelligent designer.

I have been arguing that, from the point of view of Christian theology at least, canvassing nature for evidence of a divine "plan" distracts us from engaging in sufficiently substantive conversation with evolutionary science. Evolutionists have told a story about nature that is extremely difficult to square with the notion of a divine "plan." Nature's carefree discarding of the weak, its tolerating so much struggle and waste during several billion years of life's history on Earth, has made simplistic portraits of a divinely designed universe seem quite unbelievable.[5]

To admit this much, however, is not necessarily to conclude that there is no "point" or purpose to the universe. We must remember that science as such is not equipped, methodologically speaking, to tell us whether there is or is not any "point" to the universe. If scientists undertake nevertheless to hold forth on such matters, they must admit in all candor that their ruminations are not scientific declarations but at best declarations *about* science. Moreover, in hazarding such reflections, they will probably be influenced by any number of temperamental or ideological factors extraneous to science as such.

Thus, any respectable argument that evolution makes the universe pointless would have to be erected on grounds other than those that science itself can provide. And yet, even though science cannot decide by itself the question of whether religious hope is less realistic than cosmic pessimism, we must admit that any beliefs we may hold about the universe, whether pessimistic or otherwise, cannot expect to draw serious attention today unless we can at least display their consonance with evolutionary science. We must be able to show that the visions of hope at the heart of the Abrahamic religious traditions provide a coherent metaphysical backdrop for the important discoveries of modern science.

Inevitably, such a proposal will seem outlandish to the many intellectuals who intuitively consider evolutionary biology to be consistent only with a "tragic" interpretation of the universe. It is difficult for experts in the sciences to make out in the physical universe a solid basis for the steadfast hope that prophetic religions require. Alfred North Whitehead himself admitted that the ancient Aeschylean sense of tragedy has always been intertwined with modern science.[6] And even though a pessimistic interpretation of the cosmos is more the product of myth than of science, physicists and evolutionary biologists have generally displayed their ideas in such a way that tragedy seems to be their most natural setting. In particular, the Darwinian notion of impersonal natural selection, when combined with the second law of thermodynamics and the possible "heat death" of the universe, seems to require on our part nothing less than an honest pessimism about the future of the cosmos.

"Cosmic pessimism," the modern synthesis of science and tragic mythology, still poses the most serious cultural challenge to religions based on hope in a promising future. But the Abrahamic religions forbid our surrendering to the seductive lure of the seemingly more "realistic" stoicism around which so much of modern science has congealed. How then can we expect those whose minds have been steeped in this amalgam of science and pessimism to embrace the conviction that the cosmos and its evolution are fundamentally shaped by God's promises?

One prominent religious response to this question says that we should tolerate a sense of despair about the physical universe but look toward a state of immortal personal survival after death in a spiritual "heaven" detached from the material world. Although this solution is quite unbiblical and barely conceals the strain of cosmic despair that underlies it, more than a few believers have found considerable solace in its dualistic segregation of a supernaturally perfect realm "up above" from the imperfect and finally futile natural world "down here." The division of reality into the spheres of spirit and matter—and of humans into soul and body—provides a powerful answer to our personal longing for the eternal, and it apparently renders religiously innocuous the sober modern scientific conjectures about the destiny of nature, including the prospect that the material universe may be headed toward final catastrophe. Dualism, in other words, releases theology from the obligation of seeking a genuine consonance between religion and contemporary science.

However, any religious faith professing to abide within the framework of the biblical vision of hope for the future cannot be content with such a settlement; for the Bible clearly invites us to see *all of reality,* including the physical cosmos—and what we would now recognize as the entire sweep of its evolution—as profoundly stamped by the promises of God, participating along with humans in the quest for future fulfillment. If St. Paul's words about *the whole* of creation "groaning" for redemption mean anything at all, it is that from a religious perspective we can no longer consign nature to the realm of final futility.

However, if we are to envision a divine promise as so fundamental to the definition of the universe, doesn't this place theology in an even more intellectually tenuous position than ever? Modern science's long affair with tragic pessimism still persists, and we cannot expect that scientific culture will casually renounce so stable a union. The Darwinian discovery of life's epochs of struggle, waste, and suffering, along with contemporary physics' layout of a universe eventually dissolving into permanent deep freeze, is hardly suggestive of a world whose fundamental being is informed by divine concern for its future. How, by any stretch of the theological imagination, can we claim seriously that the natural world may be viewed more realistically within the framework of God's love and promise than within that of tragic pessimism?

Before we can deal with this question we must restate what we mean by the notions of God's love and promise. Curiously these two themes, though central to biblical faith, are often barely visible in formal discussions of science and theology. Too often, it seems to me, our conversations about science and God tend to drift along vaguely without much agreement on what kind of "God" we are talking about. Perhaps out of a spirit of openness to dialogue, theologians often allow scientific skeptics to define the terms of the debate, even though this generally means trimming off features that faith considers essential to its pictures of God. Moreover, in their efforts to find common ground with scientific skeptics, theologians sometimes tend to concede ideas about divine power and intelligence that may be quite out of keeping with actual religious experience. This accommodation has led many articles and books on science and religion into lengthy and uninteresting defenses of religiously pallid notions of God as a "designer" or "planner" of the universe, while the richer and more nuanced images of God given to religious experience hover helplessly in the background.

For example, in Christian theologians' dialogues with evolutionary scientists, it is easy to lose sight of faith's primordial experience of God as self-emptying love, and to focus instead on a much more abstract representation of the "deity," such as "intelligent designer." Unfortunately, the experience of God that occurred in connection with such events as the life and death of Jesus—an encounter with ultimacy that Hans Küng rightly calls a "revolution" in the whole human story of God-consciousness—is taken only minimally into theological engagements with science.[7] Especially in debates about the compatibility of religion with the randomness, struggle, and suffering in life's evolution, theologians typically find themselves guarding some bleary notion of divine "power" and "rationality" rather than bringing patently to the front faith's more troubling images of the compassionate mystery that pours itself out into the world in unrestrained and vulnerable love.

Moreover, as I have been emphasizing in previous chapters, our treatises on God and evolution can easily become so sidetracked by obsession with the notions of order, plan, and design that we may ignore altogether another fundamental feature of biblical faith, namely, the experience of God as one who makes promises and who relates to the cosmos not by compelling it from the past but by opening it to an enlivening and unpredictable future.[8]

Evolution and Divine *Kenosis*

Steven Weinberg argues perceptively that it is useless to reconcile some vaguely construed and religiously uninformed concept of deity with modern science. Instead we must ask whether science is compatible with the idea of an "interested God," one who captures the hearts and souls of devout believers. After all, it is always possible to redefine the concept of "God," as Einstein himself did, in terms that will make it scientifically palatable. But if we are to be fully candid we must instead ask whether the sense of God *as operative in actual religious awareness* is consonant with contemporary scientific understanding. Weinberg claims that it is not. Contemporary physics and, especially, evolutionary science, he argues, point to an utterly impersonal and indifferent universe, one that rules out the "interested" God of religious faith.[9]

One does not have to accept Weinberg's conclusion in order to agree with him that we should connect our thinking about issues in science and religion to images and convictions about an "interested" God as these are found in actual religious experience rather than in philosophically watered down versions of theism. Of course, we cannot speak seriously about God's relationship to the scientifically understood universe without using philosophical or metaphysical language. But such discourse must remain tethered closely to the nuances of actual religious experience. For Christian theology, this would mean seeking to understand the natural world, and especially its evolutionary character, in terms of the outpouring of compassion and the corresponding sense of world renewal associated with the God of Jesus the crucified and risen Christ.

Christians have discerned in the "Christ-event" the decisive self-emptying or *kenosis* of God. And at the same time they have experienced in this event a God whose effectiveness takes the form of a power of renewal that opens the world to a fresh and unexpected future. As a Christian theologian, therefore, when I reflect on the relationship of evolutionary science to religion I am obliged to think of God as both *kenotic love* and *power of the future*. This sense of God as a self-humbling love that opens up a new future for the world took shape in Christian consciousness only in association with the "Christ-event"; and so, as we ponder the implications of such discoveries as those associated with evolution, it would be disingenuous of Christian theologians to suppress the specific features of their own faith community's experience of divine mystery. This means quite simply that in its quest to understand the scientific story of life, Christian theology must ask how evolution might make sense when situated in a universe shaped by God's kenotic compassion and an accompanying promise of new creation.

From science itself, of course, we have no right to expect any sweeping judgments about the meaning of evolution or cosmic process. Following its customary constraints, science must acknowledge that it is not equipped to discover the significance or value of anything. But from the perspective of a theological vision that takes seriously both biological science and what Christian faith understands as "revelatory" portraits of a vulnerable and faithful God, nature's evolutionary journey may exhibit levels of meaning that could never be illuminated apart from a prior commitment to such a revelatory framework.

Such an interpretative commitment, I would submit, is no more of an impediment to objectivity than is the equally a priori allegiance many scientists have to the myth of cosmic tragedy. It is now commonly agreed, after all, that some kind of commitment is a condition of, and not inevitably an obstacle to, knowledge. Even to begin scientific exploration, for example, a scientist must be committed already to such beliefs as "the universe is intelligible" or "truth is worth seeking." And these scientifically essential "faith" commitments, I believe, correspond much more approximately to religious visions such as the one I am presenting here than they do to the seemingly more "realistic" tragic modern envisagements of an ultimately pointless universe.

At the center of Christian faith lies the conviction (John 3:16) that "God so loved the world that He gave his only Son" to redeem and renew that world. Theologically translated, this text and many others like it imply that the very substance of the divine life is poured out into the creation, and that the world is now and forever open to an infinitely replenishing future. I am suggesting that those who envisage the universe as enfolded by such infinite love and promise will be able to appreciate aspects of "Darwinian" evolution that those committed to a more tragic spin on things might take as a reason for cosmic despair. St. Paul (Philippians 2:5–11) portrays Christ as one who "though in the form of God" did not "cling" to his divine status, but instead "emptied himself" *(ekenosen seauton)* and took the "form of a slave." It is to this image that Christian theology must always repair whenever it thinks about God's relationship to the world and its evolution.

Creation as "Letting Be"

As we have seen, what has been especially troubling in Darwinian science is its picture of a world in which randomness mingles with the "impersonal" process of natural selection in such a way that evolution seems to have no direction or inherent meaning. A world that sponsors such a process may seem at first to be incompatible with the existence of a loving and effective God. But perhaps this is only because our philosophical notions of divine power are usually implicitly uprooted from any grounding in the actual religious intuition of God as self-emptying love. By ignoring the image of divine humility, it is easy for us to forget that intrinsic to the divine *kenosis* is its authorization of creation's striving for genuine independence vis-à-vis its creator. Love by its very nature cannot compel, and so any God whose very essence is love should not be expected to overwhelm the world either with a coercively directive "power" or an annihilating "presence." Indeed, an infinite love must in some sense "absent" or "restrain itself," precisely in order to give the world the "space" in which to become something distinct from the creative love that constitutes it as "other." We should anticipate, therefore, that any universe rooted in an unbounded love would have some features that appear to us as random or undirected.

As I observed in Chapter 4, even in the original creation of the cosmos, the divine infinity may be thought of—in our imperfect human concepts—as "contracting" itself, foregoing any urge to direct the creation forcefully or to absorb it into the divine. An unrestrained display of infinite presence or "omnipotence" would leave no room for anything other than God, and so it would rule out any genuine evolutionary *self-transcendence* on the part of the cosmos. It is a humble "retreat" on God's part that allows the cosmos to stand forth on its own and then to evolve as a relatively autonomous reality distinct from its creative ground. In this sense, creation and its evolutionary unfolding would be less the consequence of an eternal divine "plan" than of God's humble and loving "letting be."[10] So if ultimate reality is essentially self-giving love, and if love in turn entails "letting the other be," then, theologically speaking, both the world's original coming into being and its indeterminate Darwinian transformation through time would be completely consonant with the Christian experience of God.

The world can have its own being and realize its own evolutionary potential, therefore, only if God's creative power and love consist of a kind of self-concealment. As I have noted, it is in its encounter with the crucified man Jesus—and not in philosophical reasoning alone—that Christian faith is given this key to God's relation to the world. The cross "reveals" to faith the self-absenting of a God out of whose limitless generosity the world is called, but never forced, into being and becoming. This kenotic image of God, even though inaccessible to philosophical and scientific rationality as such, nevertheless gives a surprising intelligibility to the cosmic whole in which Darwinian evolution turns out to have played so important a role.[11]

Not surprisingly, those scientific skeptics and theists whose ideas of God center primarily on the notion of "intelligent design" have found Darwinian ideas unacceptable. Skeptics have rejected a divine "planner" as incompatible with the undirected course of biotic evolution, whereas many theists have dismissed evolution contemptuously as incompatible with their notion of a designing deity.[12] A universe entertaining the degree of indeterminacy that Darwin's vision entails seems incompatible with a transcendent power and intelligence. God, the alleged "divine designer," is apparently not "in control" after all. Evolution appears to be a mindless lottery rather than the "mighty act" of an omnipotent God. And the enormous amount of time evolution takes seems to rule out the existence of God, since a truly intelligent designer would surely not have "fooled around" for so long (fifteen billion years or so) before bringing about human beings. The enormity of cosmic time simply adds to the suspicion that intelligence is something that emerged only recently, perhaps only in the evolution of the human species.

However, the God given to a faith shaped by the "Christ-event" is not first of all an infinite embodiment of what we humans narrowly understand as rationality, intelligence, or design, but an outrageously "irrational" and mysteriously humble love that comes to meet the world from out of the realm of an open and incalculable future. A theology attuned to this image of ultimacy suggests to us a way of rendering theologically meaningful the very same scientific data that have led a more "rationally" based theistic preoccupation with design to repudiate Darwinian theory, and that have led scientific skeptics to a tragic interpretation of nature.

The Creator's power (by which I mean the capacity to influence the world) is made manifest paradoxically in the vulnerable defenselessness of a crucified man. And such an expression of divine "power" is not only consonant with, but ultimately explanatory of, the curious world that evolutionary science now presents to us. The randomness, struggle, and seemingly aimless meandering that the evolutionary story of life discloses as the underside of its marvelous creativity is consistent with the idea that the universe is the consequence of an infinite love. The key to such an interpretation lies in faith's staggering discovery that a truly effective power takes the form of self-emptying compassion.

If God were "powerful" only in the restricted sense of possessing the capacity to manipulate things coercively, then the facts of evolution might be theologically problematic. But an infinite love, as the Roman Catholic theologian Karl Rahner has made clear, will not manipulate or dissolve the beloved—in this case, the cosmos. For in the act of seeking intimacy with the universe, God forever preserves the difference and otherness of that beloved world. God's creative love constitutes the world as something ontologically distinct from God, and not as a simple extension of the divine being. Consequently, the indeterminate natural occurrences that recent physics has uncovered at the most elementary levels of physical reality, the random events that biology finds at the level of life's evolution, and the freedom that emerges with human existence are all features proper to any world that is permitted and even encouraged to be distinct from the creative love that underlies it.

In order for the world to be independent of God, and therefore to undergo a genuine *self*-transcendence in its evolution, a God of love would concede to the world its own autonomous principles of operation—such as the "impersonal" laws of gravity, natural selection, and self-organization. This "self-distancing" of God, however, is in no sense apathy but, paradoxically, a most intimate form of involvement. In other words, God is nothing like the otiose and remote first cause of deism; for it is out of a longing to relate deeply to the world that God foregoes any annihilating "presence" to the world. This retracting of "presence," however, is the very condition of dialogical intimacy. God's will is that the world become more and more independent, and that during its evolution its own internal coherence intensify, not diminish.[13] But this "absent" God is "present" to and deeply united with the evolving world precisely by virtue of selflessly allowing it to achieve ever deeper autonomy—which occurs most obviously in the evolutionary emergence of human freedom. The God of self-giving compassion is in fact the only God that normative Christian faith can claim legitimately ever to have encountered, and yet this founding intuition about the nature of ultimate reality all too seldom enters into our thoughts about whether the universe has a "point" to it, or whether the evolution of life can be reconciled with religious hope.

God, Cosmos, and the Future

The God whom Christian faith identifies with infinite love is also one who—as a resurrection faith attests—opens up a new future for humans and for the whole of creation. Hope's intuition about the coming of an always new and creative future is no less central to Christian faith than is the paradoxical divine "power" that became manifest in the defenselessness of the Crucified. And so I have been suggesting that we connect our understanding of nature's evolution to the sense of God as the world's "future."

From the perspective of theology, in fact, it is the "coming of God" in the mode of a renewing future that *ultimately* explains the novelty in evolution. Even though cosmic pessimism would view the random or contingent events that allow for evolutionary novelty as utterly devoid of meaning, to a biblically informed faith these indeterminacies are essential features of any universe open to new creation. The fifteen billion years of cosmic evolution now appear, in the perspective of faith, to have always been seeded with promise. From its very beginning this extravagantly experimental universe has been bursting with potential for surprising future outcomes.[14] And the undeniable fact that life, mind, culture, and religion have emerged out of the barely rippled radiation of the primordial universe gives us every reason to suspect that the cosmos may still be situated no less realistically within the framework of promise than of tragedy. Even prospects of eventual cosmic doom are not enough to defeat the proposal that nature's present indeterminacies are the repository of promise. The so-called "heat death" that may be awaiting the universe is not inconsistent with the notion that each moment of the entire cosmic process is taken perpetually into, and preserved everlastingly in, the boundlessly redemptive future that faith names as God.[15]

To fit the whole of nature into the framework of a religious hope based on the sense of openness to surprising future outcomes is not nearly so great a stretch as it may once have seemed; for today we are beginning to notice just how much of nature's concrete complexity and indeterminate creativity the linear mathematical methods of modern science since Newton had left out. Scientific abstractions appealed greatly to the Cartesian ideal of complete and immediate clarity, and they gave us enormous power to analyze and manipulate our natural environment. But the full actuality of the natural world had meanwhile slipped out of the grasp of science.[16] And we have begun to realize only recently that the intellectual appeal of cosmic pessimism is supported not so much by nature itself as by abstract mathematical representations that inevitably overlook the elusive complexity and indeterminacy that open the cosmos to a genuinely novel future.

What modern science had passed over is now emerging palpably in the so-called sciences of "chaos" and "complexity." Nature, as we can now picture it (especially with the help of computer imaging), is composed of intricate adaptive systems that cannot be understood adequately simply by dissecting them into their constituent law-bound particulars. The makeup of the universe, from immense galactic clusters all the way down to infinitesimal quantum events, exhibits an unpredictably self-creative and self-organizing character to which the linear mathematics of mechanistic science is inadequate. Although materialist dreams are still around, significant doubts about the abstract ways of reading nature, which previously had fueled our fatalism, are now beginning to spread within the scientific community and are even spilling out into public awareness. The prospect of precise scientific prediction of final cosmic catastrophe is shakier than ever. If, as physicist John Houghton notes, science cannot even tell us where a billiard ball will end up a minute from now without taking into account the motion of electrons in outer space, it is hardly in a position to settle the question of cosmic destiny either.[17]

Although it may not be prudent for us to draw any theological conclusions directly from the new sciences of chaos and complexity, we cannot help but notice how severely they have challenged the quaint claims that impersonal laws of physics are running the universe to ruin and that we can make long-term predictions about the fate of the cosmos. It seems entirely plausible that the universe of contemporary science is more congenial to promise than pessimism.

Story and Promise

Obviously neither science nor faith is in a position to predict the actual details of the cosmic future, but it is of great interest that science—especially since Darwin and, more recently, Einstein—now places the cosmos within a narrative setting in which the universe is a "story" open to an unpredictable future. The universe, as it turns out, is not eternal, nor is it just a set of abstract laws, nor a mere backdrop for human history. Rather, it is a creative project yet unfinished, and because it is unfinished it still has a future.

Currently most scientists agree that cosmic evolution began in a hot "big bang," after which the universe began to expand and cool, giving rise to atoms, stars, and galaxies. Eventually elements and compounds cooked up in some now burnt-out stellar ovens came together to form our own planet. After another billion years or so the

Earth's surface cooled sufficiently to allow primitive forms of life to appear. Biological evolution on Earth, according to the most recent estimates, began about 3.8 billion years ago, but like most other episodes of cosmic process it was apparently not in a hurry. In its unfolding it was often hesitant, sometimes explosive, and almost always extravagant. After experimenting with less-complex forms of life, it eventually blossomed out into plants, reptiles, birds, and mammals. Not long ago, in our own species, evolution was endowed with self-consciousness.

The story has not been linearly progressive. For vast periods of time little happened, and much of the history of life's evolution can be captured in the image of a randomly branching bush. But all great stories have quiescent interludes, blind alleys, and unintelligible shoots; and a more sweeping view of cosmic evolution shows clearly, at least to those who care to notice, a narrative trend toward increasingly complex forms of natural order. Without too much difficulty, we can make out a kind of story line along which nature has traveled from trivial to more intricate and eventually sentient, conscious, and self-conscious states of being. Although neo-Darwinian biologists often highlight what they take to be the aimlessness of evolution, if we step back and survey the life-process within its larger cosmic context, it is hard even for the most entrenched pessimist to discount altogether the obvious "directionality" visible in the overall movement of the cosmos from simplicity to complexity. And to those of us who have been encouraged by faith to look for signs of promise in all things, it would seem egregiously arbitrary not to remark at how, at any past moment in its history, the cosmos has remained open to surprisingly beautiful future outcomes.

Astrophysics, for example, has instructed us recently that an incredible number of stunning physical coincidences had to have been present in the earliest micromoments of the universe in order for life eventually to appear and evolve. And although it may be unwise for theology to take the physics of the early universe as the basis for a new natural theology, the current scientific information is remarkably consistent with faith's conviction that the physical universe had always held at least the *promise* of emerging into life.[18] Though known to us only retrospectively, the early phases of the universe clearly contained the prospect of evolving toward such indeterminate outcomes as life, mind, and even spirituality. Cosmic pessimism, therefore, does not seem to provide a sufficiently comprehensive metaphysical format for organizing our current scientific understanding of the universe. Until not too many years ago, it may have been considered scientifically acceptable to think of the physical universe as inherently hostile to life, and to view life and evolution as absurdly improbable eventualities toward whose accidental appearance on our small planet nature was intrinsically "unfriendly." But today it is much more "scientific" to acknowledge that physical reality has always been positively disposed toward the emergence of life and consciousness, much more so than we had ever suspected prior to the emergence of contemporary scientific cosmology.[19]

Thus, if it is now evident that the ambiguous cosmic past held such enormous promise as the eventual emergence of life and mind, can we claim confidently that the *present* state of the cosmic story is not also pregnant with potential for blossoming into still more abundant new creation? Science by itself cannot answer the questions most important to faith. But in the panorama of cosmic evolution disclosed by science, faith is still permitted, perhaps even encouraged, to think of the cosmos as being called into yet newer ways of being.

A tragic perspective, of course, will simply assume that the world's future states are not really new but are instead the same old simplicity now just "masquerading as complexity." However, it is unthinkable that novel events could arise only out of the fixed past. Novelty must arise, of course, *in connection with* what is and what has been, for otherwise we would not grasp it as truly new. But it would not really be new if it were simply the algorithmic unfolding of a fully deterministic past. New possibilities can arise only out of the region of time that we refer to as the *future*. And since the future is such a boundless reservoir of novelty, we cannot assume that, simply because it is not fully present to us now, it is reducible to bare nonbeing (as both philosophy and science have often implied). Because of its faithful and inexhaustible resourcefulness, we must concede to the future some modality of *being*. Indeed, the biblical vision of reality's promise implies even that the future is the *most real* (though obviously not yet presently actualized) of all the dimensions of time. The future claims the status of being eminently real not only because it always shows up even after every present moment has slipped away into the past, but ultimately because it is the realm from which God comes to renew the world.[20]

However, as I have also emphasized, the future in its overflowing abundance is always hidden. By definition it cannot be fully captured in any fleeting present experience, or become fully spent in the fixity of the past. In its perpetual transcendence of the past and present, the future inevitably hides itself. Thus, I have envisaged God's self-concealment in an unavailable future as coinciding with the paradoxically intimate divine "absence" associated with the notion of *kenosis*. God's humble self-withdrawal, in other words, takes the form of God's being the inexhaustible "futurity" whose continuous arrival into the present is always restrained enough to allow the cosmos to achieve *its own* independent evolution. As biblical faith makes clear, God's "glory" is at present kenotically veiled, and where it does manifest itself, at least according to John's Gospel, it is, paradoxically, in the picture of the "lifted up" and crucified Christ.

From a biblical perspective, of course, the whole "point" of the universe is to manifest God's "glory"; but for the present, God's glory is revealed characteristically in a *kenosis* that endows the world with a surprising degree of autonomy.[21] The self-emptying God refrains from overwhelming the universe with an annihilating divine presence but in the mode of futurity nonetheless nourishes the world constantly by offering to it a range of relevant new possibilities—such as those depicted by evolutionary science. At the same time, God's compassionate embrace enfolds redemptively and preserves everlastingly each moment of the cosmic evolutionary story.

Conclusion

Thus, in theology's conversations with contemporary science, it is more helpful to think of God as the infinitely generous ground of new possibilities for world-becoming than as a "designer" or "planner" who has mapped out the world in every detail from some indefinitely remote point in the past. The fundamental difficulty implied in the notion of such a "plan" for the world is that it closes the world off to any real future. Referring to some often overlooked ideas of Henri Bergson, Louise Young comments insightfully on the openness of evolution to the future:

> As we view the groping, exploratory nature of the process—the many favorable mutations, the tragic deformities—it is apparent that we are not witnessing the detailed accomplishment of a preconceived plan. "Nature is more and better than a plan in course of realization," Henri Bergson observed. A plan is a term assigned to a labor: it closes the

future whose form it indicates. Before the evolution of life, on the contrary, the portals of the future remain wide open.[22]

We might also say that God is more and better than a planner. A God whose very essence is to be the world's open future is not a planner or designer but an infinitely liberating source of new possibilities and new life. It seems to me that neo-Darwinian biology can live and thrive quite comfortably within the horizon of such a vision of ultimate reality.

8

Religion, Ethics, and Evolution

THE AMERICAN PHILOSOPHER W. T. STACE once remarked that "religion can get along with any sort of astronomy, geology, biology, physics." What it cannot put up with, he said, is a purposeless universe. "If the scheme of things is purposeless and meaningless," then our own human lives are purposeless and meaningless also.[1] When I expressed my agreement with Stace on this point in a book on science and religion some years ago, the outspoken scientific skeptic Will Provine of Cornell University took me to task.[2] Belief in cosmic purpose, he insisted, is completely unwarranted. In fact, science has actually ruled out the notion of a meaningful universe:

> All that science reveals to us is chance and necessity. . . . Modern science directly implies that the world is organized strictly in accordance with mechanistic principles. There are no purposive principles whatsoever in nature. There are no gods and no designing forces that are rationally detectable. The frequently made assertion that modern biology and the assumptions of the Judeo-Christian tradition are fully compatible is false.[3]

However, Provine continues, this does not mean that our individual lives are meaningless:

> My own life is filled with meaning. I am married to a talented and beautiful woman, have two great sons, live on a beautiful farm with

121

lots of old but good farm machinery, teach at a fine university where the students are excellent, and have many wonderful friends. But I will die and soon be forgotten.... Haught will have a tough time convincing me that my life is meaningless just because there is no cosmic meaning for it.[4]

Will Provine is a congenial sort, and so he would not take offense if I reminded him that when I speak about purpose or "meaning" in the universe I do not have in mind what he does when he catalogs the comforts of academic and family life in upstate New York. I mean the belief, expressed paradigmatically in religions, that the cosmos is embraced by an incomprehensible divine mystery that promises an eternal significance and unimagined coherence to the sequence of happenings that make up evolution and our lives within it.

If we were firmly convinced, at every level of our being, that the universe as a whole is ultimately absurd, then perhaps we might be able to discover precarious havens of human warmth, and even attain a sort of tragic nobility, as we huddle in the cold of the cosmos. But such solace would never add up to what most humans have taken to be a meaningful life. Only a conviction that the *whole of things* is somehow redeemable from absolute nothingness can give real substance and depth to an individual's sense of meaning. And it is only in religion, not in the sciences or even in ethics, that we ever come across a sustained intergenerational cultivation of such a sense of cosmic purpose.

Provine goes on to argue that ethics needs no religious grounding either. Countless nonbelievers, he rightly reminds us, lead exemplary moral lives. To this argument, one can reply only that both believers and nonbelievers are often ethical people, and often they are not. I doubt that a comparative assessment could ever produce any clear picture. However, I am inclined to suspect that over the course of generations human moral aspiration would eventually wither and die unless it were sustained by a trust that the whole of being, including the physical universe, is the embodiment of transcendent meaning.

Again, this does not mean that one has to be a religious believer in order to be deeply moral. What it does mean, however, is that a view of reality that portrays the basic context of our lives as sheer meaninglessness will scarcely nourish a sense of moral values down through the ages to come. Ambiguous, and even barbarous, as our religious traditions may sometimes have been, I am persuaded that only their conviction that the universe itself in some way ultimately makes sense has been able to nourish, throughout a succession of epochs, the human longing for goodness. Cosmic pessimism, projecting absolute nothingness as the ultimate destiny of the universe— were it ever to become the common creed of our race—would prove to be rather shallow soil for the cultivation of ethical incentive. I should add that I hope we never set up any experiments to test this conjecture.

In any case, at least until the age of science, the main stimulus to ethical commitment was religious belief in a meaningful universe. The most exemplary lives almost always seemed to be those lived with deep trust in the general meaningfulness of the creation. Currently, though, the ageless trust in a purposeful cosmos is under siege, at least in the intellectual world. This, it seems to me, is something about which we should be seriously alarmed. On the very day I am writing these words, I have noticed that Vaclav Havel, the current president of the Czech Republic, also expresses great regret that the ancient consensus no longer holds. "I have become increasingly convinced," he says, "that the crisis of the much-needed global responsibility is in principle due to the fact that we have lost the certainty that the Universe ... has a definite meaning and follows a definite purpose."[5]

I would have to agree that without a core conviction that the cosmos is at heart an expression of divine purpose our ethical aspiration will wither and die. The ideals that define the moral behavior of all of us, including that of contemporary skeptics, have all undeniably come down to us from predecessors whose lives were shaped by *religious* trust. Our own cult of compassion, justice, humility, gratitude, the avoidance of greed and selfishness, delight in the success of others, and hope for the thriving of life—all of the virtues we still cherish most—sprang forth originally long before our own times and have remained alive in our various cultures only because our ancestors thought of these ideals as grounded *eternally* in a transcendent reality.

Once again, however, is it not the case that Darwin has made it impossible for us to feel any longer the deep conjunction our ancestors experienced between their religiously sharpened ethical aspirations on the one hand and a sustaining "moral" universe on the other? Or is it conceivable that Darwin's science can ground human morality in a new and equally compelling way. Contemporary "sociobiology" responds by claiming that we can derive our moral instincts satisfactorily from a purely Darwinian picture of the universe, even though nature itself is intrinsically aimless and amoral. E. O. Wilson and Michael Ruse, for example, claim that our ethical ideals are simply adaptive evolutionary mechanisms leading us to cooperate with one another so that our genes will survive into the next generation. Ethics, in other words, is nothing more than a function of selfish genes.[6]

The sociobiological interpretation denies forcefully that our moral values are rooted in any transcending source of values:

> Morality, or more strictly our belief in morality, is merely an adaptation put in place to further our reproductive ends.... Ethics is a shared illusion of the human race. If it were not so it would not work.... Ethical codes work because they drive us to go against our selfish day-to-day impulses in favour of long-term group survival and harmony and thus, over our lifetimes, the multiplication of our genes many times. Furthermore, the way our biology enforces its ends is by *making us think* that there is an objective higher moral code, to which we are all subject.[7]

This idea is provocative, and to its credit it does try to link human moral instinct to the evolving natural world. But it does so in too superficial and restricted a manner. Seeking the reasons for good behavior in the aimless mechanics of genetic adaptation will do little to reinforce the much needed sense today that our moral life has the backing of the universe. Sociobiology's ostensibly "scientific" grounding of human morality in the blind accomplishments of evolutionary adaptation would simply provide us, as philosopher Peter Singer notes perceptively, with new opportunities to "outfox" our genes and thus, at our own discretion, to terminate even the outward expressions of morality.[8] Thus, if we are to ground our moral life in any substantial way in an evolutionary understanding of nature, we shall have to seek an alternative to sociobiology.

The Dualist Alternative

There is a way, of course, by which we might avoid the whole issue of whether our moral passion requires the support of a purposeful universe. We might fall back once again on the ancient religious dualism that divided reality into matter and spirit. Accordingly we could claim that we humans are essentially spiritual beings only accidentally imprisoned in a material universe. In this perspective, our moral lives do not need to feel or express any close linkage to the universe. Instead, morality would consist of our struggle to detach ourselves from nature. God put us here to learn strength of soul by purifying ourselves of matter. Our bodies and earthly things are only sources of temptation that we shall eventually discard altogether.

Furthermore, to those souls who can accept a Darwinian view of nature, a distinctively human morality would consist not of cooperating with evolution but of devising ways to contradict the law of selection dominant in evolution up until our own emergence.[9] Whereas natural selection has favored only the strongest or fittest, our own ethical life demands that we resist evolution resolutely by taking care of the weakest among us. Once we humans came along, the purely natural laws of evolution no longer applied, and so now we must even do battle with them. In such a scheme, human culture in general and moral aspiration in particular have no need to seek support in the larger context of nature.

I do not need to emphasize here that in some religious circles this view of things is still entrenched deeply. Unquestionably, it speaks powerfully to many religious people. Interestingly, one can also detect the residue of this ancient religious dualism even in the attempts by skeptics such as Will Provine to salvage a purely human kind of significance out of the absurdity of an ultimately indifferent evolutionary universe. Only by positing a sharp discontinuity between human existence and the natural world can the evolutionary materialist attribute significance to our own lives while simultaneously denying it to the rest of the universe.

A number of twentieth-century intellectuals have given voice to a similar feeling of estrangement of humanity from nature. Bertrand Russell, for example, declared that the amoral universe in which we find ourselves is not worthy of us,[10] whereas Albert Camus urged us to rebel heroically against the death-dealing world into which we are born.[11] And the famous biochemist Jacques Monod, coupling Darwin with French existentialism, similarly regarded life and human consciousness as pure accidents of evolution, marooning us in a hostile universe.[12]

One might suppose that evolutionary biology, which so clearly demonstrates the continuity between ourselves and the rest of nature, would make scientific thinkers feel at least somewhat at home in the universe. But more often than not, the Darwinian accounts of life have edged the scientifically enlightened even farther out of the cosmos. Today some scientists, notably Stuart Kauffman and others studying autopoietic processes, are beginning to challenge this bias, but many others still see little connection between an evolutionary universe and human morality.[13] In fact, to some prominent evolutionary biologists, Darwin presents a specter so horrifying that human existence can be rendered meaningful only by our going to war against the ways of nature. Natural selection seems so remote from our human sense of compassion that we cannot help interpreting it as our enemy, even though we are also its offspring.[14]

A Process Perspective

Is there some alternative way, then, by which we can link our moral life substantively to an evolutionary cosmos? Can our ethical aspiration in any sense claim the backing of a universe that permits amoral and ruthless, but also creative, Darwinian processes to shape life on this planet?

In order to make such a connection, we would first have to be able to discern in the cosmic process some general aim or purposiveness with which our own lives might become morally aligned. But what possible conception of nature, consistent with scientific knowledge, might allow us to envisage our ethical inclinations as flowing with the course of evolution rather than against it? And what sense would it make to speak of an overarching cosmic purpose, if in the evolution of life nature acts in the ruthless manner Darwinians suggest? What "point" could such a universe be said to have, and why should we wish to belong to it, let alone conform to it morally?

In pondering such questions, I have found considerable help once again in the cosmology and metaphysics of Alfred North Whitehead. This great philosopher's wide vision not only weaves our own existence tightly and unapologetically into the fabric of the cosmic process but also plausibly situates the whole of the cosmic process within the accommodating embrace of an ultimate meaningfulness. Whitehead's thought captures and expresses what many religions and theologies have intuited about the creative and compassionate depths of reality, while remaining consistently faithful to scientific discovery. Without having to leave out the most challenging features of the

Darwinian theory of evolution, Whitehead's thought generously brings the entire universe into the scheme of meaning and redemption.

The cosmic breadth of Whitehead's philosophy is hardly typical of modern theological reflection, much of which has been content to rescue human existence from what theologians have silently conceded to be an inherently pointless universe. Modern theology has allowed that our own subjectivity and human history are redeemable, but it has cared little for the rest of the cosmos. However, a Whiteheadian theology—in keeping with the cosmic religious instincts of the majority of our human ancestors—thinks of divine redemption as reaching back across the immensities of time, embracing every natural event with such immediacy and intensity of feeling that nothing in the cosmic process is ever lost or forgotten.

This belief, of course, is not a property of Whitehead's thought alone. Theologian and philosopher Paul Tillich finds the same sentiment at least implicit in many religious depictions of eternity:

> Nothing in the universe is unknown, nothing real is ultimately forgotten. The atom that moves in an immeasurable path today and the atom that moved in an immeasurable path billions of years ago are rooted in the eternal ground. There is no absolute, no completely forgotten past, because the past, like the future, is rooted in the divine life. Nothing is completely pushed into the past. Nothing real is absolutely lost and forgotten.[15]

Citing Whitehead's ideas, process theology concurs fully. God not only lures the cosmos toward new modes of being but also preserves the cosmic past with a never fading immediacy of feeling. God is the ultimate repository of *all* the occasions that make up the cosmic process.[16] God is "the feeling of all feelings," gathering every occurrence into an ever expanding pattern of beauty. What appear to us as absurdity and contradiction, God's own breadth and depth of feeling can transform into a harmony of contrasts, endowing even tragedy with redemptive significance.

God, in this theological interpretation, saves the world as it passes into the immediacy of the divine experience.[17] Each occurrence in the world process, no matter how disagreeable it may be to our own moral sense, contributes novelty and contrast that may be locally disruptive at times but that can be rescued ultimately by its "relation to the completed whole."[18] In God's feeling of the world, events that from our own limited perspective appear irredeemable "contradictions" may, over the course of the world's becoming, be transformed by God into "contrasts" contributing intensity of beauty to the "wider vision." God, as Whitehead says, is "a tender care that nothing be lost."[19] It is its understanding of God's sensitivity to all events that allows process theology to agree with Tillich that "nothing truly real is ever forgotten."

And so, all the moments of an evolving world are harvested into the divine experience in an ever intensifying aesthetic pattern. Here all the suffering, struggle, loss, and triumph in evolution are finally endowed with eternal meaning. Whatever occurs in the evolving universe can contribute—at least in the long run—to the beauty that takes shape in the compassionate embrace of God. Perhaps, then, the "point" of the universe has something to do with the production of a beauty that in God's experience never fades but grows increasingly wider and deeper and abides everlastingly.

It would follow that an appropriate way of thinking about cosmic purpose in an evolutionary world, and hence of providing a firm basis in evolution for human ethical endeavor, consists in the view that the cosmos is a restless aim toward ever more intense configurations of beauty.[20] The general physical features of the universe are shaped by what we might call the "aesthetic cosmological principle." Unlike the so-called "anthropic cosmological principle," which views the physical constants and initial conditions of the universe as pointing only toward the eventual emergence of humans, the aesthetic principle suggests more broadly that the universe has been set up, as it were, from the very beginning in such a manner as to allow for the ongoing creation of beauty.[21]

The physicist Freeman Dyson suggests comparably that the universe is constructed according to what he calls the "principle of maximum diversity." This principle says that "the laws of nature and initial conditions are such as to make the universe as interesting as possible."[22] The aesthetic principle suggested by Whiteheadian cosmology expresses a similar intuition. Within the general sweep of the evolving universe, as it moves from less to more intense forms of ordered novelty, the resultant beauty may take many different forms. But what stands out—at least in our terrestrial experience—is the emergence of life, subjectivity, freedom, consciousness, and community. We do not yet know exactly what kind of "interesting" results the cosmic impetus toward beauty may bring about in other sectors or epochs of our unfathomably vast universe. But it is hard to suppress the suspicion that upon journeying elsewhere we would encounter evidence of the same cosmic discontent with the status quo that we experience here from Earth. It is also hard to imagine that in these regions any emergent phenomena similar to what we call "life" would not also be accompanied by the risk of suffering and tragedy. Once again, however, we may envisage even these occurrences as being taken into God's own feeling of the universe, where they receive a significance that forever eludes our own finite grasp.

Science itself has given us reasons for suspecting that our universe has at the very least a general kind of directionality. Nature abandoned the monotony of its earliest moments and blossomed over the course of billions of years into an astounding display of diversity and beauty. By any standards, there is an enormous difference in aesthetic intensity between the nearly homogeneous sea of radiation present at the time of cosmic beginnings and the biological and cultural complexity that prevails on our planet (and perhaps elsewhere) today. It seems to me that there is an obvious directionality here—as we survey the cosmic process over its fifteen-billion-year history. And although this directionality constitutes no proof of an intentional cosmic director, it does suggest strongly that something momentous is going on in the universe.

Science, then, has not only failed to refute the religious belief in an overall meaning to cosmic process, but also, through its ever more detailed representations of evolutionary emergence, has added recently to the list of reasons for theology to suspect the unobtrusive presence of such meaning. We do not need to specify precisely any final outcome of the cosmic process in order to conjecture with some confidence that the religious intimation of cosmic purpose is logically consistent with contemporary scientific knowledge of the details of cosmic evolution.

In fact, an aesthetic understanding of cosmic purpose is encompassing enough to permit more specific and focused proposals about what is really going on in the universe. For example, Teilhard's conviction that cosmic process aims toward increasing consciousness does not contradict, but may be subsumed under, the aesthetic cosmological principle that I am enunciating here. However, we are not obliged to make consciousness the only criterion of purpose. For even if consciousness were eventually to vanish from nature altogether in the possible heat death of the universe, the fact that it shall have existed and flourished at all adds significant beauty to the "whole picture" of things that comes to rest eternally in the empathy of God.

Such a theological portrait in no way conflicts with the perennial religious belief that the cosmos exists for the glory of God. In this envisagement, however, any notion of God as a self-aggrandizing creator is ruled out by the image of divine humility or vulnerability that offers to the evolving creation every opportunity to strive from within itself toward the attainment of wider beauty. Additionally, an "aesthetic" notion of cosmic purpose is consistent not only with the data of evolution but also with the classical theological notion that God *is* the ultimate in beauty.

If we understand God's "will" as that of maximizing cosmic beauty, then the Darwinian vision of life—even with all of its way-wardness and prodigality—fits quite comfortably within an aesthetic conception of cosmic meaning. The universe may not be directional or "designed" in the restrictive and anthropomorphic ways that we humans generally prefer. But its random experiments are completely consistent with a generic cosmic aim toward more exquisitely nu-anced beauty. Thus, even after Darwin, we can reasonably conceive of the cosmos as something other than just meaningless rambling.

When critics of teleology reject the idea of purpose in the universe it is usually for ostensibly ethical reasons. For example, they cite evolution's "wastefulness" and its "cruelty" or "indifference" to-ward the weak. Its pitiless experimentation is hardly a model for hu-man conduct. In Chapter 1, I quoted David Hull's remark that evo-lution is "rife with happenstance, contingency, incredible waste, death, pain and horror" and that therefore any supposed deity would be "careless, indifferent, almost diabolical."[23] Such a judg-ment, however, can easily overleap the fact that for the most part the universe sustains life instead of crushing it. Furthermore, even the perishing of individual organisms—including ourselves—seems to be consistent with the ongoing adventure of a larger life-process. Na-ture generally favors the flourishing of life and is by no means as in-tent upon snuffing it out as scientists may have thought earlier.

Nevertheless, nature's care is not always unambiguously evident, for there is tragedy, suffering, and, for all living beings, eventually death. And so a purely ethical perspective is not broad enough to discern the full breadth of meaning that might underlie this restless adventure that we call the universe. An ethical outlook assesses everything in terms of human conceptions of good order, and so it remains baffled and often aggrieved by the chaotic consequences of the evolutionary openness to novelty. An aesthetic perspective, on the other hand, can accommodate the very contradictions that offend our moral sensitivity. It does so by allowing for a "wider vision" and for the eventual transformation of clashes and chaos into a harmony of contrasts. The overall aim toward beauty is enough to endow cosmic evolution with a purpose to which we can in turn connect our moral instincts.

Before unfolding this suggestion, however, let me specify a bit more carefully what I mean by beauty. This is a notoriously difficult notion to define clearly, but Western philosophy has generally agreed that "beauty" is a fragile balance of form and content, or a combination of unity and multiplicity.[24] According to Whitehead, beauty can similarly be defined as the "harmony of contrasts" or the "ordering of novelty."[25] Without the novelty of contrast, there is only a monotony of sheer order. And without some ordering or harmonizing of novelty and contrast, there will be an excess of discord. Beauty requires a balanced synthesis of the two polar extremes. At times, order may suppress contrast, leveling it down to bland uniformity. At other times, variation threatens to dissolve any overriding unity, fragmenting it into incoherent particulars. Every instance of beauty, it seems, walks the razor's edge between chaos on the one side and monotony or triviality on the other. Beauty is a delicate synthesis of unity and complexity, stability and motion, form and dynamics. It precariously resolves contradictions or clashes into "interesting" arrangements that constrain variety without smearing it out. And it places conflicting elements within limits that soften the contradictions without erasing differences. Thus, a localized disharmony can in the "wider vision" become an intriguing shade that enhances the whole instead of a conflict that destroys it.

Apparently, it is toward concretizing such instances of beauty that our universe has always been oriented. Thus, we are permitted to say that from its beginning the cosmos has always had at the very least a "loose" kind of teleology. In view of the discoveries of sciences ranging from astrophysics to biology, today there can be no serious doubt that the natural world has journeyed directionally from simplicity to complexity, from triviality to more intense harmonies of contrast, that is, toward increasing beauty. Of course, it is characteristic of an unfinished, evolving universe that it will often seem to be sometimes more discordant than harmonious, at least from our own finite, local perspective. And we may be tempted to project our own limited impressions of local or present discord outward onto the entire universe, making it seem altogether pointless. But such projection, stemming as it does from hasty judgment and narrow perspective, can itself be vanquished by a wider breadth of vision.

An aesthetic understanding of the cosmos cautions us that our own points of view are inevitably fragmentary, even if they seem to enjoy the apparent support of science. Religions, on the other hand, want to persuade us that there may be a vastly more expansive vantage point on the universe, one to which we humans, even with all of our scientific know-how, do not have access. Maybe our own impressions are always only glimpses of a very small cross section of a much larger and still unfolding panorama. Perhaps also there is an ultimate reality capable of resolving all the world's contradictions, monotonies, and absurdities into a harmonious and beautiful whole that our finite vista cannot encompass. Finally, it is possible also that within this totality our own lives have a significance that we can expect to grasp only indistinctly at the present time and place.

An Evolutionary Grounding of Ethics

In any case, this aesthetic understanding of the evolving universe may allow us to connect our own ethical life to nature after all. We are not restricted to following the feeble acosmic flights of the religious dualists, nor the moral isolationism of the neo-Darwinian pessimists, neither of whom ascertain any real connection between evolution and ethics. And we can root our moral life in the cosmic epic of evolution in a manner that goes much deeper than that suggested by the sociobiologists. Wilson and his followers focus so myopically on the swirling eddies of "selfish" genes that they miss altogether the dominant and dramatic cosmic current that flows directionally from triviality toward fuller beauty. Our morality need no longer appear simply as a way of purifying ourselves of nature, or of defending ourselves against it, or as a way of ensuring the immortality of our genes. Rather, an evolutionary ethic can consist simply of our carrying forward at the human level of life the universe's incessant impetus toward the intensification and expansion of beauty. It is in this sense that we may be able to experience once again our ethical aspiration as having the backing of the universe.

At times, evolutionary scientists have cited natural selection's insensitivity toward the adaptively disadvantaged as a reason for claiming that nature provides poor guidelines for human conduct. However, before we jump to the conclusion—with both the pessimists and the dualists—that our own ethical idealism lifts us out of what we may have taken to be a morally indifferent universe, we would do well to take a look at evolution in its larger cosmic setting. Once we have done so, we shall be able to see that the universe is not fundamentally indifferent or hostile to the realization of value; rather, it has always had an adventurous inclination to expand the provinces of beauty. The fact that Darwinian process leads toward the intensification of beauty in a way that runs counter to our human standards of conduct need not blind us, as it often does, to the more generic cosmic propensity to combine order with complexity, unity with plurality, and harmony with nuance in order to enhance the scope of beauty.

It is to this deep and ageless evolutionary straining toward an intensification of beauty that we may link our own sense of meaning and morality. The purpose of our own lives, when seen in this setting, must have something to do with the preserving and enlarging of the dominion of beauty in the universe. An awareness that our own conduct can contribute at least something to the ongoing creation and expansion of cosmic beauty can give our moral lives what they have often lacked, a sense of being connected meaningfully and creatively to what is going on in the universe at large. It is thanks to the evolutionary picture of the universe, and not in spite of it, that we gain this significant moral perspective.

How, though, can our fresh awareness of the overarching cosmic aim toward beauty translate into the specifics of moral conduct? Speaking concretely, I would propose that an evolutionary ethic would pursue essentially the same virtues as those prescribed almost universally by the world's religious traditions. However, this pursuit of virtue would now be fired by a much stronger sense that our moral lives are contributing to the ongoing creation of a universe. Our actions "would matter" in a way that the acosmic ethic of detachment from nature, proposed by much traditional religion, could not possibly have envisaged. Accordingly, we would continue to idealize and practice justice, compassion, humility, love of enemies, moderation, and gratitude. But we would realize that the good life is not only one of refining our own moral mettle, or of improving the lot of humanity, or even of pleasing God. Without eliminating these motivations, our reasons for doing good would also arise from a sense that the practice of virtue contributes to the creative enterprise of intensifying cosmic beauty.

But how is this possible? In what sense may human morality contribute to the evolution of the universe? In reply to this question, I would say that it is by promoting diversity and inclusiveness at the level of human sociocultural existence—and, more broadly, at the level of the whole Earth community—that the life of virtue contributes to an intensification of the harmony of contrasts in the cosmic process, and this harmony of contrasts is the defining mark of beauty.

Take, for example, the imperative to "love justice." As the biblical prophets understood it, justice requires that the poor and oppressed be included within the same societal orbit as those who benefit most from communal existence. Incorporating those who are disadvantaged, or reaching out to minorities banished from social and political life, adds nuance and contrast that brings aesthetic depth to human community. It also brings with it the risk of disruption and cultural turmoil. But whenever humans attempt only to maintain mere uniformity in their social experiments, they risk an equally offensive banality. Every movement from triviality to more intense beauty, especially in our social life, risks going through what Whitehead calls the halfway house of chaos. Difficult is the road that opens out into wider beauty.

In Jesus' practice and teaching, justice and compassion demand that a wide diversity of people be brought into the unifying embrace of what he called the "kingdom of God." His parables overflow with shocking images announcing the inclusion of those normally left out: a father embracing and preparing a banquet for a wayward son; a hated Samaritan or an insignificant widow made into an ideal of virtue; those who sit at low places invited to the head of the table; loafers and latecomers receiving wages comparable to that of hard workers.

This disturbing inclusion of the excluded is the defining mark of Jesus' conduct also, and not just of his words. The arrival of an unprecedented *cosmic* epoch is already occurring when he reaches out to the medically ostracized, the religiously alienated, the socially rejected, and even the morally unacceptable, transporting them all to the very center of a new and more nuanced order. Again, the prospect of bringing about such a harmony of contrasts in the precincts of human relations proves inevitably to be too disruptive for the congenial cult of triviality characteristic of the established. And yet nothing could be more consistent with the aesthetic creativity of the universe itself than the attempt by humans to build inclusive community out of a wide base of diversity.

An instinctive longing for the beauty that will eventually emerge from a harmony of contrasts emboldens the prophetic biblical imagination to create visions of lions lying down with lambs or of swords being transformed into plowshares, of young and old together dreaming dreams. That the actual implementation of such ideals will inevitably precipitate moments of social and economic disorder is consistent with the larger evolutionary aesthetic principle according to which any invasion of novelty may have the effect of disturbing the orderly status quo. It is an essential mark of the aim toward beauty that it will have to risk disorientation as the price of intensification. Beauty brings with it a fragility that makes it vulnerable to either excessive monotony on the one side or destructive chaos on the other. It is in this fragility, however, that the humble, hidden presence of divine creativity is most at home and most effective.

The recurring shape that beauty takes in the emergent cosmos is that of community. By "community" I mean any complex entity—whether an atom, a cell, an organism, a colony of ants or bees, or a society of persons—that consists of a synthesis of unity and plurality, order and novelty, or contrast and harmony—the elements that compose every instance of what I am calling beauty. Accordingly, human moral action can be measured by the extent to which it advances or detracts from the precarious but creative cosmic impulse toward community. Our own moral lives remain most deeply in touch with the creativity in the cosmos when they contribute to the ongoing composition of beauty in the form of a community capable of integrating a plurality of contrasting constituents. What this means concretely has already been spelled out for us by the religious imperatives to live humbly and to practice justice and compassion. What evolutionary science in the broad cosmic sense allows us to realize is that our moral lives are themselves vehicles of ongoing evolution. In this sense, our moral endeavors can truly claim the "backing of the universe."

I am assuming here that genuine moral activity occurs not by slavish obedience to arbitrarily issued imperatives—even if these seem religious in origin—but only when the urge toward goodness surges spontaneously from a deeply felt intuition that our actions have a purpose and can make a lasting difference to the universe. Wholesome moral aspiration can come to birth in us only if we are first convinced that the good life is worth living. And that conviction in turn can be emboldened by a sense that our actions do count for something at the level of the cosmos and its ongoing creation.

It may be objected immediately, of course, that most of us are not in a position to accomplish anything so grand. This, however, is to miss the point. For what I wish to convey is that our evolutionary understanding of the universe as an unceasing adventure toward more intense beauty can give importance to even the most insignificant, everyday acts, as long as they contribute in some small way to the sustaining or the development of the many communities that embrace us—not only human groupings but the entire Earth community and the wider universe as well.

Why This Kind of Universe?

This way of understanding ethical life and cosmic purpose still begs the irrepressible question of why the world has been set up in accordance with the "aesthetic cosmological principle" in the first place. Did things have to be this way? Why so much diversity? Why is the world's creation of beauty spread out over billions of years and over such an immensity of spatial magnitude? Why so much evolutionary drama, including not only the invention of unpredictable beauty but also an enormous amount of struggle and loss? And, if God is a reality, why did life have to take so long to become complex enough to be endowed with consciousness and the capacity to love?

These are humanly unanswerable questions, of course, but an aesthetically based theological cosmology would consider all of the puzzling features of the cosmos revealed by modern science to be consistent with the notion of a God who seeks to maximize beauty. Moreover, if this God's very essence is love, and if divine "power" is inseparable from divine love, then God acts effectively not by forcing the divine will onto the cosmos but by inviting it to unfold its creative potential freely and spontaneously from within. God longs for the well-being, self-coherence, and aesthetic adventurousness of the cosmos.

Viewed in this manner, the sometimes troubling Darwinian picture of life is completely consonant with a God whose essence is that of self-giving love. A God whose power is manifested most fully in humility and defenselessness—for Christians, in the death of a crucified man—would not be able, precisely because of the constraints to which love subjects itself, to bring a universe into being in the magic of a single instant. Love must apparently leave space and time for the beloved to emerge as its own distinct reality. Thus, we should not be surprised at the gradual, experimental, and extravagant manner of life's coming about ("extra-vagant," literally "wandering beyond").

The notion of God as defenseless and vulnerable love provides, as I have been arguing, an *ultimate* explanation of nature's evolutionary character. And it does so without having to candy over the deviations, disorder, and tragedy that Darwinian science has uncovered in its portrayals of the life-story. Those who appeal to the idea of "intelligent design" as the explanation for life usually ignore the accidental and often painful elements of evolution, seeing them as incompatible with their concepts of good order and omnipotence. In their fixation on the ideal of abstract order, they fail to appreciate the power resident in a love willing to risk the disorder and deviation that actually occur in the evolution of cosmic beauty.

A Note on Original Sin

Thus far I have said nothing about "original sin," which for many Christians is the most difficult religious teaching to square with Darwinian evolution. I have delayed any discussion of it until now because I consider it to be far less important than the question of how to think about God in a neo-Darwinian context. Moreover, I have waited until this point because I wanted first to present the outlines of an aesthetic understanding of cosmic evolution that might allow us to grasp the meaning of original sin in a fresh way.

Obviously an evolutionary understanding of life cannot be reconciled in a literal sense with the story of a primordial couple, Adam and Eve, rebelling against God in the Garden of Eden and passing down the consequences of their disobedience through our genetic history. The science of evolution cannot and should not be made to conform literally to the mythic biblical accounts, and vice versa. To resort to this artifice would be in fact to miss any deeper meanings resident in the sacred stories.

What, then, might original sin mean? Superficially, it means a systematic turning away from God by human beings. But what does it mean in terms of the notions of God and cosmos that I have been setting forth in the course of this book? Rather than tracing here the complex and controversial history of the notion of original sin, I would prefer now simply to suggest a way of interpreting it from the point of view of the aesthetic-evolutionary perspective sketched above.[26] Other frameworks would understand it differently, but in this setting original sin means that each of us is born into a still unfinished, imperfect universe where there already exist strong pressures—many of them inherited culturally over countless generations—for us to acquiesce in an indifference to God's creative cosmic aim of maximizing beauty. Original sin consists of all the forces that lead us away from participation in this most essential and vitalizing pursuit.

Original sin is not the same as actual sin. In actual sin, we concretely manifest our indifference to the divinely aroused aesthetic cosmological principle, either by actively destroying that which is good and beautiful, reducing it to disorder and chaos, or by tolerating unnecessary forms of monotony when the creation of deeper beauty is called for. Thus, to use Whiteheadian terminology, there are two ways in which we can show our disregard for the cosmic orientation toward beauty: either by promoting "the evil of discord" or by accepting complacently the "evil of monotony."

It is not difficult for us to point to concrete examples in our world of both of these forms of evil. The evil of discord shows up in physical violence, terrorism, war, ecological recklessness, disease, predation, many other forms of destruction, and finally death. Wherever there is disintegration of community—in the broad sense defined above—we encounter the evil of discord. As an example of the evil of monotony, on the other hand, we need only take note of the many ways in which a "community" cuts itself off from the opportunity to attain richer beauty. In the human sphere this kind of evil occurs whenever sociopolitical, economic, or ecclesiastical experiments seek the establishment of unruffled order by excluding an enriching diversity, whether of minorities, the unemployed, of women, children, or any group that does not seem to "fit in."[27] In aesthetic-cosmological terms, injustice, which always purchases unity (or, strictly speaking, uniformity) at the price of diversity, is the epitome of the evil of monotony. Think of the stubborn persistence, age after age, of class distinctions or caste systems that impoverish so many humans, or of all the political and religious purges and "ethnic cleansing" designed to eliminate vital multiformity from our social life. Though the evil of monotony is apparently devised to prevent chaos, it is our attraction to this evil that so often leads to the evil of discord.

"Original sin" points not to some vague genetic flaw inherited biologically but to the much more serious contamination each of us contracts immediately simply by entering a world in which the banality and ugliness of evil are tolerated so easily. Original sin is a notion indicative not so much of our actual evil acts or of our willful neglect but of the intractable *situation* that has come to prevail as a result of the human family's cumulative indifference to its creative mission in the cosmos (this indifference includes not only our neglect of the imperative to create just human community but also our failure to conserve and foster the wider diversity of the Earth community).

Moreover, even though the potential to do evil is already a part of our genetic makeup, it is theologically inappropriate to identify original sin simply with the instincts of aggression or selfishness that we may have inherited from our nonhuman evolutionary ancestry. Even though these tendencies are part of our evolutionary legacy, the substance of "original sin" is the culturally and environmentally inherited deposit of humanity's violence and injustice that burdens and threatens to corrupt each of us born into this world.

However, the awareness of this sinful state of affairs can occur to us only if we also already have at least some sense of what the "ideal" (nonsinful) situation would be like. Religions can make us deeply aware of our flawed condition only by providing us with vivid symbolic portrayals of an "essential" condition, a place or situation somehow "beyond" us, free from the suffering and evil that beset us now.[28] In a pre-Darwinian world, it seemed appropriate to represent this essential or ideal world as a prehistorical Garden of Eden, a dreamworld now lost. Accordingly, it was understandable that "original sin" came to be thought of as an event occurring in the remote mythic past, exiling us from the primordial paradise.

However, after Darwin we can render the notion of original sin no less meaningful if, instead of placing the paradisal realm somewhere in the vague mythic or historical past, we locate the "essential" or ideal world "up ahead" in accordance with what I have been calling a "metaphysics of the future." We saw earlier the strain that evolution puts upon a traditional metaphysics of *esse* or upon any "metaphysics of the past." A number of contemporary religious thinkers are now proposing, therefore, that we think of the "essential" realm in terms of the coming of the future into our lives. The "really real" lies not up above us, nor in the dead past, but in the "up ahead." It is not from a mythic past but from an infinitely resourceful future realm that we are exiled in the state of sin and in need of redemption. "Original sin" can therefore still express meaningfully the sense of our estrangement from the ideal; only the "ideal" world is the enlivening new creation yet to come, not a once perfect world to which we now seek nostalgically to return. That from which we are exiled is not a temporally past paradise but the Absolute Future that seeks always to transform and renew the world.

By making this adjustment in the ideal or "essential" world's temporal coordinates, moving it from the mistiness of the ambiguous past to the always faithful future, we not only render the notion of original sin completely compatible with evolutionary science but also give a significance to cosmic evolution—and to human history within the cosmos—that the traditional schemata were unable to offer.

Evolution implies that we live in an unfinished universe, and we can easily overlook the invigorating and even explosive spiritual implications of this fact. The sense of a universe still being created, as implied in evolutionary science and now amplified by big bang physics, opens up to us the gracious horizon of an indeterminate future for the world; a static, eternal, finished, or perfect universe could not possibly permit the graciousness of this horizon. The fact that creation is not yet completed endows all of cosmic reality, including our own lives, with a significance that would be inconceivable if the cosmos had been produced instantaneously in a state of finished perfection.

As Teilhard de Chardin rightly insists, the notion of an instantaneous creation is not only theologically incoherent but also spiritually deadening—even though this very assumption has dominated our religious thinking for centuries. For if the creator had produced a world already finished *in illo tempore*, we could assume reasonably that such a world would have to have been perfect. Then the evil that obviously exists in what we had taken to be an originally perfect cosmos would be a secondary imperfection. But the introduction of this imperfection would in turn require the search for a culprit to explain how things got as messed up as they have become.[29]

Our myths and religions are full of scapegoating quests for victims to sacrifice for the sake of restoring some imagined lost world of perfection. And our human obsession with redressing the origin of evil leads easily to an equally compulsive need in our spiritual lives to make repetitive acts of reparation for our own alleged complicity in spoiling what we have taken to be an *initial* perfection. Moreover, the assumption of an original perfection leads our theologies to support the inveterate human tendency to expiatory violence, the implicit objective of which is to restore things to an hypothesized primordial integrity.[30]

Evolutionary science, however, has rendered the assumption of an original cosmic perfection, one allegedly debauched by a temporally "original" sin, obsolete and unbelievable. Simultaneously, it has also abolished, at least in principle, the whole cosmological framework in which motifs of reparation and expiation have become so deeply entrenched in our cultures and our classical spiritualities. Part of Darwin's great gift to theology, therefore, is to have provided it—at last—with a cosmological setting proportionate to Christian faith's revolutionary good news that the age of expiation is over and done with, once and for all.

Evolution's implications for theology are enormous, and many of these have already been expressed in process theology and other forms of religious thought. But an often overlooked theological consequence of our new awareness of living in the not-yet-perfected universe that evolution logically implies is that the obsessive repetitiveness of expiation sanctioned by the longing for a lost paradise can no longer plausibly dominate our religious sensibilities. An evolutionary picture of the world allows us to appropriate, with complete intellectual honesty, the good news announced in the Letter to the Hebrews, namely, that redemption is once-and-for-all (*ephapax*). As Gerd Theissen has argued, the central message of this piece of scripture is that expiation is now religiously antiquated.[31] Christ entered the temple once and for all. There is no longer any point to our self-punishment, nor to the sacrificial violence that lies at the foundations of our social and political institutions. Evolutionary science shows clearly that there never was, speaking literally or historically, an original cosmic perfection. If such a notion still has figurative meaning, then nothing is to prevent us from locating the ideal world, the "essential" realm to which it points, in the domain of the eschatological future, as the goal of an energizing hope, rather than in the cosmic past as something whose loss makes the world process and our own creative participation in it inherently futile. And if the eschatological future now becomes the most important dimension in our reconfigured theology after Darwin, then there is no need to prolong our search for victims to blame for the world's present lack of harmony.

Christian faith's conviction that in Christ God has put an end to the epoch of expiation sits much more comfortably in an evolving, unfinished world open to the future than in cosmologies that posit an eternal perfection that hovers judgmentally over and paralyzes our current projects. An evolutionary world provides the cosmic setting in which the taste of new creation can now flavor all of our actions and aspirations. Genuine hope for the future can survive only in a universe that forbids perpetually repeated reparations for the loss of a timeless primordial perfection. Perfection, evolution helps us to see, lies in the eschatological future, not in the indefinite temporal past, nor in an eternal present immune to the travails of becoming.[32]

Pre-evolutionary pictures of the cosmos could all too easily represent the physical universe as a deviation from, rather than as an exciting journey toward, the fullness of being. Evolution, on the other hand, instead of banishing meaning from our lives and the cosmos, as many have interpreted Darwin's "dangerous idea," now allows us to experience our lives and the whole cosmic process as a purposeful struggle to realize the promise of new being. Likewise it casts a fresh light not only on life's struggles but also on its delights. Whereas in a pre-evolutionary world the transient beauty and bliss we experience could easily be disheartening reminders of what could have been, in an evolving—and therefore unfinished—universe, they are joyful harbingers of new and unprecedented epochs of creation yet to come. Nature is essentially promise.

Spiritual life, therefore, no longer needs to be dominated by nostalgia for what has been lost but can be structured primarily by anticipation of what might be. In a pre-evolutionary universe, religious life is, consciously or unconsciously, a longing to restore rather than a creative contribution to the birth of something truly new. In the classical perspective (generally speaking), life had a goal, of course, and there was something to look forward to, but the kind of spiritual aspiration that a static universe tended to promote was what Teilhard aptly labeled the "optimism of withdrawal."[33] It exalted as the end or purpose of our lives the prospect of being saved *from* the world. This ideal may have energized individual hopes, but it implicitly diminished the value of the natural world as a whole. Spirituality was ruled by the expectation of retrieving what had been forfeited rather than by the adventure of participating in the coming into existence of surprisingly new forms of being.

It makes an enormous difference to our spirituality, therefore, that we now recognize the universe's present imperfections and ambiguities as the inevitable consequence of an incomplete labor of creation, and that we not interpret the fact of present disorder as evidence of an ancient or prehistoric disruption of an initial wholeness. The doctrine of original sin still has meaning, of course, in pointing to the fact that each of us is born into a world where the accumulated effects of despair and sin have diminished and destroyed what is good and have restricted what is possible. Yet in refuting the notion of an initial instantaneous creation of a perfected universe, evolution implies that this world is still very much in the making. The good news that accompanies evolutionary science, therefore, is that all beings—including, in a special way, us humans—are gifted with the opportunity of making unique and unrepeatable contributions to an ever innovative cosmic adventure, one that aims always toward fresh and more profound forms of beauty. Perhaps only an evolving universe can really have a purpose to it and therefore fully excite us to moral achievement.

Conclusion

Evolution, I would emphasize once again, in no way requires that we abandon our hierarchically construed religious traditions; but, in place of the nostalgia for a primordial perfection and "forgotten truth" that permeates so much pre-evolutionary spirituality, it does demand that we reconfigure the ancient hierarchies in accordance with the logic of hope in new creation. Here biblical faith can be our best guide. Its dominant theme of promise implies that we need think no longer of "ultimate reality" primarily as the highest "level" or even as the "deepest dimension" of reality. Rather, we may think of God as our Absolute Future.[34] Setting the ancient hierarchy on its side, as it were, and introducing a processive leitmotiv into it, we can picture our emergent universe as being lured forward toward the transcendence of an indeterminate and inexhaustibly resourceful but never static future. The "ultimate" dimension in this eschatologically restructured hierarchy remains hidden and unavailable, as before. But we may understand God, the Absolute Future, as the source of new being, that is, as the source of the destabilizing and always surprising "informational input" that slips into each present. And we may view "revelation" as the unmerited arrival in the present of this informative future.

Moreover, in this vision of things the unavailability of God is not the consequence of our having forgotten a primordial revelation or of having lost touch with some nebulous *Urzeit* to which we must now return through a life of expiation. Rather, the absence or incomprehensibility of God is simply a mark of the essential futurity of reality. It is characteristic of the world's Absolute Future that it escapes confinement in any present temporal moment. And yet this transcendent future, precisely in its reticence, is all-explanatory. It is out of the hidden but endlessly abundant future that the world is brought continually out of nothingness and placed in evolution.

9

Evolution, Ecology, and the Promise of Nature

A LL OVER THE EARTH, and especially in the most impoverished lands, sources of freshwater are diminishing, forests are being destroyed, soil is eroding, deserts are spreading; the land, air, and water are being poisoned, and species are disappearing at an alarming rate. Patterns of excessive consumption and the pressure of increasing human numbers are making these problems even worse in many areas. The news is not all bad: For example, there has been some reforestation of areas in the eastern United States previously ravaged by bad agricultural practice; some municipal recycling programs are having success; industrial polluters are beginning to acknowledge that good business practice is not opposed to sound environmental policy; the quality of water and air in various places is improving; and there is an emergent ecological sensitivity in many lands.

Still, the picture is generally bleak. Pollution, global climate change, the thinning of the stratospheric ozone layer, the loss of topsoil and sources of freshwater, and numerous other ills pose unprecedented dangers to plant, animal, and human life. Holmes Rolston III, one of America's best environmental ethicists, writes:

> As a result of human failings nature is more at peril than at any time in the last two and a half billion years. The sun will rise tomorrow, because it rose yesterday and the day before; but nature may no longer be there. Unless in the next millennium, indeed in the next century, we can regulate and control the escalating human devastation of our planet,

we may face the end of nature as it has hitherto been known. Several billion years worth of creative toil, several million species of teeming life, have now been handed over to the care of this late-coming species in which mind has flowered and morals have emerged. Science has revealed to us this glorious natural history; and religion invites us to be stewards of it. That could be a glorious future story. But the sole moral and allegedly wise species has so far been able to do little more than use this science to convert whatever we can into resources for our own self-interested and escalating consumption, and we have done even that with great inequity between persons.[1]

A sincere appraisal of the ecological data available today could easily cause us to lose heart. Doesn't realism require an honest pessimism as we ponder the planet's future? Runaway ecological decline has gained such momentum in some regions that many people have already surrendered to the prospect of final catastrophe. For solace they have retreated into their private pleasures; or, if they are religiously inclined, they have taken consolation in their belief that this world was never meant to last anyway. Having set their sights on a better home "beyond" Earth, they remain quite untroubled by ecological problems. Meanwhile, religious believers who are sensitive to the fact that something is radically wrong with our relationship to the natural world cannot always recite convincing theological reasons for taking ecological responsibility seriously.

At least to some extent this is the fault of those of us who are theologians, since until recently we have attended only superficially to nature. In the early modern period, for example, we virtually handed the natural world over to science, reserving for theology the task of pondering matters such as human destiny and the meaning of history. To a great extent, theology lost touch with the universe. Today, however, the theology of nature is making a comeback of sorts, stimulated in great measure by natural science. And we Earthbound theologians have begun to weigh, perhaps more deliberately than ever before, precisely why the life-systems of the planet are worth saving.

The religious basis for an ecological theology is certainly not lacking in the scriptural and traditional sources. We have discovered anew the relevance to our contemporary ecological predicament of the biblical creation theology, of the theme of God's incarnation in the world, of a sacramental vision of nature, and of the necessity of practicing the virtues of humility, detachment, compassion, moderation, justice, and gratitude. In our theological sources, we can now discern a wealth of ecologically relevant material that had previously escaped our notice.

But have we yet looked at our sources deeply enough? Without in any way minimizing the ecological significance of the items just mentioned, I shall propose here that ecology, no less than evolution, needs to be situated within the biblical scheme of hope and promise. An ecological theology consistent with the interpretation of evolution set forth in the previous chapters also requires a metaphysics of the future. Even though biblical faith includes at its very foundation a sense that the world is continually being shaped by promise, theology has yet to draw out explicitly the ecological significance of this so-called "eschatological" vision of reality.

A major reason for this oversight is that eschatological concern, which means preoccupation with *future* fulfillment, seems at first glance to be ecologically dangerous. After all, if we cast our attention toward the future, whether we think of it in a this-worldly or an other-worldly way, will we not be inclined to discount today's tribulations, averting our eyes from the depressing devastation in nature as presently experienced? Some sensitive religious ecologists are even embarrassed by the Bible's concern for the future. They see no way of integrating "eschatology" into their ecological vision and ethics.[2] We must ask, though, whether it is appropriate for a biblically based ecological theology to ignore what may well be the most distinctive feature of the Abrahamic religious traditions.

The term "eschatology" comes from the Greek "eschaton," a word that literally means "last." Traditionally, "eschatology" denoted the kind of religious speculation that deals with the "last things"; and the "last things," at least in traditional theology, meant death, heaven, hell, and purgatory. In a wider and more original sense, however, eschatology has to do simply with "what we may hope for." In the Bible, especially the prophetic writings, there is an overwhelming sense that the world and its history are defined by God's promise, and so we are encouraged to hope for the fulfillment of this promise.[3] Eschatology seeks to arouse complete trust in the God who makes promises, who is faithful to these promises, whose "reign" will bring about a "new creation," and who comes to meet us out of an always surprising and ultimately fulfilling future. In the resurrection of Jesus, Christian faith discerns the future fulfillment of the whole universe already made manifest in advance.[4] Eschatology, then, quite clearly lies at the very heart of biblical faith. Hence, we must ask whether we can ever have a distinctively biblical ecological theology if we leave out this central theme of hope for future fulfillment.

Authentic faith, if we follow the spirit of the Bible, is openness to a divine promise that points us in the direction of a fulfillment yet to come. It eagerly anticipates the arrival of "the reign of God" and the "new creation." It affirms that God's initial creation *(creatio originalis)* continues even now *(creatio continua)* and will be brought to fulfillment in the future *(creatio nova)*. Eschatology is the extension into the future of a fundamental faith in the God who is still creating "the heavens and the Earth." However, even though the belief that all of creation is oriented toward future fulfillment in God is fundamental to biblical faith, contemporary theology has yet to clarify just how this eschatological tenor can also be the basis of an ecologically responsible theology.

A Christian Ecological Theology?

A distinctively Christian ecological theology would begin with the question of whether there is an *essential* connection between the classic sources of faith and ecological concern. It would ask if there is an inner momentum in the biblical vision of the world that might intrinsically, and not just as a historical accident or afterthought, lead us to care for the nonhuman natural world. Some environmentalists doubt that there is. The Australian philosopher John Passmore, for example, states that Christianity is irreformably anti-ecological. Belief in God and the "next world," he argues, removes any serious obligation to safeguard "this world." The most appropriate framework for environmental concern, he claims, is a pure naturalism, a philosophy that denies the existence of God and views "this world" as all there is. Only after we have acknowledged that we are all alone in a world devoid of "supernatural" protection will we begin in earnest to assume responsibility for Earth's well-being. Embracing this planet as our only and final home will motivate us to take much better care of it than would a Christian supernaturalist optimism.[5]

Occasionally ecologists issue even more passionate disavowals of religion and, especially, of Christianity. "Religion must die," says one. "It is the fundamental cause of virtually all social, economic, and ecological problems." Another told Gerald Barney, a Christian environmentalist: "You have done some very important work, but just think of how much more you would have done if your parents had not exposed you to the pernicious influence of Christianity!"[6] Such statements, however excessive they may be, indicate that the Christian tradition has given at least the appearance of being ecologically problematic. Can we, then, expect our theology to convince both unbelievers and believers that Christianity is *essentially* supportive of ecological responsibility? Are there sufficient resources in the tradition for an ecologically positive theology?

My argument here will be that we need look not merely toward those texts in the Bible and tradition that *explicitly* proclaim the goodness and glories of nature, although it is important to seek these out as well. Rather, we may find the core ingredients of an ecologically responsive theology at the very centerpiece of biblical faith, namely, in its consistent confidence that all of reality exists within the embrace of God's promise. There is, of course, a plurality of voices in what I am vaguely calling the "biblical tradition," but what stands out in this complex record of religious sentiments is a constant expectation of future fulfillment.

Of course, prominent features in scripture and tradition other than eschatology must also enter into the shaping of an ecological theology. For example, there is a powerful creation theology not only in Genesis but also in the Psalms, the wisdom literature, and the Prophets. Likewise the cosmic Christologies of John and Paul, along with other segments of the Bible and tradition, interpret creation as a gift deserving of our reverence, wonder, and gratitude. And, of course, there is an emphasis on the "stewardship" that humans must exercise with respect to nature.

Additionally, the exhortations to practice the virtues of love, humility, moderation, detachment, justice, and gratitude are of perennial relevance to ecological ethics. Since human arrogance, greed, injustice, and hunger for power have led us to ruin the blessings of creation, only the practice of true virtue can keep us from further pillaging nature. Hence, to the extent that Christianity shares in the wider religious world's calling to live virtuously, it answers any accusations that it is ecologically irrelevant. Environmental abuse is not the fault of religion so much as the consequence of our failure to heed the religious vocation to live the life of goodness.

Another essential ingredient of ecological theology—especially typical of Eastern Christian and Roman Catholic spirituality—is an emphasis on the "sacramental" character of nature. In a sacramental outlook, nature's beauty and diversity tell us something about what God is like. Nature itself, in other words, is symbolic or revelatory of God. As Michael and Kenneth Himes have written: "The essence of a sacrament is the capacity to reveal grace, the agapic self-gift of God, by being what it is. By being thoroughly itself, a sacrament bodies forth the absolute self-donative love of God that undergirds it and the entirety of creation." Thus, "every creature, human and non-human, animate and inanimate can be a sacrament."[7]

By featuring nature's inherent transparency to the divine, sacramentalism keeps us from turning our world into nothing more than raw material for human projects and consumption. If nature somehow participates in the very holiness of God, this should shield it from our exploitative and destructive tendencies. "By its nature," the Himes brothers argue, "a sacrament requires that it be appreciated for what it is and not as a tool to an end." Thus, they continue, the sacramental vision "provides the deepest foundation for reverencing creation."[8]

In summary, the Bible's creation theology and its injunction to faithful stewardship, together with the call to follow the virtues and the incarnational and sacramental aspects of faith, provide substantial resources for an ecological theology. For some ecological theologians these are sufficient. However, in my own judgment, although these are all essential aspects of the larger project of formulating an ecological theology, a much deeper foundation lies in the future-oriented, promise-filled, hope-inspired quality of biblical faith. In my view, an ecological theology will understand nature's inherent worth to be grounded not only in its being a sacramental disclosure of God but also, and no less fundamentally, in its character as *promise* of the future perfection of creation. The notion of nature as promise brings together into a coherent vision the three domains of ecology, evolution, and eschatology.

The Promise of Nature

As scholars have rediscovered in this century, biblical "eschatology" means not simply survival in the "next world" but more fundamentally a sense that the totality of being is shaped by God's gracious promise. Eschatological faith affirms that the same promise that brought Israel into being has always encompassed the totality of creation. Eschatology, in its deepest and widest meaning, adds up to the good news that a splendid fulfillment awaits the *entire universe*. The divine promise first announced to Abraham is extended not only to the "people of God" but also, if we listen to St. Paul in Romans 8:22, to the "whole creation." Any ecological theology failing to root itself in this cosmic eschatological vision, that is, in faith's sense that God's promise covers the whole evolutionary sweep of creation, is incomplete and only tangentially biblical.

This means that the whole of nature and its evolution are essentially inseparable from promise. Indeed, in a literal sense, the evolving world is promise. And if through faith we can interpret the totality of nature as a great promise, we may learn to treasure it not simply for its sacramental transparency to God but also because it carries in its present perishable glory the seeds of a final, eschatological flowering. Hence, by allowing the embryonic future to perish now at the hands of our own ecological carelessness and selfishness we not only violate nature's sacramental bearing but also turn away from the promise that lies embedded in all of creation. When we interpret the evolving universe in terms of a properly biblical framework, then our ecological neglect is fundamentally an expression of despair.

To bring evolution, eschatology, and ecology together, as I am doing here, may at first sight seem to be an awkward if not unseemly proposal. As I mentioned earlier, many ecologists fear that religious concern for a future fulfillment will allow us to tolerate ecological indifference in the present. Hope for a future new creation, their argument goes, causes us to dream so extravagantly of the age to come that we lose interest in this one. If the eyes of faith are trained on the eschatological future we may be too willing to let this present world slip toward catastrophe.

We cannot ignore this objection. After all, some permutations of biblical expectation, if taken in isolation, are ecologically dangerous. For example, apocalyptic visions, when interpreted too literally and independently of other biblical forms of anticipation, look with enthusiasm toward this world's tumultuous dissolution: "The heavens will pass away with a mighty roar and the elements will be dissolved by fire" (2 Peter, 3:10). Moreover, Earth-despising brands of supernaturalist optimism seek an acosmic "spiritual" world as our final destiny, thus shrouding our present earthly abode in insignificance. Certain versions of eschatological fervor, in other words, truly appear to be an ecological menace.

Still we cannot divorce eschatology from Christian faith. As theologian Jürgen Moltmann emphasizes:

> From first to last, and not merely in the epilogue, Christianity is eschatology, is hope, forward looking and forward moving, and therefore also revolutionizing and transforming the present. The eschatological is not one element *of* Christianity, but it is the medium of Christian faith as such, the key in which everything in it is set, the glow that suffuses everything here in the dawn of an expected new day.... Hence eschatology cannot really be only a part of Christian doctrine. Rather, the eschatological outlook is characteristic of all Christian proclamation, of every Christian existence and of the whole Church. There is therefore only one real problem in Christian theology ... : the problem of the future.[9]

A major task of ecological theology, therefore, is to ensure that looking toward the future "coming of God" is a condition of, and not an obstacle to, ecological responsibility. The Roman Catholic Eucharistic liturgy invites us to pray, "We hope to enjoy forever the vision of Your Glory." But exactly how is this longing compatible with caring for the present natural world? And when we pray, with the earliest followers of Christ, "Maranatha; come Lord Jesus," how can this most characteristically Christian petition become for us an incentive to love rather than ignore the natural world? If it is accurate to say that all of Christian theology must be erected on the foundation of hope in the "coming of God" and on God's promise of "new creation," can an ecological theology find nourishment in such a setting?

I believe that it can. For in spite of the fact that the advent of God takes the form of a dramatic reversal of "this present age" (as apocalyptic literature powerfully imagines), the central thrust of biblical hope is that we may look toward a future *for* the world, not a future completely apart from it. Essentially, eschatology is hope for the fulfillment and new creation of *this* evolving cosmos, and not a wish to substitute another world for the one we live in now. A complete discontinuity between "this present age" and "the age to come" would hardly be consistent with the good news of the coming of God's reign; such discontinuity would amount to a denial of the inherent goodness of creation and of God's incarnation in our present world. Just as believers can assume some continuity between their personal identities now and a glorified existence in the "age to come," they may also be permitted to assume that the coming of God's reign transforms or transfigures, and does not abandon or obliterate, the natural world whose life-forms have come about by way of the process of Darwinian evolution.

An evolutionary perspective allows us to see that the biblical distinction between "this present age" and the "age to come" is not nearly so ecologically problematic as it might otherwise seem. A problem arises only when we forget the temporal-historical bearing of these expressions and translate them imaginatively into "the natural world" on the one hand and the "supernatural world" on the other. This latter dichotomy could easily suppress the biblical sense that all of reality, including the present age and all that pertains to it, is *already* defined by promise. In transfigured status, then, the present cosmos along with all of its prior evolution will continue to remain deeply implicated in the world's eventual eschatological fulfillment. Without a hope that nature has such a future, our present ecological commitments might indeed have entirely too flimsy a footing.[10]

Eschatology, I must now make clear, is the basis of ecological concern not only in the sense of encouraging us, as the Bible always does, to hope against hope, or in the sense of inspiring us to make the world ready for the coming of God. An even deeper reason why eschatological faith can be said to arouse ecological concern is that it invites us to see everything in our experience, including the natural world, as *essentially promise*. And the very fact that something is a promise means that it is not just a gift. Rather, it is a gift that carries the future within itself—brought to us ahead of time, so to speak. Bearing the glow of the future, therefore, an evolving cosmos always has a uniquely precious significance, one that a purely sacramental perspective may not be able to profess explicitly.

Although we may already have thought of nature as a gift, have we thought sufficiently about nature as a promise? I would suggest that our ecological theology must go beyond the bare announcement that nature is a gift; for if we view nature only as gift and not also as promise, it is still too easy for us to think of it as something we may consume or use up. Such a "religious" reading provides little protection against the complete exhausting of nature's resourcefulness. On the other hand, the intuition that God's gift of nature is at heart the gift of a promise may provide us with a deeper and more lasting reason to preserve our precious resources than would the sacramental vision all by itself. For unless we protect and nourish the natural world here and now, we may lose touch with the future that it bears within it and that ultimately explains its evolutionary character.

In the Bible there is already an explicit connection between nature and promise. One of the most obvious examples, of course, is in the story of Noah where the miraculous beauty of the rainbow becomes a token of God's eternal fidelity (Genesis 9. 12–17). Likewise, in the Abraham narratives there is the suggestion that the experience of precarious green growth in the desert, along with the nomadic anticipation of fresh patches of fertility, may well have provided the original basis of biblical faith in the future. The first sparks of what would eventually flame out into the passionate prophetic hope for the coming of God may have occurred in our remote biblical ancestors' encounter with the fragile thriving of life at the frontiers of their own wanderings. In addition, the prophetic pictures of future *shalom* were often framed in pastoral imagery. So, too, for us today the well-being of nature remains an essential condition for arousing our own hope in the future. It is the future already latent in the glories of nature produced painstakingly by evolution that invites our best efforts at conservation and sustainability.

If we fail to protect those natural processes in which science has detected the long story of evolution and the continual eruption of new forms of life, we will eventually lose our native taste for any *final* renewal of all things. To keep hope for new creation alive, we need to secure the integrity of what evolution has already produced. Our own hopes will surely die if we allow Earth's ecosystems to disintegrate. Today, as a matter of fact, the hopelessness that many people experience, especially in impoverished and environmentally devastated areas, is a symptom not only of economic injustice but also of the deeply felt human estrangement from a natural world that often seems itself to be near death. For hope to survive, nature must thrive. Hints of a final renewal of life would be unavailable to us if we divested the natural world here and now of the gift of its vitality and biodiversity. Evolution, ecology, and eschatology, therefore, form a much tighter fit than either agnostic naturalists or traditional theologians have usually detected.

Thinking about life on Earth from both a Darwinian and a sacramental perspective, Thomas Berry is fond of saying that by diminishing or losing the richness of the biosphere we will also impoverish any sense of the God whose being is symbolically revealed to us

through the extravagant diversity and beauty of nature.[11] Likewise
Jürgen Moltmann has shown how much our sense of the Spirit of
Life (the Holy Spirit) depends upon our feeling the power, complexity, and integrity of the biotic levels that support our own existence
here and now.[12] We might also argue, from an *eschatological* perspective, that if we lose touch now with nature's beauty we also risk
losing our sense of the "power of the future," the renewing energy
that faith perceives most explicitly in the resurrection of Christ.[13]

Evolution, Ecology, and the Lure of Naturalism

Construing nature's evolution in terms of the biblical theme of
promise has two additional implications for ecological theology and
ethics. First, such an interpretation helps restrain the strong human
temptation to worship or divinize either particular aspects of the
natural world or the "cosmic whole." And second, putting nature into
an eschatological and evolutionary perspective allows us to accept
realistically its limitations without letting these lead us to despair.
Let us now examine each of these two implications more closely.

(1) An eschatological-evolutionary ecological vision resists the ab-
solutizing of nature to which an exaggerated sacramentalism may be
prone. Although some naturalists, understandably, now highlight
the ecological importance of Neolithic and native peoples' sacramental approach, I would argue that an unrestrained resacralization
of the world could lead us back to the suffocating bondage to natural objects and occurrences from which the biblical prophets tried
valiantly, and often unsuccessfully, to liberate religion. Biblical faith
is distinctive for its awareness that the human spirit cannot find fulfillment in any given state of nature. Resourceful as the natural
world is, biblical faith looks beneath it and beyond it for the ultimate wellspring of nature's munificence. It finds the source of this
bounty in the transcendent power of a creative, renewing Spirit that
is distinct from nature itself but that is, nonetheless, the ultimate energy of its evolution. At the same time, in conjunction with evolutionary science, an ecological theology can open up to us the horizon
of a future that draws us out of complete servility to the rhythms
and cycles of the seasons.

However, precisely because of this apparent loosening of our ties
with cyclical nature, today some ecologically sensitive people think
of the Bible as fundamentally hostile to our contemporary need to

restore a sense of reverence toward Earth. Some even propose that ecological ethics now demands a return to the prehistoric "paganism" that the Bible uprooted. It was our exile into the terrors of history, they argue, that caused us to lose touch with the cosmos in the first place, and it is the sense of ourselves as historical rather than natural beings that now renders us oblivious to our fundamental connectedness to nature.

Although initially such an accusation may seem persuasive, it overlooks two important points. First, the prophetic-eschatological vision did not abandon nature to insignificance but took it up into the momentous story of a divine promise of a final perfecting, not abandoning, of creation. This assimilation into a promissory history, instead of cheapening nature, gives it unprecedented significance. Some feasts of Israel, and later of Christianity, inserted what had previously been pure celebrations of nature's beneficence into the broader scheme of God's promise of new creation. That the earlier celebrations gradually became overlaid with the motif of promise, one could argue, turns out to be ecologically salutary rather than ruinous.

Second, as evolutionary thinking itself clearly implies, even science now agrees that nature and history are inseparable notions. Carl Friedrich von Weizsäcker pointed out some years ago that the most significant discovery of modern science is that nature itself is inherently historical, indeed that the cosmos has always had a historical character.[14] To say that nature is historical means that even physical reality seeks to transcend or "go beyond" itself. Not only humanity but nature too is a self-transcending reality. Evolutionary biology, geology, physics, and now even astronomy have shown that the cosmos itself is a restless adventure. The irreversibility of cosmic process stands out decisively in the laws of thermodynamics and in the "big bang" cosmology to which most scientists subscribe today. The evolutionary complexion of almost all of the sciences now dictates that we simply cannot return again to the vision of an ahistorical, eternally unchanging cosmos that appealed to earlier generations of philosophers and scientists, and that still has a romantic fascination for some ecologists.

In what sense, though, is this evolutionary-historical reading of nature pertinent to our attempts to construct an ecological theology? In answer to this question, it could be argued that because of recent science's discovery of nature's fundamentally historical character, we may with more confidence than ever locate *the whole cosmos,* and not just human affairs, within the horizon of the promise that molds the experience of Israel, Jesus, and his followers. Envisaging all of nature as participative in the story of a divine promise does not require that we ignore the ecologically important notion of nature's sacramentality. But nature's sacramentality must always be overlaid with eschatology.

Viewing nature historically and as promise still allows us to attribute to it the special kind of intrinsic value that a sacramental perspective also allows. A promise, after all, is something to be treasured and valued. When we receive a promise we cherish it instinctively as a token of the promiser's fidelity. We do not just throw it away in our haste to get to the fulfillment it pledges. Perhaps, then, we could learn once again to experience nature itself as a great promise, as a medium in which the future is always seeking to become present. Such an outlook might give a more fundamentally biblical slant to our ecological ethics than is typically the case.

To summarize, it is my belief that evolutionary science is especially important to ecological theology. Unlike the previous static views of the world, evolution invites us to picture nature as the unfolding of a promise, a promise that has been internal to the universe from its very inception. Nature, when understood as essentially promise, would have intrinsic, but by no means ultimate, value. In gratitude, we might treasure it and care for it in such a way that we would not forget what it betokens, but we would not have to look upon it in a pantheistic manner, as though it were our Ultimate Environment. At the same time, we could realize that if we end up trashing nature, we will lose touch with our Ultimate Environment, the promising God who comes to meet the world from out of the future.

An evolutionary reading of biblical faith, in other words, invites us to relate to nature as we would to any momentous promise. We do not have to embrace it as an end in itself, or as the final and most encompassing horizon of our existence. But we can still value it and nurture it nonetheless. Without the dynamic, future-oriented perspective that eschatology provides it would be too easy for us to make nature itself the full and final context of our lives. But if we experience nature as essentially an evolutionary promise, we can accept it realistically as it is, in its unfinished character. It merits our veneration but never our prostration. An eschatological faith in combination with evolutionary thinking liberates nature from the burden of having to function as the final fulfillment of our deepest human longings.

(2) This brings me to the second point. Appreciating nature as promise rather than perfection is especially intolerant of those destructive ecological practices that expect the Earth itself to be limitless in its resourcefulness. Appreciating our rich planet as promise rather than paradise allows us, at least in principle, to come to terms with its limitations. Modernity unfortunately has not yet accepted the Earth's obvious finitude, and this idolatrous attitude is a major factor in our current ecological crisis. An eschatological-evolutionary grounding of ecological theology, on the other hand, allows us to accept the Earth's present limitations; for in the light of our conviction that full perfection lies only in the eschatological future, we do not expect any present state in nature's unfolding to bestow upon us the limitless being toward which hope orients us.

Moreover, our theological vision of nature as promise allows us to face up not only to the natural world's inherent limitations but also to the troubling ambiguity and suffering we find in its evolution. Indeed eschatology—with its hope for a final redemption—is really the essence of any good news religion may have for those who are tormented by the issue of evolutionary travail. Eschatology and hope are broad-minded enough to acknowledge the ugliness and unresolved cruelty in any present state of evolution, without requiring that we accept these conditions as final. A sense of nature as promise can also reconcile us to the fragility and perishability of natural beauty. For we do not expect perfection from a promise, but only from its fulfillment. And so, living with a sense that nature is promise rather than perfection allows us to tolerate its transiency and its defects, including instances where it seems indifferent to us.

The End of Evolution

My point thus far has been that, when looked at from a biblical perspective, nature-in-evolution has the character not just of sacrament but also of promise. The cosmos in its present state is neither essentially a testing ground for the hereafter, as the separatists claim, nor a final sacramental epiphany of God's presence.[15] Rather, it is at heart a foretaste of future perfection, of "the kingdom which will have no end" that constitutes the good news of faith. My argument is that if we want our ecological theology to connect deeply with biblical religion, and not just with incidental or tangential aspects of it, then we need to make the notion of nature's promise central to such a theology. An eschatologically transformed evolutionary vision might still see the natural world around us as sacramental, but any sacramentality present in an evolving world would be transfigured by the sense of a God whose being is essentially future.[16] No particular present, then, can represent the divine infinity exhaustively. Thus, the natural world deserves neither neglect nor worship, but simply the kind of care we would tender toward any significant promise.

However, such a view might still be taken too narrowly and anthropocentrically. For that reason, we must reflect further on what it means to say that the whole cosmic story—and not just human history—is defined by God's promise. The entire universe is heir to God's pledge of fidelity. But if the totality of nature and its long evolutionary history are God's creation, and not our own, we can assume that it has levels of meaning and value that we humans may never grasp fully. Prior to our own appearance, for example, the cosmos had already brought forth countless surprising evolutionary developments, most of them having little or nothing to do directly with our own existence. We need not assume that during the prehuman evolutionary span of fifteen billion years the only meaning the galaxies and stars in the heavens, or the diverse living creatures on Earth, had was to foreshadow the coming of human persons. Nor can we plumb the possible depths of significance the cosmos may have for God as it moves into the future, perhaps eventually without us. The universe may well hold the promise of outcomes in the future that, like many of those in its past, are not narrowly definable in terms of its being simply a home for our own species.

Therefore, during the present phase of the world's unfolding, at a time when humans are the dominant evolutionary species on Earth, we have the responsibility not only of ensuring our own species' survival but also of leaving ample room for the future of other forms of life. We are obliged to adopt styles of living that leave open the possibility of yet more incalculable outcomes as the still unfinished creation of the cosmos continues into the future. Even if these outcomes have little relevance to our own lives and interests at the present moment, a robust creation faith demands that we rejoice in the prospect that other natural beings have a meaning and value to their creator that may be quite hidden from our human powers of discernment. This universe, it bears constant repeating, is ultimately God's creation, though we have been granted a role in its aesthetic intensification. It has taken some billions of years for nature to attain the ecological richness and beauty that existed prior to our appearance. So when in our own time we allow pollution, resource exhaustion, and the annual extinction of thousands of species to fray the delicate tissue of life, we are surely aborting the hidden potential for a larger and wider-than-human future that still lurks in the folds of the Earth's complex ecosystems.

Since nature's beauty, vitality, and creativity are an irreplaceable intimation of the new creation promised not only to us but to the whole universe, we must protect them with all of our moral energy.[17] And if we truly hope for the *complete* unfolding of God's vision for the universe, we will take immense delight, here and now, in saving the natural world for the sake of its future in God, even when we see no advantages for ourselves in doing so. Those who are sensitive to the element of promise in nature will mourn the poisoning of land, air, streams and oceans, and the destruction of ecosystems everywhere, not only for the suffering this causes us humans but also because such negligence leads logically to the termination of terrestrial evolution, and surely also to a frustration of God's own creative envisagement of the future. It is not only the human present but also the cosmic future that is diminished by our ecological devastation.

Ecology and Immortality

Eschatology, however, refers not only to our collective human destiny and to that of the universe but also to the prospect of our personal survival beyond death. What is the relationship between this aspect of eschatology and an ecological theology?[18] Traditional theology's treatment of personal destiny in terms of "immortality of the soul" seems, to many at least, to raise serious questions about honestly reconciling Christian faith with evolution and ecology. The idea that we have immortal souls destined for a heaven beyond this world seems to imply that the material universe out of which our bodies have evolved is itself worthless, at least in the final analysis. The influence of Greek philosophy on Christian thought can easily lead us to think of ourselves as essentially immortal souls exiled in material bodies, and this dualistic vision, though perhaps consoling to individual humans, hardly seems good news for the rest of creation. For why should we invest our moral energy in saving a material world if it seems finally superfluous anyway? Is there any reason for "saving the Earth" other than simply to have a training area for working out our personal salvation?

The doctrine of bodily resurrection, as distinct from the idea of the "immortality of the soul," implies that the whole physical universe—and every episode in its evolution—somehow shares in our destiny. It is extremely difficult to imagine how we could completely disassociate any *bodily* form of being from the rest of the physical universe and the entire story of its evolution, even eschatologically. But our theology has yet to draw out the evolutionary and ecological implications of the doctrine of bodily resurrection.

To exist in a bodily way means, at the very least, to be bound up with a wider universe in a network of innumerable relationships that all contribute something to our embodied existence. Ecology, evolutionary biology, genetics, geology, chemistry, physics, and astronomy now convince us that all entities in the cosmos are made up of complex, dynamic interconnections. Indeed, the way things are tied together with one another in space and time—and this is as true of us humans as of other beings—is what gives them their identity. Reality, as both science and philosophy have concluded recently, is fundamentally relational.[19] If you take away an atomic particle's surrounding energy field, for instance, it vanishes. A living cell removed from its setting in a complex organism composed of other cells is no longer a living cell. Likewise, if you were suddenly torn out of your own natural and social environment, your own identity would change dramatically. Ecologically speaking, each human person is a deeply relational center tied dynamically into an evolutionary environment that includes numerous other complex living and nonliving systems. And so, inevitably, any changes to that environment somehow reconfigure the identity of the personal centers connected to it.

But what happens to each personal center at death? All efforts to answer such a question are quite speculative, of course, but if we understand human personality ecologically, that is, in terms of its complex relatedness to the wider evolving universe, then our dying need not mean a decisive break with the cosmos. Rather, it may be the occasion for entering into an even deeper relationship with it. Although this idea may seem novel to many Christians, it is entirely consistent with their tradition's hope for bodily resurrection.

Theologian Karl Rahner conjectures that in "personal" death we would not break our bonds with the universe but instead enter more deeply into relationship with it. Death, of course, is a *natural* occurrence, one that seems to go hand in hand with evolution, and therefore one to which we must submit passively. Yet from the personal center built up by all the relationships we have had to others and to the natural world during our lifetime, we can freely transform our dying, Rahner believes, into a radically *personal* passage toward deeper participation in the universe.[20] The Christian creed's belief in the doctrines of God's incarnation and the resurrection of the body emboldens us to think of death in terms such as these. Since in Christ God has already taken on the flesh and materiality of the world, a deeper relationship to the cosmos occurring in our own death would not be a distancing from, but a movement toward deeper intimacy with, an eternally embodied deity.

Death so conceived could still be a decisive moment of liberation. Apparently it was the promise of such definitive freedom that made the Greek idea of the soul's immortality—often imaged as release from prison—so attractive in early Christian efforts to unfold the implications of Jesus' redeeming career. But evolution and ecology together now make possible other ways of understanding our personal participation in the liberation promised by Christian faith. Understood in a manner consistent with ecological sensitivity and recent science, as well as with the Pauline intuition that God's redemption is cosmic in scope, our individual death need not mean a total separation of the self from nature. Hoping for a complete severance of our identities from the natural world that constitutes and nourishes us would be good news neither for us nor for the evolving universe to which faith believes God has unreservedly communicated the divine selfhood. Resurrection, if it is truly *bodily*, could mean a person being set free from a limited relationship to nature in order to take on an even deeper intimacy with it, a relationship that Rahner calls "pancosmic."[21]

A theology of death sensitive to ecology and evolution would interpret dying in Christ as a transition from our present relatively shallow associations with the world to an ever deepening solidarity with the entire universe and its future in God. Perhaps one way of understanding the doctrine of the "communion of saints" would be to see it in terms of the deeper presence those who have already died have to us through the mediation of the world that gave birth to them and to us.

My point, then, is that ecology is now inviting evolutionary theology to think of death, and of what may await us beyond death, in a way that allows the entire world of nature to have some share in our own destiny. Or should we not put this another way? Perhaps God's primary concern is that of creating and saving an entire complex *universe?* If so, we should rejoice that we are privileged to be a small part of a much grander and indefinitely wider-than-human story of God's creating and continually renewing the immense cosmos out of which we have evolved and to which we shall always in some sense belong.

How then can we prepare for death in a way that helps us to love rather than escape the Earth? Saints and philosophers have often advised us that the appropriate way to live our lives is to prepare for death. But does our preparation for death have to mean the detaching of ourselves from nature, as it often has in the past? Cannot preparing for death mean instead the intensifying of our capacity to relate to the still evolving world? Such a preparation would certainly not be devoid of its own kind of asceticism. After all, it is not only liberating and enlivening but also generally quite painful to expand the circle of our relationships. Perhaps the pain of death consists, at least in part, of our undergoing the transition from a relatively narrow range of relationships "in the present age" to the wider web of relations that would pertain to a perfected creation. Such a prospect would fit an evolutionary spirituality that consists not so much of separating ourselves from the Earth as of deepening our sense of being forever a part of it and its future in God.[22]

For Christians, at least, the main paradigm of such a widening of relationship is Jesus. The Gospel portraits of Jesus picture him as one who constantly sought out deeper connections. He was concerned especially with relating to those who seemed relationless: the sinners, the religiously despised, the sick—and the dead. A central motif of his life was that of embracing those who no longer belonged, all in accordance with what he took to be God's will. Jesus' life, then, is the model of our own ecological concern. From a Christian point of view, our ecological sensitivity and action can be seen as a manifestation of the radically inclusive Spirit of Christ now extending out over the long stream of life, and not just over the human species, calling all of creation into the kingdom that will have no end. The Spirit of Life, the Holy Spirit, groans not only in our own hearts but in the depths of the still emerging and unfinished universe as it seeks to be brought into final unity with God in Christ. An ecological theology, as conceived in both a Darwinian and a Christian context, extends Jesus' inclusive compassion for the unincluded toward all of nature, no matter how unintelligible, alien, or forbidding it may seem to our narrow human sensibilities.

It is no longer as difficult as it used to be to picture the entire universe as sharing in the "redemption of the children of God." The total cosmic process, as we now understand it with the help of science, is in some very real way interior to our very existence. The rest of the physical world is not just accidental to our being but constitutive of it. Recent astrophysics has even shown that the structuring of matter during the earliest moments of the universe's existence fifteen billion years ago was already so specifically defined as to promise the eventual evolution of living and thinking beings at least somewhere in this vast cosmos.[23] We now realize, much more clearly than did the Greek philosophers who gave our theology its earliest categories, how intimately our mental and spiritual existence meshes with the larger story of the physical universe. The latest scientific thinking no longer pictures our unimaginably immense cosmos as indifferent to life and mind but as actively cooperating in their production. Hence our own existence is neither cosmic exile nor evolutionary accident. The thrust of much recent science, and especially evolution, is that we truly belong to the universe.[24] Theologically this would mean that the revelatory promise that gives us our hope extends backward to cosmic beginnings, outward to the most remote galaxies, and forward to the future of the whole creation. And if all of nature shares in the promise, then this should be more than enough reason for taking care of it here and now as we wait "in joyful hope" for its fulfillment in God's new creation.

IO

Cosmic Evolution and Divine Action

A THEOLOGY OF EVOLUTION MAINTAINS that whatever the immediate causes and mechanisms operative in Darwinian process may be, the *ultimate* explanation of evolution and of the cosmic process that sponsors it is God. However, as we have seen, the intelligibility of such a claim may not be transparent immediately, especially since so many scientific thinkers now consider the mechanism of natural selection of random genetic mutations to be adequately explanatory of life and its diversity. For some, Darwin's theory itself provides the *ultimate* explanation of life.[1]

It is part of the task of a theology of evolution, therefore, to provide an understanding of how divine interaction with the cosmos might influence the process of evolution. If, in the course of evolution, unconscious matter is to give rise to life, consciousness, freedom, and culture as a consequence of God's influence on the cosmos, how then are we to understand divine action, especially with respect to the *prebiotic* physical universe? If inanimate matter is to move "upward" toward life, mind, and "spirit," what properties must the physical universe possess that would allow it to be drawn into these configurations?

If physical reality were essentially mindless, as is normally thought to be the case, would it not be inherently unresponsive to any supposed divine power of attraction? In that case, the only option left open to thought would be that life and mind are the products of a purely mechanical and algorithmic sequence of events, as Daniel

Dennett attempts to lay out in his book *Darwin's Dangerous Idea*. But if theology rejects this alternative as inadequately explanatory of evolutionary emergence, then we cannot help asking what hidden features the universe *did* have, prior to the emergence of life, that permitted it to be so moved by God that eventually it began to behave in the strange and novel ways we behold in living organisms and in thinking, willing, loving, and longing persons.

Whitehead's answer is to extend "subjectivity" and therefore responsiveness into those regions of the cosmic process that most modern thought has taken to be mindless and unfeeling. For even here, Whitehead argues, the fundamental constituents of the cosmos—he calls them "actual occasions"—are endowed with at least some measure of "feeling" that would allow them to respond in a hidden way to the persuasive presence of God. This almost negligible, but nonetheless real, capacity to "experience" the lure of an ultimate source of order and novelty is what allows the natural world to evolve over the course of time toward more intense forms of emergent beauty. To theologians looking for concepts by which to explain how matter has become alive, conscious, and even religious in the course of evolution, Whitehead's "panexperientialism" can be very attractive.[2] Indeed we might wonder what reasonable alternatives could possibly be left available for a theology of evolution.

However, even to many theologians, Whitehead's panpsychist (or panexperientialist) solution is simply unbelievable. At a recent conference of scientists and theologians, I was reminded once again of how much resistance there is to Whitehead's attributing "subjectivity" to nonliving nature. Yet what other philosophically coherent options are available to evolutionary theology today? And in framing a coherent conceptual framework for understanding how evolutionary emergence can occur, can any of these be serious rivals to Whitehead's?

The pure materialist, of course, will claim that nothing more is needed to explain the evolution of life than the bonding properties of atoms, plus chance, plus natural selection and an ample amount of time to experiment with various arrangements. However, materialist evolutionism leaves out any satisfactory account of how or why subjective experience and eventually consciousness entered into the cosmic picture and became so dominant. The plausibility of materialism's account of evolution is contingent upon our accepting the assumption that nature is inherently devoid of subjectivity, and that the evolutionary emergence of mind is a pure fluke, having nothing to do with the essence of the universe. As I noted earlier, materialist interpretations of evolution, such as Dennett's, have so far shed no light whatsoever on the question of why living beings have developed something like an "inner sense."

Acknowledging this omission is of utmost importance when it comes to asking how God acts in nature so as to be the ultimate explanation of evolution. For by ignoring the possibility that the cosmos includes a pervasive dimension of subjectivity, the conventional scientific "explanation" of evolution pushes out of view the very feature of nature that a theology of evolution might point to as the primary zone of divine influence. In a Whiteheadian idiom, nature's receptivity to the novel informational possibilities proposed to it by God could consist only—at least in some extended or analogous sense—of a *subjective* capacity to experience and *respond* to the pull of these possibilities.

Evolutionary materialists would, of course, scoff at such a proposal. However, materialism's decision to ignore or deny the reality of subjectivity—explaining it away as though it were purely epiphenomenal—is itself congruent neither with common human experience nor with the empirical spirit of science itself. Although abstracting from subjectivity may be appropriate for the method of physical science itself, the materialist judgment that nature is *essentially* mindless goes far beyond science and becomes a matter of belief. Most of what Dennett has written on evolution and consciousness follows from this belief rather than from anything in science itself.

Materialist metaphysical assumptions, according to which the category of "mind" has no essential place in nature, have caused scientific thinkers to ignore, if not explicitly reject, the peculiar reality of subjective experience, which, though not completely objectifiable, is nonetheless something we all indubitably experience. Moreover, the usual renditions of evolutionary thought have suppressed, or attempted to explain away, the fact of the emergence over time of more and more intense versions of subjectivity. In particular, they have failed to show how the evolutionary intensification of subjectivity even to the point of human self-consciousness could be sufficiently accounted for in terms of a purely materialist understanding of Darwinian adaptation. After all, unconscious modes of life, and forms of life that have not attained the level of self-awareness, are no less reproductively fit—and are perhaps even more so—than self-conscious ones. Once evolutionary materialists have committed themselves to the assumption that only mindless matter can be "really real," they are destined either to ignore the emergent reality of mental interiority or to squeeze it into categories shaped by a method of inquiry that has decided from the start to abstract from it altogether.[3]

It has, of course, always been a mark of modern science to leave out of its purview the whole realm of subjectivity. Perhaps this omission is a legitimate methodological contrivance. But science is supposed to be based in experience, and so we have every right to ask, with Whitehead, why there is no room in science's understanding of evolution for the emergence of the most obvious experience any of us has, namely, the sense of our own selves as experiencing subjects. The fact that we cannot objectively or publicly communicate all of what it is to have subjective experience does not make it any less true that subjectivity is part of nature. Our own interiority, the set of "data" most immediately available to each of us, gets left behind mysteriously in science's understanding of the evolving universe, almost as though it is not really there.

Even if science is permitted to abstract from nature's emergent subjectivity, however, the theological search for an *ultimate* explanation of evolution is not required to do so; for it is especially in the ongoing cosmic intensification of inwardness that genuinely novel forms of being enter into the evolving universe. The emergence of novelty occurs most obviously to us humans in the recent evolutionary arrival of our own kind of consciousness, but no one will convict us of being outrageously unempirical if we assume that other living beings also have an "inner sense." Michael Polanyi, in fact, has argued persuasively that our ineradicably personal understanding allows us to recognize instinctively that the attributes of striving, achieving, and failing that are characteristic of other living beings can occur only if these features flow forth from a *subjective* center that cannot register itself in the purely impersonal categories of modern natural science.[4]

Noting science's inability to represent subjectivity, the great Jewish philosopher Hans Jonas argues similarly that an "inner sense" enters into the cosmos with the most primitive forms of metabolism, and from there continues to increase. Though it is hidden from scientific objectification, this inner sense is embodied even in life's most primitive forms, and it contains embryonically all of the "great contradictions" that we humans eventually experience in our-selves. Our own feeling of being torn between freedom and neces-sity, self-sufficiency and dependence, or "connectedness and isola-tion" is continuous with a kind of sensitivity that appears in the earliest instances of life's evolution. Thus, from its very beginning, life exists within what Jonas calls a "horizon of transcendence":

> This theme, common to all life, can be traced in development through the ascending order of organic capabilities and functions: metabolism, motility, and appetite, feeling and perception, imagination, art, think-ing—a progressive scale of freedom and danger, reaching its pinnacle in man, who can perhaps understand his uniqueness in a new way if he no longer regards himself in metaphysical isolation.[5]

By attributing an inner sense even to the earliest forms of metabo-lism, both Jonas and Polanyi think that they have extended subjec-tivity far enough down into nature to defeat the mechanistic inter-pretations of life. Obviously the seam of subjectivity that has woven itself into the cosmos since the first dawning of metabolism can never be laid out in objective terms without our losing something in the translation. But Jonas emphasizes rightly that no cosmology is accurate that presents to us a universe devoid of subjectivity or inner experience. Subjectivity is an *objective* fact of nature.[6] Even though for billions of years the cosmos may have been actually devoid of in-ner experience, Jonas argues, we cannot ignore the fact that the early universe had at least the potentiality for giving rise to subjectivity eventually. Jonas considers it important for *cosmology* that inner ex-perience was always a cosmic possibility and that even in actuality it extends far beyond the realm of the human into the nonhuman or-ganic sphere, down to the most primitive stirrings of life.

The Whiteheadian will detect immediately the aroma of vitalism here, but Jonas does not want to allow for the "free run of mecha-nism in the inanimate world" that vitalism, in Whitehead's interpre-tation, typically does.[7] Jonas, in fact, is trying very hard to overcome any kind of dualism that makes the universe appear so pervasively dead and alien to human experience. He claims that a sound philo-sophical interpretation of life, by acknowledging the "inner dimen-sion" that exists far beyond the human realm, can "restore life's psy-chophysical unity to its place in the theoretical totality, lost on account of the divorce of the mental and the material since the time of Descartes.... The resulting gain for our understanding of the organic realm will then also be a gain for our understanding of the human realm."[8]

But what about the preanimate phases of cosmic evolution? Jonas argues that these, too, cannot be said to be altogether unconnected to mind. In a sense, he seems to be claiming, evolution has never had a completely presubjective stage. He refers to the preliving period of cosmic reality as "mind asleep," or as mind in the state of "latency," and this, he thinks, is a long way from claiming that the cosmos outside of humans and other living beings is essentially mindless. Differing here from Whitehead, for whom he has great respect, Jonas does not find it credible for us to extend active subjectivity down any further into the makeup of nature than metabolic processes.[9] Metabolism is so sharply discontinuous with the rest of natural occurrence that at life's first appearance we must draw a clear line in cosmic evolution between potential and actual interiority. With the first instance of metabolism, evolution has forthwith crossed a threshold, on one side of which there is no actual subjective experiencing and on the other side of which there is.

Still, this barrier, Jonas claims, does not necessarily plunge us back into a strict dualism in which the major portion of reality is consigned to the realm of utter mindlessness. Even its potentiality for mind keeps the prebiotic epoch of cosmic evolution from being absolutely mindless. Mind has in some way always been entangled with the material world. Jonas thinks that attributing a potentiality for subjective experience to nature prior to metabolism is enough to overcome the alleged dualism of mind and matter.

Even if this is so, however, a theology of evolution is still left with the question of how God can influence the whole cosmos—especially in its unconscious zones—so as to be in any sense effective in its evolution. What sort of causal link do we have to conceptualize as occurring between God and the early, not-yet-sensate universe in order to explain how the latter's nonmetabolic processes can be moved effectively in the direction of life and mind? It is easy enough for us conscious beings to suspect that when we are grasped inwardly by timeless values we are being addressed by and responding to the lure of God. And if *all* living beings may be said to have a dimension of inwardness in some way analogous to our own, as Jonas claims they do, we may conjecture that these could also, in some unconscious way, feel and be responsive to the novel possibilities proposed by God.

But even if we were to concede this much to Jonas, how are we then to understand God's interaction with an earlier cosmic epoch, one still at the stage of being only potentially alive yet actually destitute of life? If we are to avoid falling back on the mechanistic assumptions that Jonas allegedly wishes to overcome, do we not have to attribute some sort of *actual* responsiveness to nonmetabolic process itself, as Whitehead does? At a time in cosmic history when matter was still not yet alive even to the point of primitive metabolism, how could it have been susceptible to the influence of God without possessing, at least to some degree, an "inwardness" that Jonas is not willing to concede to it? Are we left to understand things the same way the mechanists do, in which case Jonas's account of life would be leading us back toward vitalism at best?

Jonas does not like this option either. The mere potentiality for becoming alive and developing an inner sense is for him enough to place the entire universe on the subjective side of the Cartesian divide. If we look at the many instances of inner experience that have actually emerged in this big bang universe, we can say that even its bare *potentiality* for inwardness is enough to make "matter" something other than what mechanists generally take it to be. Even so, Jonas does admit that "it is an especially hard demand on thinking that what is emphatically nonindifferent, as subjectivity certainly is, should have arisen from what is entirely indifferent and neutral. Thus it is also hard to suppose that this arising itself was an entirely neutral contingency whose occurrence involved no favoring preferment of any kind."[10] Interestingly, Jonas does not refer here to the so-called "strong anthropic principle," a notion that he would probably reject. But he does agree that it is "reasonable to assume ... a preferment in the womb of matter, i.e., to interpret the witness of subjective life, which is will through and through, as not being utterly alien to that which brought it forth, namely matter."[11]

Jonas even goes on to say that we might ascribe to matter a "tendency, something like a yearning" that leads it in the direction of inwardness.[12] There is no plan or logos in the early cosmos, but there is a "cosmogonic eros." And this implies that "right from the beginning matter is subjectivity in its latent form, even if aeons, plus exceptional luck, are required for the actualizing of this potential."[13] The presence of a "cosmogonic eros" in the early universe also means that finality or striving for a goal, such as we find in living organisms, "cannot be entirely foreign to nature, which brought forth precisely this kind of being. Finality must itself be 'natural'—in keeping with, conditioned by, and autonomously produced by nature. It follows from this that final causes, but also values and value distinctions, must be included in the (not utterly neutral) concept of the cause of the universe."[14]

Moreover, the mere presence of human beings in the cosmos today tells us something about the distant "in the beginning." "As facts of the universe, human beings must be analyzed and evaluated cosmologically.... The existence of inwardness in the universe, and along with it the anthropic evidence of reason, freedom and transcendence, are ... cosmic data. As such they belong together among the generically indispensable elements of a cosmology."[15]

Jonas's Evolutionary Theology

Do we have in Jonas's thought, then, an understanding of nature that might rival Whitehead's in allowing theology intelligibly to make a place for God as an explanation of evolution, but one that does not put as much of a strain on conventional standards of scientific plausibility as Whitehead's panexperientialism seems to do? Is a *potentiality* for inwardness perhaps enough to give purpose and significance to the whole universe without our having to project any *actual* inwardness into cosmic regions and epochs where most scientists and philosophers would intuitively deny its presence?

By attributing inwardness to nonmetabolic regions or phases of the cosmos, do we perhaps confront in Whitehead a way of thinking about physical reality and evolution that is finally irreconcilable with science? And is it not sufficient for a theology of evolution to suggest with Jonas that the early universe had a potentiality for subjectivity, rather than to insist that it was *actually*—even though minimally—endowed with it? Especially in light of the life-and-mind favoring constants and conditions that recent physics associates with the first microseconds in our big bang universe, do our efforts to overcome the dualism of mind and nature need to fall back any longer on some kind of panexperientialism, which for scientific thinkers has been perhaps the main stumbling block to their accepting of Whitehead's metaphysics?

Jonas, who is certainly familiar with and in many ways appreciative of Whitehead's thought, finds panexperientialism both intellectually unacceptable and theologically unnecessary. It is instructive,
therefore, especially for those of us who are attracted to some aspects of Whitehead's thought, to watch where Jonas's theological
reasoning takes him from here. One gets the impression that Jonas
himself would claim that his own theological speculation, by not
having to appeal to "panpsychism" in the explanation of evolution,
is much easier to harmonize with conventional neo-Darwinian scientific accounts of evolution than is process theology.

Influenced by Jewish Kabbalistic thought as well as by the provocative and moving writings of Etty Hillesum, who died during the
Holocaust in 1943, Jonas pictures a cosmic creation in which God, in
the beginning, undergoes a self-divesting of mind and abandons
"Himself and his destiny entirely to the outwardly exploding universe and thus to the pure chances of the *possibilities* contained in it
under the conditions of space and time."[16] Why God underwent this
self-divestiture is an impenetrable mystery, but it is precisely this
mystery that helps Jonas hold together belief in God on the one hand
and the standard neo-Darwinian accounts of evolution on the other.
The idea of God is necessary, according to Jonas, simply to explain
the naked existence of the world. But in order to be the *ultimate* explanation of evolution there is no need for the self-divesting and now
powerless Origin of all things to interact with or lure the world directionally in the way that Teilhard de Chardin's well-known God-
Omega does. Nor is there any need for God to present each cosmic
moment with relevant new possibilities in the way that Whitehead's
God does. Rather, Jonas says, "*only* in the endless play of the finite, in
the inexhaustibility of chance, in the surprises of the unplanned, and
in the distress caused by mortality, can mind experience itself in the
variety of its possibilities. For this the deity had to renounce His own
power. Be that as it may, from then on things proceeded only in an
immanent manner, with no further intervention of transcendence."[17]

Jonas wants to avoid any notion that evolution is a directional
road of progress, and in this respect he is much closer to Stephen Jay
Gould than to Teilhard de Chardin. Rejecting all Hegelian thoughts
about the progress of nature and spirit—a myth shattered by the
horrific events of this century—and also distancing himself from
Teilhard's evolutionary optimism, Jonas states that "creation had no

power at all to bring forth antitheses out of itself, but had to tread its long path through space and time, bound to the gradual, cumulative transformations permitted by the self-developing and consolidating law of nature, external chance, and its inner endowment."[18] In other words, a theology of evolution does not have to supplement the scientific accounts by looking into prebiotic processes for any *actual* inwardness that might, as a condition for emergence, subjectively "feel" the lure of divine persuasion. Instead Jonas's theology can seemingly embrace much more literally than Whiteheadians the Darwinian picture of nature evolving as a product of impersonal chance, necessity, and the immensity of time and space.

For Jonas the hypothesis of a self-renouncing God also helps us understand why the cosmos is so large and so old, as well as why the amount of life and subjectivity it carries is so vanishingly minute in comparison with the dominating deadness of the heavens.

> Only a universe colossal in space and time, in accordance with the rule of mere possibilities and with no intervention of divine power, offered any chance at all for mind's coming to pass at any time or place whatsoever. And if this and the self-testing of mind in a finite world were the intention of the Creator, then he had to create precisely an immense universe and leave finitude in it to its own career.[19]

Jonas, I think, would claim that in the science and religion exchange today his own understanding of God and the universe has an apologetic advantage over the Whiteheadian. For in order to interpret the evolutionary emergence of life and mind as the consequence of a divine intention, Jonas does not have to ask scientists to envisage any *actual* responsive inwardness or subjectivity in the inanimate tracts of cosmic process where science, common sense, and most philosophy can apparently discern only mindlessness. Of course, in the absence of any actual subjectivity chronologically antecedent to primordial metabolism, a spatially immense and temporally protracted universe is required in order to allow life to come about and bring forth mind all on its own by purely Darwinian processes. But that is exactly the kind of universe that Jonas thinks science has given us. Theology should work with this scientifically respectable version of the cosmos rather than fabricate one suited more immediately to its own spiritual tastes.

In order to will the evolution of mind, Jonas argues, God first had to will life and inwardness. But in order for these to be possible, God had only to guarantee a universe of sufficient spatial magnitude and temporal duration to possess at least the potentiality for eventual inwardness. So God, the primordial mind, renounced itself in order to make room for such a universe, one that, without divine intrusion and also without having to be subjectively responsive to any hypothesized divine persuasion, might eventually give rise to metabolism, subjectivity, and human consciousness.

Jonas's picture of God and evolution bears some degree of similarity to the kenotic theology that I have been proposing as the ultimate explanation of creation and evolution.[20] However, his position is distinctively different in that it requires no ongoing interaction between God and the world during the course of evolution and human history. It should be noted that Jonas's emphasis on divine noninterference is motivated not by a deistic desire to render the notion of God irrelevant to the day-to-day workings of nature but by the need to make room for an idea of God that would be compatible with appalling events in history such as the Holocaust and, in nature, with the ruthlessness of Darwinian evolution. A God who is helpless to influence the course of natural or human history beyond the initial moment of creation cannot, after all, be held accountable for the contingent evils that do occur in the world.

Such an understanding of God, though it gives us no basis for hope in an inevitably happy outcome to cosmic process, is nonetheless for Jonas an ennobling one. The very helplessness of God provides incentive for humans to exercise their own responsibility more zealously than classical theism's notion of providence would permit. Here Jonas sympathetically cites a prayer from the diary of Etty Hillesum:

I will help you O God.... Only this one thing becomes more and more clear to me: that you cannot help us, but that we must help you, and in doing so we help ourselves. That is the only thing that matters: to save in us O God, a piece of yourself. Yes, my God, even you in these circumstances seem powerless to change very much.... I demand no account from you; you will later call us to account. And with almost every heartbeat it becomes clearer to me that you cannot help us, but that we must help you and defend up to the last your dwelling within us.[21]

One can sense in Jonas's attraction to these words his own sensitivity to the important theological directive that if we say anything at all about God today we should not say anything that we would not also be willing to repeat in the presence of the burning children of Auschwitz. If we wish in any way to challenge Jonas's theology, therefore, it seems appropriate that we at least run our own alternatives past the same guidepost.

In a manner that seems to reflect the influence of Whitehead (though he is not cited), Jonas goes on to speculate that "God renounced his own being" so as "to receive it back from the Odyssey of time weighted with the chance harvest of unforeseeable temporal experience: transfigured or possibly even disfigured by it."[22] In a manner reminiscent of Whitehead's notion that God's "Consequent Nature" is sensitive to and transformed by what goes on in the world, Jonas speaks of God as accumulating a "patient memory of the gyrations of matter"[23]:

> In the temporal transactions of the world, whose fleeting now is ever swallowed by the past, an eternal presence grows, its countenance slowly defining itself as it is traced with the joys and sufferings, the triumphs and defeats of divinity in the experiences of time, which thus immortally survive. Not the agents, which must ever pass, but their acts enter into the becoming Godhead and indelibly form his never decided image.[24]

Jonas, Whitehead, and Evolutionary Theology

Can a theology of evolution be enriched by an encounter with Jonas's intriguing philosophical and theological proposals? Let me respond by making the following five sets of remarks.

(1) The first thing to say is that evolutionary theology can be appreciative of what is entirely too rare in philosophy today, namely, Jonas's firm insistence that the experience of inwardness provides data not only for psychology but also for cosmology. This alone makes his thought important as we look for alternatives to modernity's catastrophic exiling of mind from nature.[25]

According to Whitehead, however, our own experience of subjectivity is much more consequential for cosmology than Jonas allows. Our "inner experience" provides us with clues as to how *all* occurrences in nature are to be understood, including those that take place in premetabolic processes. Contrary to most modern philosophers, Whitehead has generously permitted human experience, including religious feeling, to provide us with categories for understanding the cosmic process in which our own subjective and conscious lives are fully embedded. It is only through the most arbitrary kind of abstraction that modern philosophy has decided to exile our own mental life from what it has taken to be an "essentially" or "fundamentally" mindless universe. "This sharp division between mentality and nature," Whitehead insists, "has no ground in our fundamental observation. We find ourselves living within nature. . . . We should conceive mental operations as among the factors which make up the constitution of nature."[26]

Yet it is not just our own human mentality but a "subjective" quality at the heart of every occasion in the cosmic process that for Whitehead permits the interaction of God and nature. This may sound implausible in the intellectual culture of our time, as Jonas's own thought implies, because scientific method, which has influenced the thinking of all of us, leaves out reference to the subjective. However, for Whitehead any proposals to understand divine action in the evolving natural world that ignore the fact of nature's *actual* subjectivity will be so abstract as to be irrelevant.

Since the beginning of the modern age there have been many attempts to understand how God might act in the world as construed by natural science. But most of these endeavors have sought to relate divine action to a cosmos that has been already denuded theoretically of the capacity to experience any causal influence other than a mechanical one. In theology's endeavors to keep up with the times it has implicitly conceded the adequacy of abstract and impersonal scientific accounts of nature, and in doing so has embraced a cosmic picture from which nature's "subjective" capacity to receive God's influence has already been erased. In spite of his disclaimers, it is this mechanistic version of natural philosophy that Jonas's theological speculation also builds upon.

A cosmos devoid of any actual "subjective" aspects prior to the evolutionary appearance of life leaves theology only two unsatisfactory ways of understanding the relationship of divine action to prebiotic process. A cosmic domain completely opaque to internal relationship with God would either have to be manipulated externally by the deity, in which case—as Jonas demonstrates—God would be directly responsible for the suffering and evil that occur in evolution, or, if we accept Jonas's option, God would be helpless to influence the world at all, other than by giving it its "naked existence." The latter proposal renders God innocent of evil, but it throws us back on an incoherent mechanistic understanding of the very universe that, in the course of evolution, gave birth to subjectivity. Attractive as Jonas's theological alternative might seem as far as theodicy ("justifying" God in the face of evil) is concerned, it cannot explain how subjectivity gets inside the natural world in the first place.

Teilhard de Chardin, like Whitehead, argues that there is a subjective element that runs throughout the whole of evolution in varying degrees of thickness. There is always a "withinness" that corresponds by degrees to the outward complexity of all beings—from atoms to humans. Built into the cosmos at every level is a responsiveness that allows nature to be influenced by God. No less than for Whitehead, nature in Teilhard's thought is never, concretely speaking, actually mindless or spiritless. In an evolving universe, "matter" is not the equivalent of mindlessness. It is a term that denotes a *tendency* in nature toward diffusion or multiplicity that in its extreme state would be the equivalent of nothingness. "Spirit," on the other hand, designates the opposing disposition of evolution toward increasing unity and consciousness. It cannot be said accurately, therefore, that the cosmos, at any point in its evolution, is essentially spiritless or devoid of "withinness." Teilhard overcomes dualism not by insisting that subjectivity inheres in each atomic constituent of reality but by arguing that withinness or spirit—and therefore a kind of "responsiveness"—is a property attributable to states of more or less complex makeup involving many atomic particulars. A perfectly pure state of "mindless" matter could never exist, simply because "matter" as such can never exist.

Inasmuch, therefore, as "matter" is always accompanied by some degree of inwardness in Teilhard's cosmology, a theology that follows his thought may speculate that from the very earliest moments of the cosmic process the physical universe has been receptive and responsive to the presence of God. To followers of both Whitehead and Teilhard there can be no meaningful theology of evolution that seeks to relate the notion of God to a cosmos from which all strains of mind, inwardness, or subjectivity have already been wrenched arbitrarily. This does not mean that theology must reject science's *methodological* bracketing of the fact of subjectivity in nature. Science has every right to leave out all considerations of subjectivity, as

long as its practitioners remain aware of this self-limitation. However, it is precisely the refusal to acknowledge this limitation that lies
behind most areas of alleged conflict between science and religion.

In the dialogue of science with religion, theology should not be required to follow Jonas in relating the idea of God exclusively and
immediately to scientific models or mathematical constructs that
have already subtracted from nature its interior substance. Such a
methodological maneuver eliminates in advance the very feature of
nature that might allow it to be influenced by God. Most of science,
after all, does leave out the fact of inner experience in nature, and
sometimes scientists even deny the reality of subjectivity altogether.
Such a denial, however, is itself not a scientific judgment but a nonscientific decree about the scope of science. I am afraid that Jonas
has built his fascinating theological proposal on such an abstraction
rather than on nature as it exists in the concrete.

It is of utmost importance that a theology in dialogue with science
have available to it a metaphysics fully aware that science, in its attempts to be clear and distinct, has left behind what is truly fundamental in the natural world, including possibly a vein of subjectivity
inaccessible to scientific objectification. Thus, a theology of evolution
has to work with more than just the data delivered by neo-Darwinian
biology; for we can assume that evolutionary science, especially in
its deliberately mechanistic and atomistic packaging, has also left
out a great deal that would be of interest to theological explanation.
A theology of evolution must search for a general vision of reality
capable of criticizing the abstractness of neo-Darwinian biology and
of turning our attention toward what is really concrete in cosmic
and biotic processes. Whitehead, in my opinion, comes closer to providing such a vision than do Jonas and most other philosophers.

Jonas does agree with Whitehead that any cosmology that ignores
the fact of mentality, subjectivity, or consciousness is ignoring an *objective* aspect of nature. Cosmology remains incomplete until inner
experience is accorded the status of being a fundamental category in
our understanding of the natural world. To leave the "inner side"
out of our picture of nature, as modern science has always done, is
to scale cosmology down to a mere torso of what it *really* should be.
Both Jonas and Whitehead can agree on this much. Where they differ is in the scale of their attribution of subjectivity to nature. For
Whitehead any attempt to relate the notion of divine action to a
truncated representation of the "fundamental" nature of the cosmos

such as physics gives us will inevitably fail. The typical abstractions of science leave nothing in nature that could "detect" or interact with the supposed presence of God. Jonas, along with most other philosophers, parts company with Whitehead at this point.

Why so? What is the reason for this stark division between two great philosophers? Michael Polanyi would respond as follows. The fundamental reason for the expulsion of subjectivity from the cosmos lies in modernity's intellectual commitment to the primacy of impersonal knowing. This ideal arose because of the awareness that our own subjective consciousness can be distorted easily by biases and beliefs, and so it would seem to follow that the more we can keep our personality out of the knowing process, the more obtainable the goal of complete objectivity becomes. Unfortunately, in its own pursuit of this ideal of impersonal knowing, most modern scientific thought has blinded itself to the objective fact of the *subjectivity* and personality that also reside in nature. The more it has idealized impersonal knowing, the more impersonal and subjectless the "real" world itself has seemed to be. Hence we can conjecture that much of the resistance to Whitehead's panexperientialism is prepared for at least remotely by the modern epistemological assumption that only impersonal knowing can be trusted.

Probably no recent thinker has penetrated the ambiguity—and indeed the evils—of our ignoring the personal dimension of knowing more passionately and persuasively than Polanyi. It seems appropriate, therefore, that in spite of clear differences from Whitehead, we make a place for Polanyi, alongside of the process philosopher, as a contributor of concepts vital to a contemporary theology of evolution.[27]

(2) Even though Jonas is too restrained in extending subjectivity only as far down as metabolic process, he helpfully instructs the Whiteheadian not to allow panexperientialism to blur the sharp discontinuity that comes into the cosmos with the first traces of metabolism. Whatever degree of subjectivity process philosophy may attribute to nonliving physical occurrence, the earliest emergence of life still introduces a kind of inwardness utterly different from anything that went before it. What this discontinuity entails, moreover, is something that a process perspective can lose sight of easily, namely, the hierarchical structuring of the cosmos.

It is at this point that Jonas's thought links up again with Polanyi's. Like Jonas, Polanyi would not want to extend subjectivity down below the realm of living beings, lest we lose a sense of what is distinctive about life. Intuitively, humans have always segregated living from nonliving beings on the basis of our spontaneous "personal knowledge." Personal knowing, unlike objectifying abstraction, convinces us immediately that living and thinking beings follow a distinct "logic of achievement" that does not function at the level of the inanimate processes accessible to science. Living beings are radically different from nonliving beings in that they can strive "subjectively" to achieve some goal—whether it is a tree seeking sunlight, a snail crawling toward a food supply, a bird looking for a mate, or a person struggling to be virtuous. This striving to "achieve" brings with it something radically different in evolution, namely, a capacity for failing, an experience that cannot happen to inanimate entities or processes. Even at the level of the most basic metabolism there is a kind of "striving" that does not occur in inanimate processes. Because of its capacity for striving, metabolism also can either succeed or fail, as Jonas is aware, whereas success and failure are not results that we would attribute logically to invariant and predictable chemical processes. With the appearance in evolution of living entities able to succeed or fail, therefore, we may say that the cosmos opens out into a kind of being clearly distinct from anything previous.

There is a sharp ontological discontinuity here to which a reductionist materialism is completely blind. Modern scientism and most modern philosophy have failed to acknowledge the fundamental difference between those beings capable of achievement and failure and those inanimate beings and processes not so capable. This failure, according to Polanyi, is rooted ultimately in our refusal to acknowledge the ineradicably personal character of the knowledge by which we recognize the special character of life in the first place.

Is it possible that in its impressive resistance to dualism and to the abstractions of materialism Whitehead's panexperientialism, by spreading subjectivity around so generously, may also have the effect of blurring the sharp discontinuity between living and nonliving beings that Jonas and Polanyi find so crucial? Is Whitehead's concept of subjectivity, shaped as it is primarily by the notion of feeling or experience, perhaps itself too abstract to capture the distinctive "logic of achievement" that defines the inwardness of living beings, as Polanyi maintains, and the self-affirmation that Jonas finds in every living thing?

In any case, whatever contributions process philosophy might contribute to a theology of evolution, in my opinion it must make room also for a concept of emergence that is open to Polanyi's logic of achievement. Correspondingly, the notion of relationality so fundamental to Whitehead's metaphysics must not be allowed to obscure the hierarchical character of nature and evolution as both Polanyi and Jonas see it.

(3) For all Jonas's claims that his evolutionary theology has vanquished mechanism, he still concedes too much to it. In order to reconcile his thoughts about God with the standard materialistically encumbered ideas of most neo-Darwinians, he concedes to them their decisive abstraction from inwardness as far as the nonliving epochs of cosmic evolution are concerned. To say that there was a "potentiality" for inwardness from the beginning, and that this is enough to evade dualism, still leaves an enormous explanatory gap, metaphysically speaking. What is it, after all, that activates this potentiality? And what are the properties that allow nonliving matter to be brought into the spheres of life and mind?

Jonas responds in a manner similar to Daniel Dennett and materialist evolutionism: contingency + law + the immensity of space and time = evolution. However, the sheer immensity of time and space cannot be a cause of anything. Not even in combination with chance and necessity is space-time enough to account causally for the emergence and the ongoing intensification of inwardness in evolution. To explain adequately the evolution of richer complexity and subjectivity over the course of time, we would need to introduce some additional explanatory principle to those provided by Darwin. It is precisely in its evasion of any metaphysically satisfying explanation for either the fact or the intensification of inwardness that mechanistic biology is most problematic, and Jonas seems too easily to acquiesce in its avoidance of complete accounting.

Unlike the mechanists, however, Jonas perceives the intellectual need to explain the naked existence of the universe, and so he introduces the idea of a self-divesting deity to fulfill this requirement. But apparently it sufficed for God to create a universe with enough breadth of spatial and temporal dimension to allow that inwardness, though not yet either actual or planned for in the early universe, would at least not be ruled out. Instead of perceiving any need on the part of the early universe to be structured in a way that would lead it to inwardness—as do recent versions of the strong anthropic principle—Jonas rejects any initial divine ordering whatsoever. In the early universe, he says, there is eros but no logos. For Jonas, to maintain that there was any determinative order given by God to the

early universe would involve the deity too closely in the evil and suffering that the evolving universe in fact permits.

Jonas appears, therefore, to hand the task of explaining the evolution of life at this point completely over to a mechanistic metaphysics. His reasoning is not entirely unlike that of Dennett and
other Darwinians who count all the possible outcomes of evolution
as already enfolded implicitly in the earliest stages of the universe.
The immensity of time and space is then needed simply to provide
opportunity for the full unfolding of innumerable possibilities,
which—if time and space provide sufficient amplitude—might just
include metabolism and the introduction of inwardness and, eventually, consciousness into the cosmos.

Unlike Whitehead, Jonas sees no need to ground these possibilities
in anything other than a blind chain of efficient and material causes.
He seems to be so concerned that theological speculation conform to
the abstractive constraints of scientific feasibility that he can make
no room for formal and final causation as aspects of an adequate explanation of evolutionary outcomes. Whereas Whitehead would argue that relevant evolutionary possibilities reside eternally in God,
and are proposed to and "felt" by the cosmos at the relevant moments, Jonas finds it sufficient to root all evolutionary possibilities in
a purely material and deterministic process flowing from out of an
aimless past. Only after metabolism makes its unplanned debut does
freedom (fortunately) enter the cosmos. At times, then, it is hard to
distinguish Jonas's ideas from the mechanism he otherwise repudi-
ates so ardently.

(4) Jonas, nevertheless, does admit that there must have been what
he calls a "preferment" or a leaning toward inwardness already
present in the "womb" of the universe. He insists that this orientation consists not of an intelligible logos but only of an eros or a
vague "yearning" for inwardness. This distinction between eros and
logos, however, is problematic for both logical and scientific reasons.
Logically speaking, a primordial cosmic eros must in some sense be
distinguishable from sheer meaninglessness (or maximum entropy).
Otherwise we could not make a solid case for its actual presence in
nature. But if nature from the beginning possessed an eros that oriented it toward inwardness, then it must have been *patterned* in a
way that would distinguish it conceptually from sheer chaos. In that
case logos (intelligible structuring) would be prior to, or at least co-
originative with, eros after all.

Scientifically speaking, moreover, contemporary astrophysics now provides reasons for concluding that even in the earliest microseconds of its existence the universe was not in a state of maximum entropy—a condition that Jonas's theology seems to assume—but was already structured intricately according to the exceedingly narrow range of mathematical values that would allow for the eventual evolutionary emergence of inwardness and freedom.[28] For the cosmos to have an eros toward life and subjectivity, it must always have corresponded to some kind of logos as well. At this point, the Whiteheadian theologian might present the case for an understanding of God as the source of both order and novelty, of logos as well as eros.

(5) Finally, a remark about Jonas's theodicy. After the Holocaust, any notion of a God who has the power to prevent suffering in history and nature but who refuses to exercise this power is indeed religiously and philosophically unacceptable. Accordingly, Jonas gives us the notion of a God who surrenders all power at the moment of creation and is henceforth helpless to intervene. This sympathetic God feels all that happens in cosmic evolution and history and is given a specific identity and character by these events. This is a suffering God, one similar to the kenotic deity of traditional and contemporary theological speculation. Thus, when we reflect on evolution, there is much that recommends to us Jonas's idea of a self-emptying, suffering God. Moreover, Jonas, along with process theology, rightly emphasizes God's capacity to be affected by all that occurs in the world and thus to preserve its perishing occasions everlastingly. There is no absolute loss but instead at least some kind of final redemption in God.

Nonetheless, what Jonas's speculation leaves out unnecessarily is an adequate basis for religious hope in cosmic and human redemption. Without weakening his concerns about reconciling God and suffering, Jonas might have included the notion of nature's *promise* alongside his notion of nature's potentiality, yearning, or eros for inwardness. With this adjustment of perspective, the whole of the cosmos and its evolution could be linked more closely to the eschatological faith of Israel than Jonas's thought allows; for since we do not expect perfection from a promise, but only from its fulfillment, we would be able to acknowledge the evil and suffering in the world without having to surrender our need for hope.

Conclusion

I‍N CHAPTER 5 I ARGUED that evolution does not destroy the hierarchical ordering that has formed the backbone of our traditional religions. The notion of information, itself now a part of science's own understanding of nature, allows logically for distinct kinds of being and grades of value within what, from a purely physicalist perspective, may seem to be an unbroken continuum of atoms or natural history. However, if we take evolution seriously, we cannot simply retain without transformation the static and vertical representations of the "Great Chain of Being" that molded religious and cultural life prior to Darwin. We are compelled to think of nature's hierarchy more dynamically, historically, and ecologically.

In contrast to materialist evolutionism, the classical hierarchical metaphysics could easily uphold the superior ontological status of life and mind. It thereby corresponded more closely with common human experience and with the basic assumptions on which most cultures and legal systems are still based. To deny that beings with life and mind are "higher" in significance than nonliving ones is rightly considered madness. Thus, to the extent that the hierarchical metaphysics has lost ground to modern scientific materialism, Seyyed Hossein Nasr is probably correct in pointing out that values now appear groundless, that the probability of human atrocities has increased, and that the natural world is more vulnerable than ever to abuse at the hands of humans.[1]

However, without undergoing a drastic changeover, the classical hierarchy cannot easily accommodate the Darwinian discoveries. It pictures the fullness of being and truth as residing in a timeless realm

185

up above or in the mythic past, and in this view the passage of evolutionary time only pushes us farther away from some "forgotten truth" or fullness of being now out of view. Pre-evolutionary Western theism maintains that in order to stay close to the timelessness of truth we must find a way to overcome time altogether. At the conceptual level, one way of doing so has been to think of ultimate reality only in terms of an absolute being *(esse)* ensconced "eternally" above the finite temporal world, in a realm of finished perfection immune to the passage of time. By participating in religious life and devotion, we may journey part of the way up, or back, to the domain of perfect completeness. But time itself, in this venerable view of things, can scarcely bring about anything truly new. And so evolution, which requires the passage of time, would also appear to be essentially pointless.

The enormous appeal of classical theological metaphysics is that it provides a pillar of permanence to which we can always fasten our lives, and indeed the entire temporal world, in the midst of their perpetual perishing. The price we pay for such security, however, is that whatever happens "here below" in the sphere of becoming is robbed of any real consequence. When assimilated too intimately to classical metaphysics, the story of terrestrial life and its evolution scarcely seem to lead to a truly unprecedented future. Evolution in time cannot take the world into the realm of what is genuinely new but only toward what already is, or what has been virtually constituted from all eternity. And so, if the worst that time can accomplish is to veil our impure lives and minds from a lost primordial perfection, and the best it can do is bring us back to it once again, then how can time itself be intrinsically significant?

Can we be surprised, therefore, that in modern times some of the most sensitive souls have been perceptive enough to realize that a consistent adherence to such a circular vision actually robs life (and by extension evolution) of any inherent meaning? Whatever else we may think of Friedrich Nietzsche's horrifying notion that all events happen again and again in an infinitely prolonged and absurd circle, his notion of an "eternal recurrence" expresses accurately the inner meaninglessness of any metaphysics closed off to a new future. He may not have realized himself that his own picture of a universe devoid of genuinely novel possibilities was still tightly bound, ironically, to the spirituality and thought forms of the religious culture he abjured so forcefully for its lack of vitality.

Where being or truth is thought of as already complete, temporal duration can only mean estrangement and loss. In Teilhard's words, such a metaphysics can only "clip the wings of hope."[2] According to this outlook, the apparently new gets interpreted theologically as the vertical breaking through into time of what has been finished from all eternity. The gist of such a view of truth and being—no matter how much its devotees seek to polish it up—is that nothing *really* new is ever going to happen. If perfection has already been attained *en arche,* in the beginning, what is there of importance that the passing of time or the evolution of a universe could ever accomplish?

Ironically, the hierarchical cultivation of an eternal present locks hands under the table with modern scientific materialism in neutralizing the dimension of futurity to which the *promise* of evolution awakens us once again. Far removed as they may be from each other, materialism and supernaturalist theism both share a remoteness from the implicit metaphysics of the ancient Hebrews and the early Christians, which gave primacy to what is yet to come. If they were true to the spirit of their father Abraham, followers of biblical faiths would once again seek to live out of the future. From this future, they would anticipate the arrival of God and the *new* creation of the cosmos. If they followed their prophets, a posture of expectation would be the guiding theme of their lives, prayers, and thoughts. They would look to the past, of course, in order to find monuments of divine influence in the lives of their ancestors, as well as in the evolution of the universe, but they would do so only with an eye also toward the future of creation. They would trust that God watches over them in the present also, not to extricate them from time but in order to give them the confidence to wait steadfastly in hope for an unimaginable future fulfillment.[3]

Seyyed Hossein Nasr has proposed that we imagine our many religious traditions as streams cascading down a mountain through separate courses from a single font on high. Accordingly, he takes humanity's religious search to be one of finding our way back upstream, each of us taking advantage of the scriptures, symbols, and rites of our own traditions while also appreciating the maps provided by others. This admittedly compelling vision highlights the shared sense among religions that we live in estrangement from our common destiny, and that the world is in some sense a place of exile, even while also being a sacramental reflection of its divine source.

I deeply appreciate Nasr's scholarship, having learned much from his always worthwhile works. In concluding this book, however, I would propose that the sense of a sacred hierarchical cosmology— which Nasr for good reasons seeks to save—might be construed anew and no less powerfully in a manner more congruent with the very temporal-evolutionary portrayal of nature that he considers to be so spiritually corrosive. A theological framework open to cosmic and biological evolution is fully capable of accommodating the religious sense of an ultimate reality that is assumed to be the creator of nature with its differentiated grades of importance. The varying degrees of value or meaning that we attach to the distinct "levels" of nature, however, reside not so much in their being sacramental representations of a God totally outside of time—still less in their being dim reminders of a lost plenitude—as in their being *anticipations* of an excellence yet to be actualized. The various forms of life are of value in the present because they are now aglow with a future that is still to flower fully. We may value them in proportion to the intensity of their presaging newness of life and being; for if God is the Absolute Future and the one "who makes all things new," then those aspects of our world to be treasured the most are those that open the world up to the fullness yet to come.[4] And it is especially through life and its ongoing evolution that the universe opens itself to its future.

In no way is this a devaluation of the past and the present, since these too are defined by their own openness to the future. But we do not do justice to any past or present occurrence if we abstract it from its own anticipatory comportment. As it happens, the evolutionary picture of nature passing from "matter" through life to mind readily allows us to discern in its various past phases a perpetual potency for new being. Evolutionary emergence has always borrowed in advance from the future that is coming to birth in it, a future sustaining it in creative tension from "up ahead."

We know intuitively how much our own existence, by virtue of the hope that "springs eternal," is ennobled by expectancy. And so it is perfectly reasonable to read prehuman evolutionary history, at least by analogy, as itself having been brought into being and given its own appropriate "levels" of dignity by an inherent affinity to the not-yet. The creation of the world is energized not so much from what has passed as from what lies up ahead. If so, it is *through* evolution, and not in spite of it, that we, along with the whole of creation, approach the sacred *arche,* the origin that is also the end of all things. In tilting toward their future, all things are filled with worth. They participate in and sacramentally mediate the sacred, not by being diminished leftovers from a primordial paradisal integrity, nor by dimly reflecting a finished eternal present, but by bearing in their present fragility and instability an Absolute Future. The beauty and value emergent in the various phases of the evolving universe are not simply epiphanies of an eternally present perfection residing outside of time but also perishable promises of what is to come. And it is in its openness to what is to come that all of the world's past receives continually fresh redemption.

Theologically speaking, we are summoned to read all of nature in terms of the future horizon whose enticement we experience most ardently whenever we ourselves indwell the great sacred narratives of hope for the unexpected. Our biblical ancestors' sensitivity to the futurity of being was the product of a way of seeing the world that centuries of world-fleeing mystical spirituality and, more recently, mechanistic pessimism have unfortunately blunted. Evolutionary knowledge, however, now provides us with fresh opportunities to recover the ancient hopes afresh—this time perhaps in a grander, and more cosmic, version than ever before.

We may thereby, once again, align our religious existence with the natural zest for life that links us biologically to our evolutionary past. The inherent adventurousness of religion may then receive a new birth. There is a sense, of course, in which the pre-Darwinian hierarchy also allows for spiritual adventure in our existence "here below." We are, it has often been said, on a momentous journey, an *itinerarium mentis ad Deum*—guided by the great wisdom traditions—to the divine font of all being. In this pilgrimage, we must struggle constantly against the powerful currents of time and history so as to make our way victoriously back upstream to the immeasurable origin of all. Understandably, many different versions of this formula for religious life have comforted and challenged people all over the Earth for thousands of years.

Hence it is only with enormous respect for the courage and adventure of classical spirituality, and indeed in a spirit of trepidation and tentativeness, that I have proposed in these pages that our new evolutionary knowledge requires a radical redrafting of the coordinates on the map of such a well-trodden itinerary. However, I am convinced with Teilhard de Chardin that by conceiving of the world's sacred Alpha as also an Omega beckoning all things toward a transcendent future up ahead, we shall forfeit none of the tension, courage, and passionate longing of the classical spiritual ways. If anything, a sense of life and the entire cosmos evolving through immense depths of time toward what is radically new and utterly surprising only intensifies the religious drama. Religion here becomes more an ongoing voyage of discovery than one of recovery. And theology too acquires a new vitality while abiding with unfeigned intellectual honesty alongside of, and in concert with, the evolutionary discoveries of modern science.

A biblically inspired vision of the future provides a most suitable framework for both evolutionary science and the religious quest for meaning. The original source of all values does not reside primarily in the past, nor in the vertical timelessness of an eternal present, but in the richer realm of new possibilities that we refer to faintly as future. In this schematization, a kind of hierarchical ordering is still resident in the cosmos, but the various "levels of being" find their respective grades of value in terms of their openness to an Absolute Future. Here religious nostalgia is transfigured by hope, and pious romanticism by anticipation of the altogether unprecedented. The meaning and value of temporal existence derive from its partaking in new creation. Without the arrival of what is *truly new,* time would curl back into the closed circularity that has nauseated adventurous souls, turning them away from lifeless ideas of God. In our still unfinished universe, however, all beings may participate—in a finite and precarious way—in a future yet to be actualized, one that at its ultimate depths may justifiably be called "sacred," a *mysterium tremendum et fascinans.*

An evolutionary theology encourages us to feel with St. Paul the Spirit of God sharing in nature's own longing for the consummation of creation. Rather than attributing to God a rigid "plan" for the universe, evolutionary theology prefers to think of God's "vision" for it. Nature, after Darwin, is not a design but a promise. God's "plan," if we continue to use the term, is not a blueprint but an *envisagement* of what the cosmos might become. A design, as I have noted repeatedly, closes off the future and "clips the wings of hope." In the beginning, however, instead of design there lies "the Vision."[5] The "Word" (Logos) that John's Gospel confidently proclaims to have been present *in principio,* and on which the whole of creation is modeled, is inseparable from promise. To attend to God's "word" is always to open our lives in hope to incalculable future outcomes.

A world in evolution does not follow a strict plan but is nonethe-less given its being, value, and meaning by God's vision for it. The God of evolution does not fix things in advance, nor hoard selfishly the joy of creating. Instead God shares with all creatures their own openness to an indeterminate future. Such an interpretation does not destroy the cosmic hierarchy but by its openness to new being brings special significance to every epoch of nature's unfolding, including humanity's unique history in a still unfinished universe.

Notes

Chapter 1

1. Hans Jonas, *Mortality and Morality* (Evanston, Ill.: Northwestern University Press, 1996), 52.

2. Alfred North Whitehead, *Science and the Modern World* (New York: The Free Press, 1967), esp. 54–55.

3. Michael Behe, *Darwin's Black Box* (New York: The Free Press, 1996), 187–253.

4. Ibid.

5. David Hull, "The God of the Galapagos," *Nature* 352 (August 8, 1992), 486.

6. This principle was set forth already in the writings of the early church authors, such as St. Augustine. In 1893 it was expressed again explicitly in Pope Leo XIII's encyclical *Providentissimus Deus.*

7. E. O. Wilson, *Consilience: The Unity of Knowledge* (New York: Knopf, 1998), 6.

Chapter 2

1. Daniel C. Dennett, *Darwin's Dangerous Idea: Evolution and the Meaning of Life* (New York: Simon & Schuster, 1995).

2. Ibid., 266.

3. Ibid., 310.

4. In John Brockman, *The Third Culture* (New York: Touchstone Books, 1996), 181.

5. Richard Dawkins, *The Blind Watchmaker* (New York: W. W. Norton, 1986); *River Out of Eden* (New York: Basic Books, 1995); *Climbing Mount Improbable* (New York: W. W. Norton, 1996).

6. Dawkins, *River Out of Eden,* 131.

7. Ibid., 95–133.

8. Dawkins, *The Blind Watchmaker,* 6.

9. William Provine, "Evolution and the Foundation of Ethics," in *Science, Technology, and Social Progress,* ed. Steven L. Goldman (Bethlehem, Pa.: Lehigh University Press, 1989), 261.

10. In Brockman, *The Third Culture,* 187.

11. Ernst Mayr, *This Is Biology* (Cambridge, Mass.: Harvard University Press, Belknap Press, 1997), esp. 64–78.

12. Gavin de Beer, "Evolution," in *The New Encyclopedia Britannica,* 15th ed. (London: Encyclopedia Britannica, 1973–1974), emphasis added. This reference was brought to my attention by Holmes Rolston III, *Science and Religion: A Critical Survey* (New York: Random House, 1987), 106.

13. Francisco J. Ayala, "Darwin's Revolution," in *Creative Evolution?!* ed. John H. Campbell and J. William Schopf (Boston: Jones & Bartlett, 1994), 4.

14. Ibid., 5 (emphasis added).

15. Ibid., 4.

16. Dawkins, *River Out of Eden,* 133.

17. A. J. Mattill Jr., *The Seven Mighty Blows to Traditional Beliefs,* 2d ed. (Gordo, Ala.: The Flatwoods Press, 1995), 32.

Chapter 3

1. Richard Dawkins, *The Blind Watchmaker* (New York: W. W. Norton, 1986), 6ff. I shall discuss the design argument and natural theology more fully later on.

2. Stephen Jay Gould, *Ever Since Darwin* (New York: W. W. Norton, 1977), 12–13.

3. The claim that the cosmos has a purpose, directionality, or overall significance, as I shall argue in later chapters, does not require that we see the cosmos as "designed" in the restricted sense usually implied in the notion of "intelligent design."

4. Charles Darwin, *The Autobiography of Charles Darwin,* ed. Nora Barlow (New York: W. W. Norton), 85ff.

5. See, for example, Duane Gish, *Evolution: The Challenge of the Fossil Record* (El Cajon, Calif.: Creation-Life Publishers, 1985).

6. See Phillip Johnson, *Darwin on Trial* (Washington, D.C.: Regnery Gateway, 1991).

7. The journal *First Things,* for example, has given safe harbor to Johnson and his defenders. And in a 1998 two-hour PBS production of *Firing Line,* the noted conservative Catholic William Buckley Jr. professed his agreement with Johnson in opposing neo-Darwinism.

8. Guy Murchie, *The Seven Mysteries of Life: An Exploration in Science and Philosophy* (Boston: Houghton Mifflin, 1978). The quotations in the following paragraphs come from pages 621–622.

9. This is the interpretation given to the laws of physics by Wolfhart Pannenberg, *Toward A Theology of Nature,* ed. Ted Peters (Louisville, Ky.: Westminster/John Knox Press, 1993), 72–122.

10. An accessible example is Rudolf Bultmann, *Jesus Christ and Mythology* (New York: Charles Scribner's Sons, 1958).

11. William Paley, *Natural Theology* (New York: Boston, Gould, and Lincoln, 1873).

12. This approach is characteristic especially of the "neo-orthodox" theology associated with the famous Swiss theologian Karl Barth and his followers.

13. John Polkinghorne, "Creation and the Structure of the Physical World," *Theology Today* 44 (April 1987), 53–68. Other references to Polkinghorne in the following paragraphs are also to this article.

14. See especially John D. Barrow and Frank J. Tipler, *The Anthropic Cosmological Principle* (New York: Oxford University Press, 1986).

15. See Wolfhart Pannenberg, "Human Life: Creation Versus Evolution?" in *Science and Theology*, ed. Ted Peters (Boulder, Colo.: Westview Press, 1998), 138–139.

16. For example, see Stephen W. Hawking, *A Brief History of Time* (New York: Bantam Books, 1988), 140–141; and Paul Davies, *The Mind of God: The Scientific Basis for a Rational World* (New York: Simon & Schuster, 1992), 66.

17. Pierre Teilhard de Chardin, *The Prayer of the Universe* (New York: Harper Perennial, 1958), 120–121.

18. Pierre Teilhard de Chardin, *Christianity and Evolution*, trans. by Rene Hague (New York: Harcourt Brace & Co., 1969), 239.

19. Henri Bergson, *Creative Evolution*, trans. Arthur Mitchell (1911; reprint, Lanham, Md.: University Press of America, 1983), 13, 96, and passim.

20. See Teilhard de Chardin, *Christianity and Evolution*, 131–132.

21. Romans 8:22.

22. See Jürgen Moltmann, *The Experiment Hope*, ed. and trans. by M. Douglas Meeks (Philadelphia: Fortress Press, 1975). Teilhard de Chardin, Wolfhart Pannenberg, and Karl Rahner also think of God as essentially future. See also Ernst Bloch, *The Principle of Hope*, vol. 1, trans. Neville Plaice, Stephen Plaice, and Paul Knight (Oxford: Basil Blackwell, 1986). Later I shall take up this theme of the futurity of God more explicitly.

23. See Karl Rahner, *Foundations of Christian Faith*, trans. by William Dych (New York: Crossroad, 1984), 78–203.

24. Ibid.

25. However, this "self-withdrawal" must not be construed as an abandonment of the world such as we associate with the God of deism. Rather, God forgoes any annihilating "presence" to or compelling of the world, in order, paradoxically, to be nearer to it. One must say even that what is "withdrawn" is not at all God's "loving kindness," but instead any coercive or obtrusive presence that might suppress the autonomy of the beloved. God is present in the mode of "hiddenness," not abdication.

26. Cited by John J. O'Donnell, *Hans Urs Von Balthasar* (Collegeville, Minn.: Liturgical Press, 1992), 73.

27. See Wolfhart Pannenberg, *Systematic Theology*, vol. 2, trans. by Geoffrey W. Bromiley (Grand Rapids, Mich.: Eerdmans, 1994), 127–136: "Theologically, we may view the expansion of the universe as the creator's means to the bringing forth of independent forms of creaturely reality" (127). "Creaturely independence cannot exist without God or against him. It does not have to be won from God, for it is the goal of his creative work" (135). For a similar perspective, see also Elizabeth John-

son, "Does God Play Dice? Divine Providence and Chance," *Theological Studies* 57 (March 1996), 3–18.

28. *Summa Contra Gentiles*, III, chap. 74. I owe this citation to Christopher Mooney, S.J., *Theology and Scientific Knowledge* (Notre Dame and London: University of Notre Dame Press, 1996), 162.

29. The philosophy of Charles Hartshorne has also been influential in shaping the ideas of many process theologians. A useful summary of process theology can be found in John B. Cobb and David Ray Griffin, *Process Theology: An Introductory Exposition* (Philadelphia: Westminster, 1976). I have discussed some of the contributions of process thought to evolutionary theology more fully in *The Cosmic Adventure* (New York: Paulist Press, 1984).

30. Alfred North Whitehead, *Adventures of Ideas* (New York: The Free Press, 1967), 252–296. See also, Cobb and Griffin, *Process Theology*, 57–79.

Chapter 4

1. See Holmes Rolston III, *Science and Religion* (New York: Random House, 1987), 144–146.

2. Alfred North Whitehead, *Process and Reality*, corrected edition, ed. David Ray Griffin and Donald W. Sherburne (New York: The Free Press, 1978), 342.

3. Richard Dawkins, for example, has asserted repeatedly that the only real issue in the question of God and evolution is whether Darwin has destroyed the notion of a designing deity. The assumption here is that if design can be explained without God, then the whole edifice of theology comes crashing down. See, for example, Dawkins's recent book *River Out of Eden* (New York: Basic Books, 1995), 59–93.

4. See the studies by Donald G. Dawe, *The Form of a Servant* (Philadelphia: The Westminster Press, 1963); Jürgen Moltmann, *The Crucified God*, trans. by R. A. Wilson and John Bowden (New York: Harper & Row, 1974); and Hans Urs Von Balthasar, *Mysterium Paschale*, trans. by Aidan Nichols, O.P. (Edinburgh: T & T Clark, 1990).

5. Edward Schillebeeckx, *Church: The Human Story of God*, trans. by John Bowden (New York: Crossroad, 1990), 90.

6. See Eberhard Jüngel, *The Doctrine of the Trinity: God's Being Is in Becoming*, trans. by Scottish Academic Press Ltd. (Grand Rapids, Mich.: Eerdmann Press, 1976). The theme of divine self-emptying has been highlighted recently by Nancey Murphy and George F. R. Ellis, *On the Moral Nature of the Universe: Theology, Cosmology, and Ethics* (Minneapolis: Fortress Press, 1996).

7. Jürgen Moltmann, *God in Creation*, trans. by Margaret Kohl (San Francisco: Harper & Row, 1985), 88.

8. Readers who may suspect that my focus here on the divine self-emptying is theologically novel or marginal may note that Pope John Paul II, in his recent encyclical *Fides et Ratio*, also places the theme of God's *kenosis* at the center of theology: "The chief purpose of theology is to provide an understanding of Revelation and the content of faith. The very heart of theological enquiry will thus be the con-

templation of the mystery of the Triune God. The approach to this mystery begins with reflection upon the mystery of the Incarnation of the Son of God: his coming as man, his going to his Passion and Death, a mystery issuing into his glorious Resurrection and Ascension to the right hand of the Father, whence he would send the Spirit of truth to bring his Church to birth and give her growth. From this vantage-point, the prime commitment of theology is seen to be the understanding of God's kenosis, a grand and mysterious truth for the human mind, which finds it inconceivable that suffering and death can express a love which gives itself and seeks nothing in return" (Pope John Paul II, *Fides et Ratio*, Section 93).

9. Dawe, *The Form of a Servant*. Subsequent quotations from Dawe are drawn from pages 13–15. I have dealt at greater length with the notion of God's humility in *Mystery and Promise: A Theology of Revelation* (Collegeville, Minn.: Liturgical Press, 1993), esp. 199–214.

10. John Macquarrie, *The Humility of God* (Philadelphia: The Westminster Press, 1978), 34.

11. Karl Rahner, *Foundations of Christian Faith,* trans. by William V. Dych (New York: Crossroad, 1978), 222.

12. Macquarrie, *The Humility of God,* 34.

13. God's "self-absenting" is in fact an intimate form of presence, after all. Though withdrawn from the world in the sense that God is nonmanipulative of events, God can still be deeply present and effective in the mode of *ultimate goodness*. Indeed the self-distancing of God in the first sense is a consequence of the intimate involvement of God in the second. On this point, see the perceptive article by Ilia Delio, O.S.F., "The Humility of God in a Scientific World," *New Theology Review* 11 (August 1998), 36–50.

Chapter 5

1. See Jacob Needleman, *A Sense of the Cosmos* (New York: E. P. Dutton, 1976), 10–36.

2. For a clear and deliberately oversimplified rendition of this aspect of the so-called "perennial philosophy," see E. F. Schumacher, *A Guide for the Perplexed* (New York: Harper Colophon Books, 1978), 18.

3. In philosophy, ancient atomism and widely scattered versions of materialism may be the only exceptions.

4. See, for example, Daniel Dennett, *Consciousness Explained* (New York: Little, Brown, 1991), 33: "There is only one sort of stuff, namely matter—the physical stuff of physics, chemistry, and physiology—and the mind is somehow nothing but a physical phenomenon. In short, the mind is the brain. According to the materialists we can (in principle!) account for every mental phenomenon using the same physical principles, laws and raw materials that suffice to explain radioactivity, continental drift, photosynthesis, reproduction, nutrition and growth."

5. Henri Bergson, *Creative Evolution,* trans. by Arthur Mitchell (1911; reprint, Lanham, Md.: University Press of America, 1983).

6. Daniel Dennett, *Darwin's Dangerous Idea: Evolution and the Meaning of Life* (New York: Simon & Schuster, 1995).

7. This question has been posed recently once again by E. O. Wilson, in *Consilience* (New York: The Free Press, 1998), who answers it in the negative.

8. That there are "gaps" in the fossil record has been duly noted. However, only one in a billion bones becomes fossilized, so inevitably there will be paleologically empty intervals. Beyond this, however, the theory of "punctuated equilibria" proposed by Stephen Jay Gould and Niles Eldredge is a plausible way of saving the central core of neo-Darwinian science. See Niles Eldredge, *Time Frames: The Rethinking of Darwinian Evolution and the Theory of Punctuated Equilibria* (London: Heinemann, 1986).

9. Seyyed Hossein Nasr, *Religion and the Order of Nature* (New York: Oxford University Press, 1996).

10. Ibid., 12.

11. See, for example, Elizabeth Dodson Gray, "A Critique of Dominion Theology," in *Religion and the Natural Sciences,* ed. James Huchingson (New York: Harcourt Brace Jovanovich, 1993), 374–382.

12. Perhaps the proximate source of the notion of hierarchy is *hierarchos,* a term for a male ruler. However, I wish here to highlight the remote roots of the term, namely, *hier* and *arche.*

13. It is widely agreed that modern science is now going through an identity crisis, and one important reason for this is the growing awareness that it can no longer leave information out of its explanations of many aspects of nature, and especially of life. Whereas modern science has been concerned almost exclusively with material and efficient causes, information works nonmaterially and nonenergetically. It is a more elusive kind of influence than science has traditionally focused on, but, as we shall see, no less powerful.

14. Alfred North Whitehead, *Process and Reality,* corrected edition, ed. David Ray Griffin and Donald W. Sherburne (New York: The Free Press, 1978), 46.

15. There is now emerging, however, a fresh awareness that the shape of organisms is the consequence of factors in addition to the genetic code. See, for example, Ian Stewart, *Life's Other Secret: The New Mathematics of the Living World* (New York: John Wiley & Sons, 1998).

16. Michael Polanyi, *Knowing and Being,* ed. Marjorie Grene (Chicago: University of Chicago Press, 1969), 225–239.

17. Ibid.

18. This analogy is suggested by Polanyi in *The Tacit Dimension* (Garden City, N.Y.: Doubleday Anchor Books, 1967), 31–34.

19. Ibid.

20. Marjorie Grene, "Reducibility: Another Side Issue?" in *Interpretations of Life and Mind,* ed. Marjorie Grene (New York: Humanities Press, 1971), 18.

21. See Marjorie Grene, "The Logic of Biology," in *The Logic of Personal Knowledge,* ed. Marjorie Grene (Glencoe, Ill.: The Free Press, 1961), 199.

22. See Dawkins's comments in John Brockman, *The Third Culture* (New York: Touchstone Books, 1996), 23–24.

23. I have been using the hierarchical notions of "higher" and "lower" levels here only for the sake of simplicity. In reality, nature's hierarchical character cannot be represented adequately in such spatial terms. As I shall argue in the following chapter, we need also to appreciate the temporal, future-oriented character of nature.

Accordingly, the main "levels" (matter, life, and mind) would be graded not by whether they are spatially above other levels but by their degree of openness to the future, to the realm of new informational possibilities, the ultimate origin (or *arche*) of which is understood theologically to be God.

24. Dawkins seemingly allows for a "hierarchy of explanations" in science, but his monistic materialist metaphysics destroys any basis in principle for the logical legitimacy of such a notion.

25. Guy Murchie, *The Seven Mysteries of Life: An Exploration in Science and Philosophy* (Boston: Houghton Mifflin, 1978), 313–343.

26. See Alfred North Whitehead, *Science and the Modern World* (New York: The Free Press, 1967), 94. For Whitehead, for anything to be actual at all it must already be internally patterned (or informed), and as such it is an instance of value as well as actuality.

27. *Tao: A New Way of Thinking,* translation and commentary by Chang Chung-yuan (New York: Harper & Row, 1975), chap. 11, 35.

28. Cited by Chung-yuan, p. 36.

29. See Chapter 4 above.

30. *Tao,* chap. 14.

31. *Tao,* chap. 16.

Chapter 6

1. Pierre Teilhard de Chardin, *Christianity and Evolution,* trans. by Rene Hague (New York: Harcourt Brace & Co., 1969), 240.

2. Stephen Jay Gould, essays in *Natural History,* March 1979; August 1980; June 1981.

3. For a thorough discussion of Gould's charges and a decisive refutation of them see Thomas King, S.J., "Teilhard and Piltdown," in *Teilhard and the Unity of Knowledge,* ed. Thomas King, S.J., and James Salmon, S.J. (New York: Paulist Press, 1983), 159–169.

The renowned biologist Harold Morowitz wonders "why Stephen Jay Gould decided to do a job on Teilhard de Chardin based on circumstantial evidence, none of which is supported by the latest findings." Although Morowitz does not embrace the famous Jesuit's theology or teleology, he professes nonetheless to being an "admirer of Teilhard's biological writing." In fact, he has found Teilhard's ideas "insightful and often ahead of their time." Teilhard, for example, anticipated the theory of punctuated equilibrium, without calling it by that name, at a time when those who now take credit for it, namely, Gould and Niles Eldredge, were still "in short pants." Surely, though, it could not have been for this reason that Gould decided to pillory Teilhard in such a public way. Another possible explanation might be that Teilhard was a priest, whereas Gould is an agnostic. After all, it has not helped Teilhard's reputation in the scientific community that he was devoutly religious. Still, Morowitz reflects, "it is inconceivable that anyone with Gould's interests in fairness and civil liberties would have fingered a scientist because of his religious beliefs." Gould provocatively refers to Teilhard as a "cult figure." Morowitz asks us, however, to note the "rhetorical device" of representing Teilhard in this manner: "While there are many serious students of Teilhard's thought, they cannot be described as a cult. At the extreme they form a scholarly association. Gould is not just describing Teilhard, but setting up the reader for the attack." See Harold J. Morowitz, *The Kindly Dr. Guillotin: And Other Essays on Science and Life* (Washington, D.C.: Counterpoint, 1997), 26–27.

4. Daniel C. Dennett, *Darwin's Dangerous Idea: Evolution and the Meaning of Life* (New York: Simon & Schuster, 1995), 320.

5. Pierre Teilhard de Chardin, *Christianity and Evolution*, trans. by Rene Hague (New York: Harcourt Brace & Co., 1969), 237–243.

6. Jürgen Moltmann, *The Experiment Hope*, ed. and trans. by M. Douglas Meeks (Philadelphia: Fortress Press, 1975), 48.

7. Karl Rahner, *Theological Investigations*, vol. 6, trans. by Karl and Boniface Kruger (Baltimore: Helicon, 1969), 59–68.

8. Wolfhart Pannenberg, *Faith and Reality*, trans. by John Maxwell (Philadelphia: Westminster Press, 1977), 58–59; Ted Peters, *God—The World's Future: Systematic Theology for a Postmodern Era* (Minneapolis: Fortress Press, 1992).

9. For support of this observation see the essays in Teilhard de Chardin's book, *Christianity and Evolution.*

10. See, once again, Seyyed Hossein Nasr, *Religion and the Order of Nature* (New York: Oxford University Press, 1996), 146.

11. Dennett, *Darwin's Dangerous Idea*, 212–216; 246–250.

12. For example, John Maynard Smith, *Did Darwin Get It Right? Essays on Games, Sex, and Evolution* (London: Penguin Books, 1988).

13. In order to undertake reverse engineering, we first must be able to identify an *organizational whole* that allows for such disassembly. But such holistic recognition cannot itself be the consequence of the analytic-particulate method that Dennett takes to be the privileged road to understanding. We always start reverse engineering with what we take to be a meaningfully patterned totality. And as we move our inquiry back into the past, *the pattern itself dissolves*. The reason it dissolves is that it was there in the first place only in the mode of being *anticipated*. Pattern, form, or information is that *toward which* evolving processes move. Information's ontological status is fundamentally future. It is in this sense that Dennett's algorithmic and atomistic approach fails to account for the real novelty without which evolution could not occur.

14. Let me clarify at the outset, however, that I am not insisting that scientists, insofar as they remain conscious of science's methodological self-limitations, need to take into account explicitly the dimension of the future in their work. Science has every right to leave out any such reference, since as far as scientific method is concerned a reference to the future would implausibly attribute efficient causation to events that have not yet occurred. Nevertheless, I would argue that the inability on the part of science itself to entertain a metaphysics of the future is a consequence of the abstract nature of scientific work. In saying that science is abstract, I do not mean that science does not deal with concrete reality. What I mean is that each science has to leave out broad bands of nature's actual complexity in order to say anything clearly at all. The particle physicist as such, for example, has nothing to say about whether Darwinian selection is the only cause of all creativity in the biosphere, or about the function of mitochondrial DNA. A lot has to be left out if we are to achieve

any clear results in any science. What I am emphasizing here is that by focusing on efficient and material causes, science typically abstracts from the futurity of being.

15. I shall develop this point more fully in Chapter 10.

16. Paul Tillich, *Shaking of the Foundations* (New York: Charles Scribner's Sons, 1996), 27 (emphasis added).

17. See Dawkins's critique of "physics envy" in John Brockman, *The Third Culture* (New York: Touchstone Books, 1996), 23–24. However, as Niles Eldredge rightly points out, Peter Medawar's label "physics envy" is no less applicable to Dawkins, who, in spite of his and Dennett's claims that he is not a "greedy" reductionist, borrows from physics the atomistic ideal of explanation and applies it univocally to the "selfish genes" that, for him, are sufficient to explain life and evolution. See Brockman, *The Third Culture,* 122.

18. This formulation is one that I have put together on the basis of my reading not only of Teilhard, but also of Ernst Bloch, Wolfhart Pannenberg, Karl Rahner, and their many followers. See also Hans Küng, *Eternal Life,* trans. by Edward Quinn (Garden City, N.Y.: Doubleday, 1984), 213–214. Here Küng indicates how deeply indebted Christian theology is to the philosopher Ernst Bloch—and to Bloch's main Christian theological follower, Jürgen Moltmann—for retrieving the futurist orientation of the biblical vision of reality, one that for centuries had been buried beneath the metaphysical categories Christian theology had taken over from Greek philosophy. See Ernst Bloch, *The Principle of Hope,* vol. 1, trans. by Neville Plaice, Stephen Plaice, and Paul Knight (Oxford: Basil Blackwell, 1986); and Jürgen Moltmann, *The Coming of God,* trans. by Margaret Kohl (Minneapolis: Fortress Press, 1996). In addition, see H. A. Williams, *True Resurrection* (New York: Harper Colophon Books, 1972); and William Lynch, *Images of Hope* (Notre Dame, Ind.: University of Notre Dame Press, 1974).

19. Paul Tillich, *Systematic Theology,* vol. 3 (Chicago: University of Chicago Press, 1963), 19.

20. See the scholarly critique of Newtonian assumptions by Robert E. Ulanowicz, *Ecology: The Ascendent Perspective* (New York: Columbia University Press, 1997).

21. Peter W. Atkins, *Creation Revisited* (New York: W. H. Freeman, 1992), 11–17.

22. Steven Weinberg, *Dreams of a Final Theory* (New York: Pantheon Books, 1992), 18, 51–64.

23. John Horgan, *The End of Science* (Reading, Mass.: Addison-Wesley, 1996).

24. Atkins, *Creation Revisited,* 157.

25. See Michael Polanyi, *Personal Knowledge: Towards a Post-Critical Philosophy* (New York and Evanston, Ill.: Harper Torchbooks, 1958) and *The Tacit Dimension* (Garden City, N.Y.: Doubleday Anchor Books, 1967) for a defense of the human need to root all of knowledge in some (faith) commitment or other.

26. Again, this way of putting things is indebted to the works of Polanyi cited in the previous note.

27. Some of the philosophical and theological difficulties posed by the notion of a metaphysics of the future have been addressed already in a collection of essays edited by Carl E. Braaten and Philip Clayton, *The Theology of Wolfhart Pannenberg* (Minneapolis: Augsburg Publishing House, 1988). In spite of the paradoxes

that arise in the context of conventional philosophical discourse—most of which to-day embraces natural science's own inclination toward a metaphysics of the past—the Christian theologian must still take seriously and attempt to unpack conceptu-ally, however stumblingly, what it means for a biblically based faith to affirm that God is the "Power of the Future." For an excellent and accessible study of the spiri-tual, social, and theological implications of this metaphor, see Ted Peters, *God—The World's Future.*

28. We can speak of God's "self-withdrawal" only in terms of a paradox in which the other side of the retracting of divine presence is the most intimate in-volvement of God in the world's evolution. The notion that God is present in the mode of an always arriving future allows us to understand how God can be in-volved in the world's continual coming into being without being a datum available to present comprehension.

29. From the theological perspective adopted here, to locate the divine reality es-sentially in the future is not at all to deprive the past and present of the divine pres-ence. However, the point is that it is essentially as their future that God is present to the past and present. Put otherwise, the past and present are taken continually and forever into the divine future. As such, they never fade into absolute nothingness but are redeemed in terms of the novel patterns of beauty that emerge within the horizon of an Absolute Future. See Chapter 8 below.

30. See, for example, John Polkinghorne, *The Faith of a Physicist* (Princeton: Princeton University Press, 1994), 25–26, 75–87.

31. This is a point that Wolfhart Pannenberg has often made in his interpretation of biblical eschatology and the resurrection accounts. "By contemplating Jesus' res-urrection, we perceive our own ultimate future," he writes. And he adds: "The in-comprehensibility of God precisely in his revelation, means that for the Christian the future is still open and full of possibilities." *Faith and Reality,* trans. by John Maxwell (Philadelphia: Westminster Press, 1977), 58–59.

32. Correspondingly, the obsession with clarity and absolute transparency (such as we find in modern scientism) tends for this very reason to divest time of any gen-uine futurity. The wish for immediate clarity has led to the envisagement of time as mathematically "reversible," so as to render nature completely intelligible and pre-dictable from the point of view of the here and now.

33. As much as he deprecates the ideas of Dawkins and Dennett for being too "fundamentalist," narrow, and rigid in refusing to recognize the role of contingent events in evolution, Gould shares with them the assumption that "contingency" im-plies "meaninglessness." A metaphysics of the future, however, can interpret what is presently perceived as contingency to be an opening to a future whose meaning is yet incalculable. It seems to me that in a biblical setting what we translate as "faith" requires an anticipation of such a future resolution.

34. See Wolfhart Pannenberg, *Toward a Theology of Nature,* ed. Ted Peters (Louisville, Ky.: Westminster/John Knox Press, 1993), 72–122.

Chapter 7

1. Steven Weinberg, *The First Three Minutes* (New York: Basic Books, 1977), 144.

2. Alan Lightman and Roberta Brawer, *Origins: The Lives and Worlds of Modern Cosmologists* (Cambridge, Mass.: Harvard University Press, 1990), 340.

3. Ibid., 358.

4. Ibid., 377.

5. See Richard Dawkins, *River Out of Eden* (New York: Basic Books, 1995), 131.

6. Alfred North Whitehead, *Science and the Modern World* (New York: The Free Press, 1967), 10: "The pilgrim fathers of the scientific imagination as it exists today are the great tragedians of ancient Athens, Aeschylus, Sophocles, Euripides. Their vision of fate, remorseless and indifferent, urging a tragic incident to its inevitable issue, is the vision possessed by science. Fate in Greek Tragedy becomes the order of nature in modern thought."

7. Hans Küng, *Does God Exist*, trans. by Edward Quinn (New York: Doubleday, 1980), 676.

8. For more systematic detail, see my book *Mystery and Promise: A Theology of Revelation* (Collegeville, Minn.: The Liturgical Press, 1993).

9. Steven Weinberg, *Dreams of a Final Theory* (New York: Pantheon Books, 1992), 244–245.

10. Examples of this kenotic view of creation can be found in Kabbalistic Judaism, in the writings of Simone Weil, and in Geddes MacGregor's *He Who Lets Us Be* (New York: Seabury Press, 1975), as well as in the writings of the Christian theologian Jürgen Moltmann. See, for example, Moltmann's *God in Creation*, trans. by Margaret Kohl (San Francisco: Harper & Row, 1985), 88. A contemporary Jewish restatement of the view that creation is grounded in God's self-withdrawal may be found in Michael Wyschogrod's *The Body of Faith* (New York: Harper & Row, 1983), 9–10.

11. This self-concealment, once again, is not a divine "abdication" in any deistic sense, but instead a deep form of intimacy of God with the world. That God is "absent" from the domain of coercive power still allows that God may be present in the form of an ultimate goodness.

12. See once again, for example, Phillip Johnson's book *Darwin on Trial* (Washington, D.C.: Regnery Gateway, 1991).

13. See Wolfhart Pannenberg, *Systematic Theology*, vol. 2, trans. by Geoffrey W. Bromiley (Grand Rapids, Mich.: Eerdmans, 1994), 127–136. "Theologically, we may view the expansion of the universe as the Creator's means to the bringing forth of independent forms of creaturely reality" (127). "Creaturely independence cannot exist without God or against him. It does not have to be won from God, for it is the goal of his creative work" (135). See also Elizabeth Johnson, "Does God Play Dice? Divine Providence and Chance," *Theological Studies* 57 (March 1996), 3–18.

14. The biologist Louise Young's book *The Unfinished Universe* (New York: Oxford University Press, 1986) is an excellent example of such a reading.

15. Process thought has been particularly effective in portraying how the experiences of the temporal cosmic past can be preserved plausibly and patterned meaningfully in the everlasting empathy of God. See Alfred North Whitehead, "Immortality," in *The Philosophy of Alfred North Whitehead*, ed. Paul A. Schilpp (Evanston, Ill. and Chicago: Northwestern University Press, 1941), 682–700; and also *Process and Reality*, corrected edition, ed. David Ray Griffin and Donald W. Sherburne (New York:

The Free Press, 1978), 340–341, 346–351; and Charles Hartshorne, *The Logic of Perfection* (Lasalle, Ill.: Open Court Publishing, 1962), 24–62, 250.

16. Whitehead argues that the seventeenth-century science was dominated by the "assumption of simple location," according to which we can understand things only by leaving out any consideration of the concrete and complex web of organic connections that tie them all together. This assumption in turn was the result of a logical error, the fallacy of misplaced concreteness, that mistook mathematical abstractions for concrete reality. See *Science and the Modern World*, 51–57, 58–59.

17. John T. Houghton, "A Note on Chaotic Dynamics," *Science and Christian Belief* 1 (1989), 50.

18. And since (relatively speaking) we may still not be too far removed from the cosmic dawn, who knows what other surprising and unpredictable outcomes lie enfolded in this promising creation?

19. Such a claim seems defensible independently of the scientific status of the so-called strong anthropic principle.

20. See Jürgen Moltmann, *The Coming of God: Christian Eschatology*, trans. by Margaret Kohl (Minneapolis: Fortress Press, 1996), 259–295.

21. Ibid., 323.

22. Young, *The Unfinished Universe*, 201–202.

Chapter 8

1. W. T. Stace, "Man Against Darkness," *The Atlantic Monthly* (September 1948), 54.

2. John Haught, *The Cosmic Adventure* (New York: Paulist Press, 1984).

3. William Provine, "Evolution and the Foundation of Ethics," in *Science, Technology, and Social Progress*, ed. Steven L. Goldman (Bethlehem, Pa.: Lehigh University Press, 1989), 261.

4. William Provine, "Evolution and the Foundation of Ethics," *MBL Science* 3 (Winter 1988), 29. This is an earlier and slightly different version of the essay cited in note 3.

5. Vaclav Havel, in *Civilization* (April/May 1998), 53. This citation was brought to my attention on the META listserve administered by Billie Grassie.

6. Michael Ruse and Edward O. Wilson, "The Evolution of Ethics," in *Religion and the Natural Sciences*, ed. James Huchingson (New York: Harcourt Brace Jovanovich, 1993), 308–311.

7. Ibid., 310–311 (emphasis added).

8. Peter Singer, "Ethics and Sociobiology," *Zygon* 19 (June 1984), 142–151.

9. See Gerd Theissen, *Biblical Theology: An Evolutionary Approach*, trans. by John Bowden (Philadelphia: Fortress Press, 1985). I am not implying that Theissen himself is a dualist, but his evolutionary theology could perhaps be mistaken as such.

10. See Bertrand Russell, *Religion and Science* (New York: Oxford University Press, 1961); and *Why I Am Not a Christian*, ed. Paul Edwards (New York: Simon & Schuster, 1957).

11. Albert Camus, *The Myth of Sisyphus and Other Essays* (New York: Vintage Books, 1955).

12. Jacques Monod, *Chance and Necessity,* trans. by Austryn Wainhouse (New York: Vintage Books, 1972), 172.

13. See Stuart Kauffman, *At Home in the Universe: The Search for Laws of Self-Organization and Complexity* (New York: Oxford University Press, 1996).

14. George C. Williams, "Huxley's Evolution and Ethics in Sociobiological Perspective," *Zygon* 23 (September 1988), 383–407.

15. Paul Tillich, *The Eternal Now* (New York: Charles Scribner's Sons, 1963), 35.

16. Alfred North Whitehead, Process and Reality, corrected edition, ed. David Ray Griffin and Donald W. Sherburne (New York: The Free Press, 1978), 34–51.

17. Ibid., 346.

18. Ibid.

19. Ibid.

20. Alfred North Whitehead, *Adventures of Ideas* (New York: The Free Press, 1967), 265.

21. See Chapter 3 above for a brief description of the use by natural theology of the so-called anthropic principle.

22. Freeman Dyson, *Infinite in All Directions* (New York: HarperCollins, 1988), 298.

23. David Hull, "The God of the Galapagos," *Nature* 352 (August 8, 1992), 486.

24. See Louis Dupré, *Passage to Modernity* (Cambridge, Mass.: Harvard University Press, 1993), 17–19.

25. For the following see Whitehead, *Adventures of Ideas,* 252–296; *Process and Reality,* 62, 183–185, 255, and *passim; Modes of Thought* (New York: The Free Press, 1968), 57–63. See also Charles Hartshorne, *Man's Vision of God* (Chicago and New York: Willett, Clark & Company, 1941), 212–229.

26. For a readable recent account of the notion of original sin and its meaning in an evolutionary context, see Jerry Korsmeyer, *Evolution and Eden* (Mahwah, N.J.: Paulist Press, 1998).

27. Here we may note the contrasting example of Jesus insisting that his disciples open the "kingdom" to children, to the sick, to sinners, and so on, no matter what the cost of disruption in terms of the status quo.

28. For a discussion of the distinction between the actual and "essential," see Mircea Eliade, *Myth and Reality* (New York: Harper Torchbooks, 1968).

29. Teilhard de Chardin, *Christianity and Evolution,* trans. by Rene Hague (New York: Harcourt Brace & Co., 1969), 83.

30. For a profound analysis of the religiously inspired patterns of expiatory violence, see Gil Bailie, *Violence Unveiled* (New York: Crossroad, 1995).

31. Gerd Theissen, *The Open Door,* trans. by John Bowden (Minneapolis: Fortress Press, 1991), 161–167.

32. In a sense, an evolutionary vision makes the question of suffering all the more recalcitrant to easy answers, but (as Teilhard often pointed out) that we do not have an easy answer is itself another signal that we live in a world still being created. Inevitably, our religions and theologies must also remain imperfect and unsatisfying as long as the universe itself has not attained the fulfillment that faith awaits.

33. Pierre Teilhard de Chardin, *The Future of Man*, trans. by Norman Denny (New York: Harper Torchbooks, 1969), 45ff.

34. Karl Rahner, S.J., *Theological Investigations*, vol. 6, trans. by Karl Kruger and Boniface Kruger (Baltimore: Helicon, 1969), 59–68.

Chapter 9

1. Holmes Rolston III, "Science, Religion, and the Future," in *Religion and Science: History, Method, Dialogue,* ed. Mark Richardson and Wesley Wildman (New York and London: Routledge, 1996), 79.

2. For example, in his essay "Toward an Environmental Ethic," in *Preserving the Creation*, ed. Kevin W. Irwin and Edmund D. Pellegrino (Washington, D.C.: Georgetown University Press, 1994), Daniel Cowdin writes: "The substantive vision of the end-time, insofar as it is the norm on which we base our actions, undercuts environmental ethics" (143). A similar distrust of the messianic aspects of eschatology can be found in the writings of Thomas Berry. See his *The Dream of the Earth* (San Francisco: Sierra Club Books, 1988).

3. This is a major theme in the writings of Jürgen Moltmann. See once again his book *The Experiment Hope,* ed. and trans. by M. Douglas Meeks (Philadelphia: Fortress Press, 1975). As we have already seen, a metaphysics of the future is also a constant motif in the writings of Teilhard de Chardin, Wolfhart Pannenberg, and Karl Rahner, among others.

4. See Wolfhart Pannenberg, *Jesus, God, and Man,* trans. by Lewis L. Wilkins and Duane A. Priebe (Philadelphia: Westminster Press, 1968); a readable adaptation and development of Pannenberg's perspective may be found in Ted Peters, *God— The World's Future: Systematic Theology for a Postmodern Era* (Minneapolis: Fortress Press, 1992).

5. John Passmore, *Man's Responsibility for Nature* (New York: Scribner, 1974), 184.

6. Cited by Gerald O. Barney, *Global 2000 Revisited* (Arlington Va.: The Millennium Institute, 1993), xiv–xv.

7. Michael J. Himes and Kenneth R. Himes, "The Sacrament of Creation," *Commonweal* 117 (January 12, 1990), 45.

8. Ibid., 46.

9. Jürgen Moltmann, *Theology of Hope,* trans. by James Leitch (New York: Harper & Row, 1967), 16.

10. Even the Book of Revelation is ecologically significant insofar as it extends the sphere of God's action beyond the history of Israel and to the cosmos as a whole.

11. Thomas Berry, *The Dream of the Earth.*

12. Jürgen Moltmann, *The Spirit of Life: A Universal Affirmation,* trans. by Margaret Kohl (Minneapolis: Fortress Press, 1992).

13. Wolfhart Pannenberg interprets Christ's resurrection as the revelation in history of the "power of the future." Pannenberg's eschatological vision, his theology of revelation, and his interpretation of resurrection can provide the basis for an ecological theology that discovers the presence of God's future not only in history but

also in the history of nature. See his *Toward a Theology of Nature,* ed. Ted Peters, (Louisville, Ky.: Westminster/John Knox Press, 1993), 50–122. Moltmann also writes: "[Hope] sees in the resurrection of Christ not the eternity of heaven, but the future of the very earth on which his cross stands" (*Theology of Hope,* 21).

14. Carl Friedrich von Weizsäcker, *The History of Nature* (Chicago: University of Chicago Press, 1949). See also Wolfhart Pannenberg, *Toward a Theology of Nature,* 86–98. For further investigation of the ecological implications of our new historical view of nature, see my book *The Promise of Nature* (Mahwah, N.J.: Paulist Press, 1993), 39–65.

15. See the discussion of the "separatist" theological approach toward evolution in Chapter 3 above.

16. Moltmann, *Theology of Hope,* 16.

17. The Book of Revelation in the Christian Bible places all "living creatures" within the framework of eschatology: "Then I heard every living creature in heaven and on earth and under the earth and in the sea, everything in the universe, cry out: 'To the one who sits on the throne and to the Lamb be blessing and honor, glory and might, forever and ever.' The four living creatures answered, 'Amen,' and the elders fell down and worshiped" (Rev. 5:13–14).

18. I have developed a fuller response to this question in *The Promise of Nature,* 113–142.

19. Perhaps the most consistent and thorough treatment of the relationality of things both cosmic and personal is the ecological vision of Alfred North Whitehead, especially *Process and Reality,* corrected edition, ed. David Ray Griffin and Donald W. Sherburne (New York: The Free Press, 1978).

20. See Karl Rahner, *On the Theology of Death,* trans. by Charles Henkey (New York: Herder and Herder, 1961), esp. 18–19.

21. Ibid., 21.

22. For an extended discussion, see my book *The Promise of Nature.*

23. For details, see my book *Science and Religion: From Conflict to Conversation* (New York: Paulist Press, 1995), 12–41.

24. See Fritjof Capra and David Steindl-Rast, *Belonging to the Universe* (San Francisco: HarperSanFrancisco, 1991).

Chapter 10

1. See, for example, Ernst Mayr, *This Is Biology* (Cambridge, Mass.: Harvard University Press, Belknap Press, 1997). For Mayr—as indeed for many other evolutionary scientists today—Darwin has made theology completely superfluous to the explanation of life. Mayr does not mimic the antitheological polemics of Dennett and Dawkins—indeed his book makes not a single reference to either. Nevertheless, he places theology and evolutionary biology unnecessarily into a competitive relationship with each other. In spite of his allowance that science cannot answer our most pressing existential questions, it is clear that he considers theological explanation to be prescientific and antiscientific rather than simply nonscientific. He allows for a hierarchy of explanations *within* the sciences but not for anything like an extrascientific level of explanation. Once again, as in his previous writings, Mayr views

teleological discourse as contrary to science rather than as simply outside the arena of its competence.

2. Here I shall go along with David Griffin's helpful suggestion that we use the term "panexperientialism" rather than "panpsychism" when referring to the Whiteheadian notion that every actual entity is a subject. See his recent book *Unsnarling the World-Knot: Consciousness, Freedom, and the Mind-Body Problem* (Berkeley: University of California Press, 1998).

3. In contemporary cognitive studies this is in fact the program undertaken by the so-called eliminative materialists. See Daniel C. Dennett, *Consciousness Explained* (New York: Little, Brown, 1991).

4. Michael Polanyi, *Personal Knowledge: Towards a Post-Critical Philosophy* (New York and Evanston, Ill.: Harper Torchbooks, 1958).

5. Hans Jonas, *Mortality and Morality* (Evanston, Ill.: Northwestern University Press, 1996), 60.

6. Ibid., 165–197.

7. See Alfred North Whitehead, *Science and the Modern World* (New York: The Free Press, 1967).

8. Jonas, *Mortality and Morality*, 59.

9. Ibid., 211, n. 4.

10. Ibid., 172.

11. Ibid., 172–173.

12. Ibid., 173.

13. Ibid.

14. Ibid. Jonas does not discuss here Jacques Monod's proposal that purpose in the sense of an organism's *teleonomic* properties can be accounted for sufficiently in mechanistic terms. Any purposive functioning in living beings (which for Monod is an "objective" fact of nature) is taken to be the direct result of the blind, invariant replicative "mechanism" known as DNA. "Invariance precedes teleonomy." Jacques Monod, *Chance and Necessity*, trans. by Austryn Wainhouse (New York: Vintage Books, 1972).

15. Jonas, *Mortality and Morality*, 179.

16. Ibid., 189.

17. Ibid., 190.

18. Ibid.

19. Ibid.

20. See Chapter 4 above.

21. Jonas, *Mortality and Morality*, 192.

22. Ibid., 125.

23. Ibid., 126.

24. Ibid., 124.

25. Jonas himself was vividly aware of the ecological importance of our acknowledging inwardness to be an "objective" aspect of nature.

26. Alfred North Whitehead, *Modes of Thought* (New York: The Free Press, 1968), 156.

27. See especially Polanyi, *Personal Knowledge*. I cannot develop this proposal here, but I have done so, together with my colleague Diane Yeager, in "Polanyi's Finalism," *Zygon* 32 (December 1997), 543–566.

28. A similar point is made in Paul Davies, *The Mind of God: The Scientific Basis for a Rational World* (New York, Simon & Schuster, 1992).

Conclusion

1. See Seyyed Hossein Nasr, *Religion and the Order of Nature* (New York: Oxford University Press, 1996).

2. Pierre Teilhard de Chardin, *Christianity and Evolution,* trans. by Rene Hague (New York: Harcourt Brace & Co., 1969), 79.

3. By speaking of God as "future" I may have given the impression at times that this removes God from the past and present. This is not the case. For, as we have seen, the past and present are taken up intimately into God's future and there redeemed from absolute perishing. Rather than saying that God is in the past or present it may be more appropriate to say that the past and present are in God.

4. Such a position allows us to attribute value analogously to all beings, as do classical theology and philosophy, but perhaps we may understand the value of finite beings as consisting not so much in their being shadowy reflections of a timeless divine completeness as in their being promissory realities, anticipatory of a fullness yet to come. Their goodness comes, of course, from their participation in God, but here God is understood as creating from out of the future.

5. See Gabriel Fackre, *The Christian Story* (Grand Rapids, Mich.: Eerdmans, 1978), 198.

Index